LOOKING FOR THE KLONDIKE STONE

Looking For The Klondike Stone

"Camp Wynakee lay in a hollow of the hills..." So begins Elizabeth Arthur's luminous memoir of her five perfect seasons at a camp called Wynakee in the Green Mountains of southern Vermont – a paean to youth, to summer, and to enchanted places. Elizabeth is in her fourth year as a camper when we first meet her – at age ten, arriving at Wynakee in the back of her stepfather's Jeep, "dressed in new shorts, a new shirt, new sneakers and a new cap, like any pilgrim ready to be reborn." Possessed of a child's remarkable ability to endow the events of her days with symbolic significance, she is poised to make the most of every moment.

Hailed upon its original publication as an American classic, *Looking for the Klondike Stone* was universally praised: "stunningly good...[Arthur has] a memory easily equal to Proust's..." (*The Boston Globe*); "enchanting" (*The New Yorker*); "In prose of unfailing dazzle and profound specificity, Arthur lovingly describes every aspect of this enchanted place...electrifying as touch, warming as sun, and refining as poetry"(*Booklist*); "contains not a single false step...as delicate as gossamer" (*Boston Sunday Globe*); "Arthur's ability to convey the impressions of her childhood is eerie, almost supernatural... literary alchemy at its most magical." (*Washington Post Book World*)

With Elizabeth, we enter a world where the comforting daily routine begins with "the chimes of a great brass bell ringing and ringing in waves of deep sound across the meadows and the woods." On Klondike Day, gold-painted rocks, hundreds of them, are scattered through the hills for the campers to seek and find; one stone – and only one – is the Klondike Stone, the true treasure, whose finder, chosen by fate itself, is "cleansed, remade, newly wrought." To Elizabeth, it is the emblem of the miracle of Wynakee, where a child who has known since her parents' divorce that "things you love can vanish" might experience during a few brief seasons a measure of happiness that will nourish her for a lifetime.

Light of touch, written in a style of great lyric generosity, this is a book to remind us of the joyful seriousness and awe-filled intensity of childhood. In *Looking for the Klondike Stone* it will be forever summer in Vermont, where the pervasive magic of a place called Wynakee is elevated to the status of myth by an extraordinary child on a quest to discover the meaning of the world. It is destined for the small shelf of classic American memoirs that capture a time, a place, a life in which we all can find ourselves.

Praise For ***Looking For The Klondike Stone***

"Out of her five summers at Camp Wynakee in Dorset, Vermont, Elizabeth Arthur has made a stunningly good book. [If you prefer to read a novel] that novel had better be by someone such as J.D. Salinger or Jane Austen if it's to give you more pleasure than *Looking for the Klondike Stone* . . . Elizabeth Arthur's account rises far above articulateness. To begin with, she has a memory easily equal to Proust's or Wordsworth's (I'm thinking of "The Prelude") . . . She does a masterly evocation of Eden. More than memory, though, Arthur has amazing powers of description. As I read *Looking for the Klondike Stone*, two things happened simultaneously. One was that I got a vivid sense of what it would be like to be a little girl, how everything would look and feel and taste, what would matter a lot and what hardly at all. Seldom have I so nearly walked in someone else's moccasins. But at the same time I did some walking of my own."

Noel Perrin, *The Boston Globe*, June 27, 1993

"Like many people, I have a small select shelf of books set aside for re-reading each summer...This shelf holds *The Wind in The Willows,* Eudora Welty's *Delta Wedding*, Owen Johnson's *Lawrenceville Stories*, and now *Looking for the Klondike Stone*, an absolutely enchanting work that deserves a place by every hammock from Rehoboth to Rockaway Beach...This is a work of nearly Proustian intensity, a sort of *a la recherche du camp perdu* . . . Arthur's ability to convey the impressions of her childhood is eerie, almost supernatural. Her prose is lyrical, laced with the melancholy that comes from an adult's knowledge that paradise is always lost and wilderness once despoiled does not return. But her writing is whimsical, too, and sometimes almost surreally funny . . . The last pages of her book were so lovely, so sad and true in their evocation of beauty and childhood and loss that I had tears in my eyes and I bet you will, too . . . Those of us too old for Wynakee have Elizabeth Arthur's wonderful gift of *Looking for the Klondike Stone,* a distillation of the best summer you ever knew: literary alchemy at its most magical."

Elizabeth Hand, *Washington Post Book World,* June 20, 1993

"Elizabeth Arthur's girlhood memoir, *Looking for the Klondike Stone*, contains not a single false step. . . It is as delicate as gossamer . . . This book is a memory feast – a rich, detailed evocation of a time of wonder and innocence and daring, written after such concentrated cultivation and nurturing that for a time, at least, it convinced this portly gentleman in his mid-50's that he was inside the mind of the lively and curious eight-year-old girl. Or, perhaps even better, that he was inside the mind of a fiercely intelligent adult looking back with great honesty at the child she was."

Geoffrey Stokes, *The Boston Sunday Globe*, Sept. 19, 1993

"Arthur wins your heart instantly in this "memory feast" about her epiphanic summer-camp experiences . . . In prose of unfailing dazzle and profound specificity, Arthur lovingly describes every aspect of this enchanted place . . . Arthur's pleasure in and gratitude for these seminal times are rendered vividly tangible, as electrifying as touch, warming as sun, and refining as poetry. An inspired and magical storyteller, she makes her unforgettable memories somehow ours."

Donna Seaman, *Booklist*, June 1 & 15, 1993

"As children, we live with an emotional intensity, gathering memories of a magical time or place that sustain us in our adulthood. For writer Arthur, the five summers she spent at Camp Wynakee in Vermont's Green Mountains during the 1960's were so enchanted that, between visits, she would indulge in "memory feasts" . . . In this lovely memoir, Arthur relives a typical summer . . . Beautifully written and a joy to read, this is highly recommended."

Wilda Williams, *Library Journal*, June 15, 1993

"To fully appreciate novelist Arthur's memoir of the five childhood summers she spent at a Vermont camp in the early 1960's, readers must slow themselves to a sun-drenched amble . . . the author's hypnotic voice proves compelling."

Publisher's Weekly, May 17, 1993

"Novelist Elizabeth Arthur's memoir of the five summers she spent as a child at Camp Wynakee in the Green Mountains of southern Vermont is, like the best memoirs, uniquely personal, yet universal. It details specific moments and places that nevertheless belong to the timeless realm of childhood . . . Like Annie Dillard in *An American Childhood*, Arthur writes lyrically about the unfolding of a young girl's consciousness, her interaction with the natural world, and her quest to find her place in it."

Chicago Tribune, Sept. 3, 1993

"[In *Looking for the Klondike Stone*] gently, diligently, and without

stooping to the sentimental, Arthur traces her creative and spiritual roots to five idyllic summers in the green hills of Vermont . . . Arthur writes with flawless clarity, mixing childhood awe and honesty in equal doses. Always elegant and evocative, her prose can make even bug juice sound magical. Arthur can also be pithy and tongue-in-cheek . . . *Looking for the Klondike Stone* is a generous celebration of youth and a poignant reminder of the potential inherent in us all."

Nancy Middleton, *Belles Lettres,* Vol. 9, #3

"In this enchanting memoir, Arthur recalls her childhood summers at a camp in Vermont, evoking the passions of youth, the routines of camping, and the sense of place . . . This narrative of children's delights – campfires, woodland hikes – in a lovely landscape is also a collection of lessons on how to be parents and teachers."

The New Yorker, 1993

"A loving celebration of those special refuges of childhood that are forever the measure of happiness for those fortunate enough to have known them. . . Like the author's camp memories, better savored than wolfed down: a splendid evocation of wisdom acquired in a demi-Eden by a writer of great grace and sensitivity."

Kirkus Reviews, May 1, 1993

Collected Works

In a literary career spanning more than four decades, Elizabeth Arthur has charted a remarkable course through landscapes both physical and psychological. A writer of immense intelligence and effortless lyricism, she moves fluidly between adventure and philosophical inquiry, between realism and myth, rendering each world she creates with unparalleled fidelity and depth. Praised for their intellectual ambition, emotional precision, evocation of place, and rare ability to fuse action with introspection, her books trace a lifelong quest, both experiential and metaphysical, for the numinous.

In her first book, *Island Sojourn,* she portrays her experiences on the rocky three-acre island in a wild Canadian lake that became the *axis mundi* of her future life. Her first novel, *Beyond the Mountain,* was also a first-person narrative – this one set in Nepal and hailed upon its original publication as a masterwork of climbing fiction – while her next two novels, *Bad Guys* and *Binding Spell,* set in the Gulf of Alaska and the heartland of the American Midwest, used the third-person voice to illuminate the tragicomic nature of human life.

In *Looking for the Klondike Stone,* Arthur's luminous memoir of five summers at a camp in the edenic mountains of Vermont, she landed firmly in the pastoral, but with the astonishing *Antarctic Navigation,* she took on the challenges and rewards of an encyclopedic epic inspired by *Moby-Dick.* She followed this with *Bring Deeps* – revised and reissued here as *The Lay of Gilgamesh* – an intense, poetic novel of love and grief set in the Orkney Islands, and inspired by the world's oldest written tale. *The Forest of Katyn,* set partly in America and partly in Arthur's ancestral country, Hungary, during the First and Second World Wars, is the culmination of all Arthur learned in her lifetime – a family saga crossed with a mystery that spans centuries, genres, and the boundaries between fact and fiction.

Now collected in a uniform edition, her two memoirs and six novels will give readers the chance to encounter the full range of Arthur's singular vision as well as to trace the evolution of a remarkable artist from one end of her life to another. Arthur never stops searching for the hidden hand behind the world's voluptuousness, and whether writing about the tombs and megaliths of Orkney, the fantastic grandeur of the Antarctic landscape, or a fairy-tale-like castle set in the heart of war-torn Europe, Arthur's voice is all her own – discerning, eloquent, suffused with wonder.

ALSO BY ELIZABETH ARTHUR

Memoir

Island Sojourn

Fiction

Beyond The Mountain
Bad Guys
Binding Spell
Antarctic Navigation
Bring Deeps (UK)
The Lay of Gilgamesh (US)
The Forest of Katyn

LOOKING FOR THE KLONDIKE STONE

A Memoir

By

Elizabeth Arthur

Hollow Tree Press 2026

A HOLLOW TREE PRESS BOOK

Published in the United States of America.

Previously Published:
New York: Alfred A. Knopf, 1993

Grateful acknowledgment is made to the following for permission to reprint previously published material:
Girl Scouts of the United States of America: Excerpt from "Peace of the River" from "The Ditty Bag" by Janet E. Tobitt. Reprinted by permission.
The Estate of Keith Bissell: Excerpt from "Oh, God of All the Many Lands" by Keith Bissell and Mary S. Edgar. Reprinted on behalf of the Estate of Keith Bissell.

ISBN PB: 978-1-969498-29-9
ISBN HC: 978-1-969498-30-5
ISBN EB: 978-1-969498-31-2

In Memory of My Mother
Joan Vaczek

She, too, loved places fiercely, and
it was she who – by marrying –
brought me to Vermont.

Foreword
by Steven Bauer

I first heard about Camp Wynakee in 1981, not long after Elizabeth Arthur and I began living together in Waterville, Maine. It was the name of the summer camp Liz had attended for five glorious summers as a child, and in her retelling of her times there, it had an otherworldly glow.

I, too, had been to a summer camp. But while hers was a sleepaway camp where she spent the entire summer – from late June to late August – my sojourn had been for only two weeks. Liz had first slept in an enchanted place called the Wren's Nest, and later in a cottage called Owl's Head, with a cohort of girls her age, while I had slept with a tent mate in a Baker tent on a wooden platform in the woods. Her camp was named for its owners, Kuhrt and Helen Wieneke, while mine – a Boy Scout camp in Stanhope, New Jersey – had been named *Allamuchy* after a Lenni Lenape chieftain whose name meant "place within the hills."

Still, our camps had many things in common – a reverence for the natural world, a regimented regime (mine rounded by Reveille at 6:30 a.m. and Taps at 9 p.m.), an emphasis on water sports and riflery, and a dining hall where all the campers ate together, washing down the meal with bug juice. Both camps had Native-American-inspired honor societies as well.

For Liz, it was the Wayaku Huya. For me it was the Order of the Arrow, and my initiation, at the age of 15, was one of the highlights of my adolescence. In the aftermath of being "tapped" – by which I mean roughly shoved from behind by one of the circling dog soldiers – I and the other initiates walked in silence in single file and total darkness for what seemed miles until we reached the hidden ceremonial site.

There, in a large arrow-shaped pit in the ground, a bed of orange-red coals glowed, little flames licking at the air above. On a hillock overlooking the clearing stood a young man in full Native American regalia, wearing a feathered headdress that almost reached the ground. After some solemn words from him, we were pledged to join by reciting the Order of the Arrow Oath –

which I cannot reveal here on pain of death. But part of it reads: "I will always regard the ties of brotherhood in the Order of the Arrow as lasting, and will seek to preserve a cheerful spirit, even in the midst of irksome tasks and weighty responsibilities." This last admonition I can tell you I have consistently failed miserably at.

Allamuchy was rustic, rough, and traditionally masculine, with dirt roads, small brown-stained log cabins, clearings for tent sites, a dusty parking lot where we raised the flag each morning and lowered it at dusk. It seemed tradition-bound and ancient – though wonderful in many important ways.

Camp Wynakee, on the other hand, was co-ed, and its presiding spirit was a woman whose nurturing sensibility and love of theater imbued all camp activities. It was surrounded by a working farm, and with its horses, white-painted buildings, stone walls, and waterwheel, it was quintessentially Vermont.

Elizabeth Arthur's radiant memoir is, among other things, a story about a fortunate and perfect meeting of a person and a place. Liz was seven when she first crossed the bridge over the Mettawee River, uncertain of the world she was about to enter. She was still reeling from the dislocations of her early years – the loss, through divorce, of her adored father and the arrival of a stepfather almost Dickensian in his traits. Though he later achieves unforgettable dimensions in *Antarctic Navigation*, the memoir itself shows no real inclination toward complaint. It is too busy telling a story of recovery and transformation.

From the beginning of her very first summer as a Wren, Camp Wynakee fits Liz right down to the soles of her sneakers. Though she is dressed from head to toe in a brand-new outfit, it is the camp itself – as Liz later describes – which becomes the garment she wears. The bell that signals the day's activities is like a monastery's bell announcing the Canonical Hours. It says not only "Listen," but "I hear you" to a child deeply in need of such reassurance.

Indeed, the camp envelopes her, its activities aligned with her interests, honing her skills, sharpening her attention, and swathing her in the mystery of the senses. Even those events she dislikes or fears – social dances, horseback riding – teach her something valuable. *Looking for the Klondike Stone* emerges as a profound psychological portrait of a girl lost and, through amazing grace, found again.

In these pages, a writer with near-total recall, a masterful command of metaphor, and a deep generosity of spirit reimagines herself as a child through the transparent lens of her adult self. Its humor – and it is genuinely funny – is benevolent, based not in pratfall but in the piercing, poignant, and consistently hilarious language of its telling.

While we meet fellow campers – Wendy, Johnny B., Sarah – the memoir's focus remains on Liz's internal journey. Her pivotal moments happen in solitude. If relationships matter, they are with the camp's adults. A constellation of men fills the void left by her missing father: Uncle Kuhrt, a semi-stern figure who provides a sense of order and dignity; his son Carl, of the biceps, on whom Liz has her first crush; Seth, the one-armed mechanic, who shows her the vastness of the possible; and especially Jo-John, the reticent and enigmatic leader of the Indian lore program – an avatar of such spiritual importance that, even forty years later, Liz venerates his memory in this book.

In Aunt Helen, Liz finds a maternal figure – wholly devoted to the camp and its children, directing not only the plays in the Hayloft Theater but orchestrating the entire camp as a grand unfolding pageant. She seems to intuit each camper's needs, guiding and encouraging them toward their fullest potential.

When Liz suggests that the world would be a better place if every child had been to Wynakee, how can we possibly disagree? The camp's philosophy was rooted in a comprehensive vision of human wellness, liberty, independence, flexibility, and creativity. By granting children the freedom to choose and develop at their own pace while fostering a sense of belonging to something greater, it taught each one that they were masters of their own destiny, not victims of circumstance or chance.

For the child at the center of this memoir, every moment is alive, multilayered, and essential, a sensory feast. With Liz, we feel the sensuality of skinny dipping, the intoxicating potential of a rainy day. On our way to the Council Fire where Liz will join the Wayaka Huya, we "hear, beneath the drumbeats, the sound of the river and the leaves rustling in the maples, and a horse whinnying once or twice up on the mountain, and the movement of people's bodies producing little swishing sounds." Such layered sensory moments allow us to live through a summer at Wynakee with almost mystical intensity.

But if this is a story of recovery and transformation, a book about re-creation through language, it is most deeply and movingly a spiritual quest – a theme running through all of Liz's work. From the very first page, a governing simile frames the book: crossing the bridge over the Mettawee, she is "like any pilgrim ready to be reborn." The rebirth happens at Wynakee, but the pilgrimage is a lifelong search for the ecstatic oneness of the sacred.

At the core of the book are two elusive mysteries: the Klondike Stone – an ordinary, larger than normal rock, painted gold and in that instant transformed into a profound symbol – and the shimmering ball lightning seen only by Liz, a cryptic force almost like an avatar of God.

Liz never finds the Klondike Stone nor does she follow the ball of fire to its destination. From these "non-events" she learns that life's deepest desires gain their power precisely because they remain unattainable. What matters most is the quest, not the discovery; the process, not the product; the wish, not its fulfillment.

To read *Looking for the Klondike Stone* is to inhabit a prelapsarian world – a place without screens or phones, where transportation might mean a horse or hay wagon, and where the only town is the one we find ourselves in. Camp Wynakee – as seen through the eyes of an extraordinary child – is pristine, flawless and absolute, a place where everything is newly created – the first river, the first barn, the first horse, the first pond. Yet beneath its shimmering surface, this is also a profound story about loss. As Robert Frost wrote, "Nothing gold can stay."

Camp Wynakee was Liz's first island. Among her books, *Looking for the Klondike Stone* remains the most universal, approachable, and lovable. Its purity is unassailable. Before it, we are almost wordless.

S.A.B. 2025

LOOKING FOR THE KLONDIKE STONE

TABLE OF CONTENTS

THE PLACE IN THE HOLLOW OF THE HILLS

One

CAMP WYNAKEE lay in a hollow of the hills. Two roads could take you to it. Both began at the same small bridge, an unimportant-looking bridge, but one that was of crucial interest to me as a child. Each year, as far as I was concerned, the bridge was built for me anew, and each year, after camp was over, the bridge was once again destroyed. For those two days that framed my summer, the bridge was as important as the wardrobe that led to the land of Narnia, the rabbit hole that guarded Wonderland, or the phantom tollbooth that marked the road to Expectations. Once found, of course, the passage to any magic kingdom is easily misplaced, and the bridge across the Mettawee, a river then so clean I could drink from it, surprised me always with its brevity and with the muffled clatter of its Jeep-stirred boards. Dressed in new shorts, a new shirt, new sneakers and a new cap, like any pilgrim ready to be reborn, I sat with my trunk and duffel bag in the back of the Jeep, and chose, for my stepfather, which road to camp to take.

The road to the left was more wooded and bumpy, dirt for its entire length. It began at the bottom of a short hill, enclosed by an archway of maples that dropped their leaves on it in autumn, but in summer were a royal green. That was the Upper Hollow Road, and the road I always chose. Once we were inside it, oaks and conifers pressed close about the open Jeep, the smell of humus was strong, and the darkness of the woods only occasionally interrupted by shafts of sunlight like hanging, twisted vines. My stepfather drove fast, at my request, and as we crested the rises in the road, I sometimes came off the seat entirely, as if I were riding a roller coaster. Before the dim and sudden turnings of the road, a road just barely wide enough for two vehicles to pass abreast, my stepfather sounded his horn, a shrieking, honking horn, something like the bray of a donkey, and then, when no horn sounded back at him from the woods, took the turn with confidence.

I was perched on the edge of my seat, holding my cap on my head, and very aware of the new clothes I was dressed in, the trunk and duffel bag at my feet. I was an old camper now – this was my fourth summer at Wynakee – and so I knew just what to expect, and how to outfit myself for the coming eight weeks. For months I had been getting ready for this moment when I drove into Dorset Hollow, with the help of my mother and of the list in the camp handbook which came under the words WHAT TO BRING TO CAMP. I considered this heading and the list following it to be on the order of a scripture, and in fact, though by now I had had time to learn better, I insisted that we follow its instructions exactly. Of course, after my first summer at Wynakee, there were things that I *had*, and that we never again needed to buy. My mess kit, my sleeping bag, my trunk, towels, sheets and blankets lasted for my entire five years as a camper. But most of what was on the list had been lost, worn out or outgrown, and had had to be purchased brand new – despite the advice from the Wienekes also in the handbook, that old clothes were the most suitable attire for camp.

I considered this idea ludicrous. Old clothes would be clothes I had worn elsewhere. Old clothes would be clothes that had been purchased originally for school. Old clothes would be clothes that had memories attached to them from places and times that lay beyond the bridge over the Mettawee. Moreover, old clothes might even be bright or striped or flowered, might be *gay* in their general effect, and what I wanted to wear at Camp Wynakee was the plain and even outright somber, as a postulant or a monk might. Over the course of previous summers, I had devised my own uniform, one that was suitable for the business at hand; we had shopped for shorts, three new pairs, all brown, with a fabric that was tight and yet not shiny. We had shopped for shirts, two blue, two green, and two buff-colored, each one with a pocket on the right chest. Moccasins were optional, but of course I got them anyway, since I had serious aspirations as an Indian. Each year I also needed new underwear, new pajamas, new socks, new sneakers, a new swimsuit and a new cap. Of these, all were white except for the cap and the swimsuit, which were the bane of my preparations. Swimsuits came in colors, and had ruffles on them, and bows. I did the best I could. Caps were a disaster.

Since, after that first day driving there, I never wore my

cap at Wynakee, I cannot adequately explain why I insisted that we get one anyway, but it was probably for precisely the same reason that I also insisted we get a "musical instrument" and a "favorite game," though I was musically incompetent and games brought out the worst in me – because they were in the handbook. Actually, I have the suspicion that although the handbook also told us that we were not to bring comic books or guns, had it left the matter up to me by making these things "optional," I would have managed to convince my mother that we needed to procure some. That year I had followed my mother's suggestions and brought a harmonica and a pack of cards, which lay on the tray of my trunk under my socks. And that year, I was happy that the cap was less bad than usual – usually it had rainbows on it, or a demented smile, and we had left behind a salesgirl in Pleasantville, New York, who had never known that little girls were capable of such sneering.

No, this year the cap was blue, and it *didn't* have a string on it – which most little girls for some reason seemed to want – and I felt extremely well prepared for the summer that was just now beginning, the trunk and duffel bag packed as neatly as was possible. And this year, to my delight, we had found a new source for name tags and had been able to replace the slanting cursives which had always before adorned my clothing with nice bold block letters which said, gruffly, ELIZABETH ARTHUR. The long tapes had arrived four weeks before camp, leaving not much time to cut and place and pin and sew one of those names on every single piece of clothing, but we had done it, and now my name was attached, navy blue on white, to socks, underpants, shorts, shirts, and sweaters. There was something about this that was thrilling, having my name on everything I owned, where I saw it objectively staring back at me all the time; I saw it in the morning when I got up, and when I changed for swimming lessons and then changed back, and when I went swimming again for free swim, and when I went to bed. And each time I saw it, it reminded me once again of who I was; I was a person who went to Camp Wynakee, and that made me both special and privileged – made me, in fact, one of the blessed.

Not only that, but when the summer was over, and I repacked my trunk and duffel bag and took my now-old clothes with me somewhere else, the name tags and the equipment that I had had with me in Dorset Hollow would come with me to soften – just a little – the blow. When the summer had come to an end, and I had ten months to live through before I was again crossing the bridge, choosing the Upper or the Lower Hollow Road, I would still possess these now-sacred objects, these things that had been with me where it counted, and having them would help me remember where I really belonged. As I lay in bed at night, my Wynakee pajamas on my back, my navy blue name appearing twice, collar and waistband, I would indulge for minutes or an hour in what I called a "memory feast," which was remembering everything there was to remember about Wynakee. I seem to have always called these "memory feasts," though there must have been a time in my life when I didn't even know that I *had* a memory, much less that it could possibly matter. But with my parents' divorce, all that had changed, as I had learned that things you love can vanish.

So I had started to cultivate my memory very much as if it were a garden, learning that the unexpected images which appeared on the blackness of my consciousness could be sorted and organized and even nurtured, some of them weeded and some of them fertilized, until what was left in my mind was what I most needed to have there.

More accurately, I guess I thought of my memories as food, some of them not poisonous exactly, but certainly bitter and unpalatable, and some of them ambrosia and nectar, fit for a feast of the gods. During the ten months that I was away from home – I thought of camp as my home – I would lie in my bed in the darkness surrounded by that mind garden. Then I would walk up and down its planted rows, selecting food to eat that evening, trying not to be greedy, not to reach for everything at once. I wanted to savor the summer in small mouthfuls so that it would last the whole year, and the month of September might see me eating just the first week, just the first *day* even. I was amazed at how much of camp I could take away with me if I slowed time down in this manner, and I found that the more slowly I ate, the more food I had sitting on my table.

That was part of why it was so important, then, that I be outfitted properly for camp: it would help me survive the time when camp was over. The other reason it was important, though, was that having the proper equipment – plain and serviceable clothing, a black footlocker, and so on – let me feel even more than I would have otherwise that the whole camp was really my single outer garment. The khaki shorts and buff-colored shirts never got in the way when I was wearing, for example, the porch in the main house, where the Wienekes themselves lived, with its cool marble floor and its wicker furniture; then I would feel civilized and old-fashioned, dressed in shorts and shirt to be sure, but more truly clothed in the whole history of culture embodied in that setting. When I was wearing the dining room, I felt bright and shiny, sociable, just like all the polished surfaces that the dining room contained. I was friendly there, as it was easy to see myself reflecting, not absorbing. When I was wearing the stables, I felt animalistic, profound, unpredictable. When I was wearing the woodshed, I felt prudent, endowed with a wise racial memory. And attired in the Wren's Nest, where I lived for my first two summers at camp, I felt safe, cautious, protected like a snail during shell-time.

Of course, it was not to the Wren's Nest that we were traveling this summer, now that I was ten and in my second year as an Owl, but I still occasionally visited it, just for old times' sake and to marvel at how small it seemed from my new vantage point. Like the Crow's Nest, which housed the youngest boys, the Wren's Nest was located in the central compound, a compound that derived from another century, when what was now Camp Wynakee had been a self-sufficient estate in the wilderness of Dorset Hollow. That central compound had seven buildings, clustered around and opening onto a central courtyard, and it had more in common with an abbey or a castle than with a typical Vermont farm, as fully complete in its functions as a little town – it even had its own waterwheel which had once supplied the estate with power. There were two barns and two carriage houses, woodsheds and workshops and servants' quarters, storerooms and a stable and a tack room. There was a fine springhouse, which had once been a dairy, and a root cellar where potatoes and carrots had slowly shrunk and shriveled.

In the loosest possible way, the main house was shaped like an ell, but with its bays and gables, dormers and chimneys, breezeways and porches, as well as its three separate roofs, that description just doesn't cover it. It was dazzling. And it housed the Wren's Nest, the living quarters for the very young girls, located not far from the Wienekes' private quarters and accessible from them via several intriguing corridors; actually, during the camp season, Aunt Helen and Uncle Kuhrt didn't use those quarters, as Uncle Kuhrt slept with the Crows over the woodworking shop and Aunt Helen slept in the Wren's Nest. The Wrens had five tiny rooms, and Aunt Helen had one all to herself, though she might take a Wren there if the girl was very homesick. Somebody might be crying, and we would hear her – we who weren't – and shortly Aunt Helen would hear her also and pad down the mat-lined hall to invite the child to spend the night with her.

I think the entire Wren's Nest must once have been cooks' and maids' rooms, since they were so handy to the stoves and to the woodsheds. Also, the walls were narrow stripboards, like the wainscoting in the bathroom or hallway, which was cheaper in the 1890s than plaster. Because they were for servants, the rooms were small, and the hall was narrow, and the ceilings were low, and for anyone other than a small child the Wren's Nest would have been cramped and uncomfortable; for a small child, however, it was perfect, and for my first two years at Wynakee I couldn't conceive of living anywhere else and being happy. I would speed through the kitchen woodshed, bang open the door to the winding stair, and then pound up the steps, my bare feet slapping. To have my home so handy to the main camp, to the very heart of the courtyard, gave me the feeling that I was both virtuous and aristocratic. And this virtue, this aristocracy, needn't be supported by behavior, so I could pound as much or as little as I wished. I had, after all, done one thing right. I hadn't grown too big to be a Wren.

After I did grow too big for it, though, I really didn't mind, because Wynakee was much more than its central compound, more even than the fields and meadows which had originally served the estate. Now, four outlying farms had been absorbed into it, and it was in the four outlying farmhouses that the majority of the campers lived, the older boys in houses that lay deep in the hollow, and the older girls, of which I was now one, in either Netop or Owl's Head, each of them named after prominent nearby mountains. Netop was closest to the main camp, about a quarter of a mile up the Lower Hollow Road from the wheelhouse. It was a shingled, two-story building, the wood shingles stained a pleasant brown, with no shutters but with white-painted window frames. It was set next to the road – almost upon it in fact, as was often the way in the days before dependable snowplows – and because the road was slightly built up, the house seemed slightly set down, with the gray slate of its roof reaching toward the road in front of it.

For this reason and others, I wasn't much drawn to Netop. This was all right, as I wasn't yet old enough to live there, and as I was still an Owl when I left Wynakee, I never did graduate to that building from which oddness seemed to emanate almost like perfume. Netop was surrounded by maples and had a hunkering-down sort of air to it. And when you visited its inhabitants in their home environment they seemed a great deal too civilized. Almost effete, really. They had a couch, for example, in their common room. They called it their "common room"! We Owls had no need for such a frivolity. They had a record player as well, and a rag rug on the floor and *curtains* on the windows. Also, they had pictures on the walls, though the pictures had no frames and no glass, and were, in actuality, posters, mostly of men.

Even worse than all these specific sins was the general air of clutter that ruled the Netop house from bathroom to bedroom, top to bottom. Many of the Netops didn't even have footlockers, but closets, or cloth nailed across corners, hiding dowels from which they hung not just dresses but just about everything. In fact, it appeared to me then, as an Owl of nine, ten or eleven, that something mysterious happened to girls when they became teenagers. They acquired so many hangers, and such a need to hang things from them, that they seemed to like to hang up even things like shorts and trousers. The common room on the ground floor, and the four bedrooms, two down and two up, were all equally afflicted by this hanger problem, but the two upstairs bedrooms at Netop were also plagued by the distinctive smell of unguents which had wafted up and permanently settled there. Though Netop had its own smell – unfinished wood and damp ash composed it – and though you would sometimes get whiffs of this smell when you went to visit, above it rode this other odor, which made Netop too bold and sweet, a garment I didn't want to wear much when I was a pure Owl.

Yes, it was to Owl's Head that we were now traveling, at Owl's Head that the Jeep would stop, to set me and my duffel bag and my trunk free for the whole summer. At Owl's Head I would be living in what were surely, in my opinion, the best living quarters in the whole of Camp Wynakee. About five hundred yards up the Lower Hollow Road from Netop, Owl's Head sat in the middle of an apple orchard, well back from the road, and on an elevation. It got excellent morning sun, and in fact, the sun rising over the eastern mountains often woke me about an hour before the morning bell did. As I lay in my bed by the open window – I always tried, everywhere, for a window – I would just have time to fall asleep again after the sunrise before the bell rang, because of course we Owls had no curtains to obscure the clarity of the world, or the clarity of the way in which we saw it.

Owl's Head was big, with two large rooms upstairs, and four on the ground floor, and although like Netop it was brown-shingled, with white-painted window frames, there the similarity ended. It had been built by a much more generous-minded builder than Netop, and everything about it was spacious and airy. Because it was set in an orchard, none of the trees around it shaded it, and because it had big windows, and plenty of them, it was always bright inside even on the grayest day. It had two bathrooms, one down and one up, and both bathrooms had claw-footed tubs in which I could stretch out full length and even slide back and forth a little. Also, there were two big fireplaces that, although they were never lit, communicated the *potential* for warmth on the coldest and rainiest of days. Sometimes on sunny days, at Rest Hour, we got permission to go outside, to take our extra blankets and lay them on the long grass under the apple trees. We would eat the hard apples plucked from above us – green as they still were in August – although we were told that this would make us sick and sorry. It didn't make us sick, and we were never sorry, but loved the apples' tart, face- pinching taste.

From Owl's Head, you could see the central compound, because you could see right across both hollow roads, the meadow which lay between them, and the gray slate roofs and white clapboard walls of the main estate beyond, and at Rest Hour, or any other time, part of what made Owl's Head so marvelous was the view, and the way you could keep an eye on what was going on outside it. Inside, Owl's Head had the air of a monastery or a boot camp, but with the beds spaced more widely apart. The generous size of the rooms allowed this, allowed us to be monks of physical culture. We considered that the spacious neatness of our living quarters reflected an equivalent kind of inner spirit.

In nothing was this more evident than in the feeling we all had for our trunks, or footlockers as the Wynakee handbook called them; we seemed to feel as a group that not just what they contained, but what they looked like, had a lot to do with who we might become. My own trunk was something of a burden, since it wasn't the very best trunk it could be, but I loved it nonetheless and placing it at the foot of my bed marked the true beginning of summer. Whenever I came into Owl's Head afterwards, and saw it there in its own special spot, I felt true pride, mixed with just a tinge of apology. My trunk was shiny and black, and made, unfortunately, of cheap metal – metal which would bend with a snap if you sat on it, though it could be pushed back up – and I was secretly envious of those Owls who had trunks that hadn't been made, as mine had, especially to take to summer camp.

A few had trunks that had originally been designed to be stored in the holds of ships, containing clothes that were too elaborate to wear on shipboard. Others had trunks that had actually traveled all the way around the globe, as was evidenced by the old stickers marking the ports they had been loaded in. One camper, an older Owl, had a hoop-topped trunk with a stamped tin binding; she had inherited this, she told us, from a grandmother who had sung in an opera. Another had a wood-bound World War I footlocker, given to her by her colonel grandfather. And one had a theatrical wicker hamper with a lining of watered satin. These other trunks were not made of cheap metal; they were solid. You could stand on them, jump on them, drop them out a window, whatever might occur to you. And, of course, the hardware on the real trunks was brass, both the hasps and the central lock, while mine was tin and would not have resisted tampering by a toothpick.

Still, I was far more fortunate, I knew, than those campers who had *no* trunk, whose parents had provided them with some pathetic substitute – a large suitcase, or a box of corrugated cardboard, or a storage chest that didn't even have handles. To have to go to Camp Wynakee without a trunk or footlocker! If you didn't have a footlocker, you didn't have a top tray, and you had to root around for your gear in perpetual disorganization. If you didn't have a footlocker, you had nothing but your bunk to sit on while you were admiring your penknife or reading your mail before Rest Hour.

And what I lacked in the way of a trunk, I more than made up for in my blankets, which were as genuine and as tough as anyone might have dreamed. They were *real army blankets*, all three of them, each with my name sewn on the hem somewhere, and each seeming, I hoped, the outer expression of the inner me. Back in New York, I had colored blankets, and never felt comfortable with them even there in that other world – the gray one beyond the bounds of Wynakee's vividness – but at Wynakee we who had good army blankets pitied those poor campers who were forced to do without them even more than we pitied those who had no footlockers. The girl with the pink cotton blankets – ye gods! What a miserable spectacle. And I was happy that even among real army blankets, mine were a particularly hideous color, which made them the best of the bunch in my opinion. At Wynakee I wanted to know what was important, and clothes, bedding, hangers, gaudy appearances were not it; my blankets were a mighty armor against temptation. I hoped they would let me be like them, or that they would bring out qualities that perhaps we shared. I saw those as the qualities of toughness and clearness. Dependability, also. The qualities of the substantial.

So there I was. It was June 27 and my black footlocker

was at my feet, and my duffel bag was at my side, and I was perched in the Jeep holding my cap on, and we had just crossed over the bridge, and I was heading once more for Oz, carrying simplicity with me as my own personal cyclone. Which road to camp should we take? The two were really one, like a lariat that cinched the whole floor of the valley. The Upper Hollow Road, which I always chose, was actually lower in elevation than the Lower Hollow Road, which would have led us straight to Owl's Head. But I didn't want to go straight to Owl's Head, not yet; I wanted to go to the central compound, to the center of everything that made Wynakee Wynakee, and as we got close I strained ever farther forward, breathless to see the river, the pond, and the meadows, breathless to see the glorious white abbey and the waterwheel just beyond it.

Of course, when the summer was over, the measure of joy that I felt now would be meted out in sorrow, and I would be, I knew, the last camper to leave for the season. I would insist that I stay until the very end, when the mattresses had already been piled high for the winter, and when I had spent most of the afternoon alternately visiting all my favorite places and sobbing on a mattress near the ceiling. I knew that the new clothes would be old, that the cap would be lost, that the footlocker and the duffel bag would be packed most carelessly. I knew that when the Jeep was loaded and I had parted from Aunt Helen and Uncle Kuhrt, I would be given the choice of which road to depart by. And I would choose, I knew, the other road, Lower Hollow, because from the Lower Hollow Road, which was high, we would go by Owl's Head, and thus I would get one last glimpse both of it and of the entire valley. I would stop crying then just for a moment, long enough to gulp, "Please can we stop?" to my mother, who would touch my stepfather on the knee and so arrange it. Then, with the Jeep vibrating under me, and the first maples beginning to turn golden, and the bridge waiting at the far end of Dorset Hollow, I would look down at lovely Wynakee, cupped like a white blossom in green leaves, fallen from the blue sky.

Two

I REMEMBER Aunt Helen best standing in the wings of the Hayloft Theatre, and I remember Uncle Kuhrt best standing in the hayfield by the rifle range; Aunt Helen and Uncle Kuhrt were everyone's surrogate parents and they were naturally the most important people in camp, although their sons Karl and Kuhrt Jr. ran them a close second. Uncle Kuhrt was a man of average height, maybe just under six feet tall, and he was perhaps in his late fifties when I remember him. He had a lean, muscular body, and a weathered, rather stern face, and a skull that would have been coveted by any phrenologist. Uncle Kuhrt was balding, but his hair had receded in the neatest manner, had in effect simply cleared more space for the immense expanse of his forehead. The shape of the dome that was thus exposed was perfectly formed like an upside down egg. And that extraordinarily high forehead, like the term "egghead" it might have inspired, did give an impression of prodigious braininess, since it was hard to understand what the purpose of all that extra space was if not to contain extra brains. This impression Uncle Kuhrt maintained by scarcely ever opening his mouth, but shooting piercing looks at us children whenever the opportunity arose for it, and by never fussing with any part of himself – for example, he kept his remaining hair short, and it was soft and white and never acted up. Occasionally, he stroked his bald head with a gnarled hand.

Uncle Kuhrt was not just lean, but slim – his shoulders and hips were narrow – yet he had feet that were quite large for a man of average size, and he always wore old-fashioned sneakers, basketball sneakers with a black line around the top of the rubber, just where it met the white of the canvas. These sneakers protruded from his pants cuffs, and I used to study them surreptitiously, because I had never otherwise seen sneakers on an older man, and I thought they represented a radical, even a wild, streak in his nature, one that I was never lucky enough to see him actually express. As for pants, he wore simple khakis, or sometimes white pants like painter's pants, but without the loops; whatever pants he wore, they tended to be a little too long, and the cuffs would come down at the back right to the ground, or almost to it, and cover part of each of the heels of his shoes. At the waist, these pants were fastened with wide leather belts, belts almost too wide to fit through the belt loops that the pants-makers had provided, and when fastened they gave the impression of a man slimmer even than his pants, and one who wore clothes without vanity. Perhaps he was, now that I think of it, my Wynakee wardrobe model, since his shirts were, like mine, nothing but functional – short-sleeved button-down khakis, or sometimes striped T-shirts if he was feeling buckish.

I don't know whether Uncle Kuhrt had been in the army, but I do know that he had a military turn of mind; his expectations were high, and were constantly disappointed, but since he had expected them to be, he rarely made a fuss about it. Both Aunt Helen and Uncle Kuhrt had strong physical presences, and a force of character that was always evident, but Aunt Helen was much gentler, and had a number of different moods, while Uncle Kuhrt seemed, at least to a child, something of a one-note man. He had an M.S. in education and psychology, I believe, and had taught and coached all his life in public schools, colleges, and camps; he was presently a professor of health and physical education at a college in Pennsylvania with the unlikely appellation of Ursinus. His general outlook, it seemed to me, was that of a coach, one whose team was the entire camp, and it was his main job to make sure that it developed the proper team spirit, which he did *not* accomplish by leading cheers, or singing songs, or by haranguing the campers.

No, he believed in developing character in the teams' individual members, and from that, as he saw it, the rest would follow; we would all improve as people, in the company of our peers, and we would care about them as a result of it. And so the camp sports program, which was Uncle Kuhrt's special interest, never took the form that it might have in the hands of a different man; a different man, with Uncle Kuhrt's background, would have divided the camp into two "teams," and then pitted them against each other as if they were in a ground war. To Uncle Kuhrt, however, winning was secondary to the primary goal of all sports, which was to improve individual confidence, to develop healthy bodies, and to hone the capacity for empathy toward others.

No, the camp as a whole was Uncle Kuhrt's team; he was at the job of coaching it morning, noon, and night, and he made absolutely no distinction between the boys and the girls in this task of his, which was what made me like him the most of all. If he caught someone running in the dining hall, he would grab the child, boy or girl, by the shoulders, then give it a light smack on the rear with the palm of his hand, sending the child back into the lobby to try again. If there were personal items to be distributed at our daily Lost and Found, he would distribute them as fiercely to the girls as to the boys. And when it came to actual sports, ball sports or archery or riflery, his expectations were identical whatever your gender.

However, as he was the head of the male counselors, as well as the personal counselor of the Crows, I and the other girls naturally saw a little less of him than did our male counterparts, and it was, I think, something of a disappointment to him that he had to leave a lot of the character-molding of the girls to his wife, while he concentrated on the sex that was rather more challenging. At any age, from five to twenty, boys were likely, he had apparently discovered, to manifest undesirable tendencies without any warning; undesirable tendencies were purposeful cruelty to animals or to fellow campers, laziness or sloppiness, and overt competitiveness. Being rude or talking back to elders were also, of course, undesirable, but not as great a sin as laziness, sloppiness, or competitiveness, and these certainly weren't a patch on cruelty.

Sudden fights among the boys, though rare, did occur from time to time, and Uncle Kuhrt, though reproving the fighters, never took them too seriously. No, in his view anger was natural, and even healthy, as long as it was channeled immediately – it was when it went underground and became a desire to torment that it was terrible – and as for competitiveness, this, too, was natural, though the overt expression of it was unacceptable, since the main points of any activities were joy and self improvement. Laziness and sloppiness were only venial sins, but they, too, should be arrested while a child was still young through letting children learn the satisfaction of work and accomplishment. "When a child has learned the joy of work, then happiness is the by-product, not the goal"; this was carved in a plaque which had been nailed to the hay barn, and though, needless to say, not all children paid equal attention to it, this was not for lack of trying on Uncle Kuhrt's part.

Not that he was a slave driver; even the boys who actually lived with him in the Crow's Nest, above the woodworking shop, had plenty of time to play – to go for pokes along the river, to storm other boys who were holding the treehouse, to simply sit in the sun and chew a grass stem and think. Both of the Wienekes believed that it was crucial to give children time alone – "time to be alone," as they said, "but not lonely" – and in this, if nothing else, they would have been extraordinary educators, but they were also extraordinary in their refusal to make rules. Wynakee had few rules – no running in the dining hall was one of them – and most of even those few were somewhat flexible. But the one unforgivable sin, the one thing for which Uncle Kuhrt and Aunt Helen would show no understanding, was the teasing or harming of our animal companions.

I don't know how it was done, with sixty campers of such diverse backgrounds, but every year, within days, Uncle Kuhrt had communicated this single law. Whether they were caged, or wild, or fully domesticated, there was to be no mistreatment of animals, and by animals he meant everything from horses to fish. We were allowed to kill flies, though the childhood sport of wing-pulling was not tolerated, but there was no butterfly collection at the Whatsit, Wynakee's nature hut; and though there was fishing in the Mettawee, the fish were released back into the water, after a careful lesson on disattaching the hook without harming the fish's jaw. Turning turtles over, hitting snakes with sticks, or any similar common amusements among children elsewhere, were at Wynakee regarded as the most shocking of crimes, and when an occasional child persisted in any such cruelty, he was quickly reined in, not by the Wienekes, but by his fellow campers.

So Uncle Kuhrt was our coach in the hardest game of life, the struggle to discover the qualities we could be proud of, the struggle to find a way to be happy about who we were, to be good at things without becoming arrogant. On the whole he was a terrific coach, though of course for some children he was scary – and indeed, one reprimand from him would last you for life – but he was never violent or mean. Always reticent, he made terse suggestions, never on any occasion indulging in long speeches, and when he approved of something, he would say, "Good work" or "You did it, Jones"; sometimes, under such circumstances, he would even smile. His lips were narrow and held close together, but when he smiled a fan of wrinkles lit up his eyes.

Aunt Helen was very different, in all except her fundamental strength – she, too, was not a person you would try to mess with – but she had a much wider range of interests than her husband and more varied responsibilities, and, without question, she was Camp Wynakee's guiding creative force. I would say that when I knew her she was fifty, though it is possible that she was younger – she had an open, youthful face, still unlined. Whereas Uncle Kuhrt was casual on the outside and formal on the inside, Aunt Helen was, to some extent, just the opposite. She had her hair "done" every week, I suppose at a "beauty parlor" nearby, and she would never have questioned the propriety of either the phrase or the custom; her hair was always neatly coiffed, and it set off her fine, high forehead. In addition, she often wore jewelry, even on regular camp days, costume pearls in double or triple strands, and she also wore dresses, short-sleeved and cotton, with hems that came down exactly to midcalf, and flat white shoes or flat brown shoes, with stockings. I never saw her in heels, and I never saw her with makeup, either, but she had cardigan sweaters with little pearl buttons, and her watch was like a bracelet with a small watch face as its centerpiece. She sometimes wore clip-on earrings, fairly large, and always her wedding ring, a thin gold band which she would turn when she was sitting and thinking.

Altogether, Aunt Helen looked exactly like the person she actually was, the headmistress of a private school in Pennsylvania, but she was also more than was revealed by her profession or her appearance, since she had graduated from college with a degree in English and dramatic art. It was she who had devised not just the drama program at Wynakee, but all the rituals with which the camp was blessed – the Council Fire and the Indian Honor Society, the Evening Activities, the creative activities, and the special events, of which the most special was Klondike Day. It was she who had conceived the idea of painting rocks gold and scattering them once a year through woods and meadows, she who had thought of turning Wynakee into a Wild West town for a single day each summer, and she who had dreamed up the Klondike Stone, which, though it never found me, will lie long in the hills of my imagination.

When I arrived at Camp Wynakee, that first summer when I was seven, Aunt Helen was standing out on the greensward by the three young birches; I climbed out of the Jeep, and Aunt Helen opened her arms and I walked right into them and let her hug me. This was odd, because I was not then a particularly demonstrative child, and certainly never so with perfect strangers, but I trusted Aunt Helen instinctively, and there is no doubt that she had what was called in her day "a way with children" – of any and all ages. She was, in many respects, a reserved woman – you were the child, after all, and she was the grown-up – but though, like Uncle Kuhrt, she felt this distinction was important, she also thought that children had marvelous abilities. Their natural weaknesses might be fairly similar, but their natural strengths were not all alike, and she thought it was Wynakee's task to give its campers gentle encouragement so that they could find out what they were best at, and pursue it in later life, when Wynakee would be behind them. Whereas Uncle Kuhrt used the team as his model for his conception of the camp, Aunt Helen used the play, or the model of the living theatre, and her campers were not team members, but fellow actors in a great drama, which was the drama of the human species. Yes, she was the grown-up, but *her* campers weren't just children, they were young adults who had shown up at her audition, and it was her job as director of the play to discover what part they should take in the play of the future.

So from the moment camp opened, Aunt Helen established a separate relationship with each individual who had come to this open audition, and she began to assess us in action, making no sudden and erroneous judgments, giving no one person an unfair advantage. One boy was good with tools, but inept at sports; he had a bad stutter, too, and was very shy because of it. Maybe she should cast him as a carpenter, or a handyman of some sort. Maybe, in fact, she should apprentice him to Wynakee's own handyman. With Seth, the boy – Charles Evans, and a name like that didn't help – would not feel so awkward and shy, since Seth, too, had a handicap to deal with, and when Charles – would he like to be called Charlie? – saw how well Seth could function with just one arm, surely it would give him a new measure of confidence. So Charles, now Charlie, was taken out of the regular camp routine, for as short or as long a time as he wished, and assigned to Seth as an all-round helper, which Seth didn't need, but could use; in this role Charlie flourished.

Or here was a child, Toni Angela Vanetti, who was obnoxious beyond any description who had been carelessly raised, ignored and then spoiled; to Aunt Helen, it was only natural to sweep her into the Hayloft Theatre, though she had no real talent or aptitude for it. Eventually Toni, who at first found this fun, being cast in major parts in our weekly plays, came up against a role that was too hard for her, and when she was supposed to be moving her audience to tears, instead found them laughing and snorting, which made her almost instantly a less obnoxious human being. Aunt Helen's methods were rarely this ruthless. But she did not hesitate to take action when she thought that ruth was not really what was called for, and as the casting director of Camp Wynakee's twenty-four-hour living theatre, Aunt Helen did an astonishing job of treating everyone differently.

Aunt Helen's own role, for which she had been cast long since, was not fundamentally, then, that of camp director or counselor, it was not even, I think, that of mother to her own sons, or wife to her husband; she was, to her bones, a teacher, and a teacher at the top of her form who passionately believed in and facilitated learning. There are camp directors, no doubt, and perhaps they are in the majority, who think that summer is the time to go on vacation, but for Aunt Helen, as for me, Wynakee was real life, and one strove to be one's best there. For her, striving to be the best meant bending over backwards to maintain an absolute impartiality toward all her charges; for her, striving to be the best meant remembering that good teaching is, finally, allowing your students to discover the lineaments of their own characters.

All this made it a little alarming when Aunt Helen decided, early on, that I was one of those campers who had unlimited potential, and not just in her own specialties, English and drama, but in, as she put it, "anything I set my mind to." I knew better. I was inept in almost all physical activities, a total loss on the playing field, actively frightened of balls; I had as much artistic ability as a cat walking in wet cement, and I never did learn how to dive – at least, not "headfirst." While I adored working with tools, I wasn't particularly good at it, and ended up in the infirmary several times after woodworking shop; as for horses, I was scared to death of them, even more scared than I was of balls, and though I rode three times a week for five years, it was always torture.

Despite these enormous handicaps, I was flattered that Aunt Helen was so determined to make me "well-rounded," another of her phrases, since there were, frankly, quite a few children who she seemed to sense from the start would be angular no matter what level of effort she applied to them. But when it came to effort, it was *my* effort she regarded as crucial in this quest to let me do anything I set my mind to, and in that one way she was playing to a strength that I actually did have, which was the capacity to make an effort if I wanted to. In fact, I was a fanatical sort of child – obsessive, perhaps, you would call it – very determined, and always trying to go one step beyond; another way to put this would be to say that I did everything in extremes, from hating to loving, from refusing to try to trying. And while this quality never did make me a diver, or a rider, or an artist, or a carpenter, or a competent player with any size, shape, or weight of ball, it did – joined with Aunt Helen's belief in me – allow me to find what I was good at, which was sticking with things long after everyone else had given up. Not things that took any particular talent – I don't mean that, not at all – but things that took no talent, that took only discipline and will, like going for the flag in Capture the Flag when it was already dark out, and the bell was about to ring anyway, and everyone else was resigned to another dreary draw.

But although Aunt Helen was no doubt wrong in her

global assessment of my potential, she was right in one call that she made as my teacher, and she made it within the first two weeks of my first summer at camp, on the very first overnight that we had that season. Her son Karl had decided to lead a beginning campers' trip into the woods just a few miles from the main compound, and, at seven, I was regarded as young even for this beginners' adventure – not too young, but most of the campers were older than I. Although I had a new sleeping bag – sleeping bag was on the WHAT TO BRING list – and a mess kit and a rucksack, also on the list, for some reason it didn't occur to me to volunteer for this overnight, so Aunt Helen took it upon herself to do it for me. In the two weeks that she had then known me, a seven-year-old freckled girl, she had cast me as a woodsman, though she herself did not love camping, and not only did she not lead overnights, but as far as I know she had never even been on one. She insisted, however, that I give this one a try. This was an intuitive and inspired call, because in the woods I found the physical skills and aptitude that I could not count on finding in the daily round of life, and with the tools of campcraft, matches and wood and mess kit, tent and sleeping bag and rucksack and penknife, I seemed for some reason to be a natural. And though I remember Aunt Helen best in the Hayloft Theatre, and Uncle Kuhrt best on the riflery range, what I remember best about the two of them together was that they made Camp Wynakee possible.

Three

THAT IS WHY I have begun with them, because without them Camp Wynakee would not have existed – the Wynakee that was a culture, and an experience, and a creation of mind – but when I was actually attending their summer camp, it was not the people who were its most powerful spirits. It was the place, the ground, the landscape, the buildings and the sky. When I said that I wore the camp as a garment, for which my other garments were meant to clear the way, I was reaching toward, but not arriving at, something that was even bigger. Wynakee felt like part of my own body, like my eyes and feet and hands, its trees my lungs, its water my blood, its buildings my imaginings.

In fact, to me every pasture at Wynakee, every garden, every grove, every body of water, every building and covered walkway was the prototype, the original. All other such things in the world were merely workmanlike copies. The river at Wynakee was clearly the primal river. The stables were the oldest stables. The ferns that clustered in great banks by the wheelhouse were the most genuine ferns in the universe. As for the buildings, with their white clapboard and gray slate, with their gables and dormers reaching toward the mountains, they were obviously buildings that had gone up when the earth itself was made. And it wasn't just the design of the buildings, or even their situation, that drew me to them and to the whole valley we both dwelt in. It was the temperatures which ruled them, the play of light and shadow, their distinctive and often electrifying odors.

Yes, that last was very important, because the look of buildings can be captured in photographs, the sounds of places can be recorded on tape, and the touch of rock or flower or wood is the same today as it was always, but temperatures and smells are not divisible from what they're part of. Thus only Wynakee could ever smell and feel like Wynakee – no copy could ever possibly persuade – and as I think of Wynakee now, just skimming it with my mind's body, I can smell its combination of flowers and earth and wood and damp. I can smell the hay and the smoke and the stone and the water, the freshly cut grass and the horse manure, animals dead and alive; all this comes back to me as I journey around Wynakee's boundaries, pausing and then moving on, buildings to woods. There is the smell of the steam in the kitchen, the smell of pancakes for breakfast, and the thin smell of the bug-juice, a fruit punch we drank at lunch; the machine shop smelled of oil and metal parts, and enormous buzz saws, of something singed, of metal struck, of motors being built. It also smelled of sweat soaked into the fabric of cotton, and of dogs curled up in a patch of sun; next door the wood shop smelled of sawdust and wood, of old wood and wood newly opened, of wood drying and wood burning and wood being cut. There was the smell of dry rot, from the floorboards laid right on the earth, and the sharp smell of metal, the brave smell of iron clamps being tightened and relaxed again.

I can also smell the old carriage house, which did not house carriages any longer, but where two old Model Ts and an antique tractor were kept, and these were all stored beneath canvas tarpaulins, so that we had creosote and canvas and mustiness, while in the woodshed next door where the wood at the bottom of the stacks was rotting, there was an odor of earth which I found quite marvelous, something like that other marvelous odor, the smell, in new earth, of a freshly dug grave. In the wooden walks between the woodshed and the main compound there was moisture and dryness, mixed like egg whites folded into batter, and at the end of that walkway a toilet with a cement floor underneath it, which always reeked of urine and wet cement. In the center of the compound, the Farm Court, onto which all the shops and sheds gave way, there was the smell of gravel and dry earth, and sun on stone, and a fringe of grass and also the glass in the windows heating together in the sun.

And just around the corner, I can smell the Whatsit, another old carriage house, and a place where campers brought their discoveries to put them in cages or pots or aquariums or to preserve them in books, or hang them from walls depending on their natural family. The Whatsit had many huge fungi in it, which had once grown on dead trees, and into which the campers who had found them had carved initials. The fungi were white, the initials dark, and the fungi had a remarkably subtle smell, something like food and something like wine and something like green growing things, and, in addition to the fungal aurora borealis, there was in the Whatsit the smell of toads, so tart, and frogs, so sour, and grasshoppers, very toasty. Perfumed flowers found their way there, forever, as we thought, and were pressed, and dried, and labeled. Butterflies, as I have said, could be brought there only if they were found dead, and they gave off a sad odor.

But although the smells of Wynakee come back to me

with a force which cannot be evoked by anything that can be imitated or captured, it is the shapes those smells inhabited which really formed my world, or the muscles and bones of my greater body. Here the purest sensations recede, and fragments of stories come to mind. Here I have my camp, and here I also have its history. As I learned that history over the years, when what became Wynakee had been built in the late nineteenth century, there were few other habitations in Dorset Hollow, and the nearest town, Dorset, ten miles or more away, was in no position to supply the large estate with power. So Wynakee's builders had constructed the waterwheel, one of the few ever built in southern Vermont, and set it on the banks of the Mettawee, which was a small river for this purpose – they had to dam it and lay underground pipe to the wheel from the resulting pond. This pipe was made of wood, and over time was to rot, so that by my last year at Wynakee the wheel had stopped for good. But when I first arrived it still turned, and in its turning it was like an iron Ferris wheel, a circle of amazing grace. It fascinated me, as it fascinated all the children, and though it no longer powered the whole estate, the mere potential for power, for self containment, even for utopia, was enough to make it mesmeric. Here, where the wheel threw its water down and down, the business of living and dying had once been reverently carried on; here was a place where many stories must have been turned, though under them lay always the senses' shadow.

The wheelhouse itself, like the rest of the buildings in the main estate, was sided with white clapboard and had dark shiny green shutters, and it also had multipaned windows, and a gray slate roof that was steeply and elegantly angled. Inside, where we were allowed rarely, and then only when Seth was at work there, the walls were of roughly planed lumber, as were the floorboards, and set in the midst of this unfinished wood interior was an extraordinarily finished artifact of nineteenth-century wizardry. There were transformers, in great banks, and batteries, also in rows, and teeth and gears and belts, and off in one corner, where all this ingenuity was connected to the great wheel itself, a hole in the floor through which one could see the river flowing. Outside again, the well-worn marble stoop, along with the great banks of ferns and the enormous chimney, combined to give the impression that this was a small country church or schoolhouse, at least until you went around the corner and saw the concrete pad and the wheel again.

Before the wheel stopped turning, I spent much of my free time sitting on a nearby embankment or on the bridge across the river, watching the great flat platforms of the wheel gather the river on their surfaces and spill it back again within its banks below. At this, the river would rush away, exploding skywards with the thrill of the ride, then tearing off, seeking the vastness of the sea; sometimes, when the wind was blowing, I would walk to one special place where a cloud of spray would fly back and almost hit me. Here, the odor was literally intoxicating – I now know that the air around it held ozone – and it was simply impossible for me to understand why everyone in the world didn't get their power from water this way, simply. After the wheel stopped, we who had known the wheel when it was still turning had at least the satisfaction of memory, and the small consolation of being able now to climb on it whenever there were no counselors looking. One year the whole camp posed for its annual picture tucked on the wheel, and on the concrete wings of the pad it sat on, and that picture became for me the very epitome of the camp, the Wynakee people sitting upon their great mandala. But our mandala was not of fate, it was rather of choice – a circle of which we had all decided to be a part – and the waterwheel reminded us, turning or still, far or near, that using need not mean using up.

Although the waterwheel was, without question, the symbolic center of Wynakee, it was not the active center and never had been, not even in the 1890's as it was set a fair distance from the central compound. If one approached this central compound from the river to the south, one walked through a huge mown field and then came upon the triangular greensward where the three birches grew, and where there often was a colt or filly running loose. The Wienekes raised, trained and sold Morgan horses. There on the greensward we could touch the youngsters' soft noses, finer than the finest velvet. The colts were shy, of course, but with their mothers grazing nearby, they would keep their trembly legs from fleeing outright. Sometimes they would even fold those legs awkwardly beneath them, and lie down to rest beneath the trees.

To the west of the main house was the First Barn, in style and detail almost as lovely as the house itself; it had a cupola, for example, a pyramidical cap perched on the apex of its dormer dotted roof. At the end that faced the river the roof was a perfect cross, the two gables intersecting precisely in the middle, and below this you could see the window of Seth's apartment – Seth who with one hand could fix anything. Below his apartment was his shop, where he kept all the camp vehicles running, and which was one of the few places in camp where no campers were invited; but in the evening he would come out onto the ramp in front of his shop, and there prop his back against the wall and smoke his pipe in the evening sun.

In the same barn as Seth's apartment was the woodworking shop, which was one of my favorite places in camp, and above the woodworking shop the Crow's Nest, where the youngest boys lived in a lofty dorm, and where it was rumored that they all slept in *bunk beds.* These possible bunk beds, or putative bunk beds (which we who had never seen them could hardly quite believe in), were found nowhere else in camp, and were not common in children's homes then; they therefore had a great dramatic force about them. In fact, these bunk beds – the Crows two-deep – generated an aura of urgency about the boys who slept in them. They seemed to us like travelers from an antique land, where events were immediate and often frightening. The person who slept on the bottom of a bunk bed (or so we somehow imagined) would get a clear view of the upper person's inner organs, while the person who slept on the top would have to be prepared at any moment to jump down, like someone hurtling into the sea from shipboard.

The bunk beds, important as they were in contributing to the general sense that the little boys lived in a constant state of emergency, would not have had quite the same force, however, if they had not been linked in the Crows' lives to the amazing, astonishing fire pole. This fire pole ran from a hole in the floor of the Crow's Nest down to the shower room which lay below it, and which we Wrens, when we were Wrens, used also, as we had no showers of our own, nothing like the claw-footed bathtubs of Owl's Head. The shower room was stark; it was cold; it was clammy; it was gray; it was in every way absolutely revolting. But it became a place of greatness as we Wrens filed into it, when we studied, with awe and perpetual disbelief, that fire pole. We were dressed in our swimsuits, and we had terry-cloth robes, towels, and bars of soap – which we never shared, because Aunt Helen believed that germs could be transmitted on soap from child to child – but all this paraphernalia of cleanliness, which just moments before had made us feel aristocratic, suddenly lost all its resolution, confronted with the fire pole.

It wasn't that we didn't think that we could slide down it ourselves, if someone would only give us half a chance, and it wasn't that we didn't understand that it was really there for fire – there, at least, for a real emergency. No, it was that, in practice, the Crows got to use it twice a week, when they had to take a shower after we did, and there was something so appalling, and at the same time so exciting, about the fact that for boys, bathing was considered an emergency. It wasn't so great for us, either, having to strip naked in that cold room, having to stand under that communal and unenthusiastic shower head, but for boys apparently it was terrible, something that could only be regarded as a continual, if biweekly, crisis. On shower days they would slide down the fire pole shrieking and hollering, and showing off generally, as indeed they normally did, but in this case we almost respected them for it – all that bravado in the face of terror, which was the only thing we could conceive was waiting for them. We, who had already showered, and were now outside in the courtyard, our hair squeaky and flat against our heads, held our wet towels and our germy soap bars in our hands as we lingered, listening to the hollers turn to whimpers as the boys stepped under the now-cold water.

The sense that the little boys lived in an uncivilized, even savage world was also captured by their other special place, the treehouse, located to the north of the Second Barn – which held the dining room and the Hayloft Theatre – in the sloping field that led toward the tack room and stables. Also in that general vicinity there was a playhouse for the girls, used, as I recall, just once a summer, when the photographer came and two girls were asked to pose there, petting a rabbit and staring rather glassily at the camera. The treehouse, however, was anything but redundant, even in a place as full of wonderful spots as Camp Wynakee, but unfortunately, like the Crow's Nest, it was supposed to be off limits to girls, an injustice that to this day, I find, still rankles.

That isn't to say I didn't go there often, and some of the other girls occasionally visited it also, but since it was officially the boys' treehouse, it took cunning and even wheedling to get there, and certainly some male friend, or occasionally some male rival, who was willing to stick up for you against the others. Having a girl there, once she'd arrived, climbing the rope ladder with its wooden rungs, was not in itself vastly satisfying, but having invited a girl there, against the tradition and perhaps a bit of peer pressure, had a great charm for those boys who indulged in it. And if the girl was like me, outraged to have to beg, there was an even greater charm to the whole experience, since – once tired of such a girl – it was more fun to make her get down, as she could be counted on to be mad instead of tearful.

I had one friend, fortunately, who didn't indulge in anything so complex, but would just invite me up to the treehouse when it was empty, and Johnny B., as he was called for some reason, let me stay there as long as I wanted, looking at the mountains and feeling the sway of the wind. The treehouse was just like a real house in that it had a roof and four walls and was not just a platform, as some treehouses are; on nights of the full moon several lucky Crows might get permission to sleep there, hauling their sleeping bags up on a rope with them. The treehouse was in an old maple, and it was sturdy, with a perfect fork, but even a huge old maple will bend with sufficient wind, so the nights had to be very still; in the days this didn't matter, and I was in the treehouse several times when a storm blew in.

I don't know exactly how it happened that Johnny B. and I became friends, but we were the same age and we both had blond hair and freckles, and while neither of us was exactly pudgy, we were not exactly sleek either, so perhaps physical resemblance had something to do with it. Johnny B.'s family lived in Connecticut, or somewhere even farther away, and so he was never visited once in the whole summer, which probably was part of the reason why he, who had one sister, formed such a fast friendship with a girl. So fast was this friendship that while I made my crafts projects for my mother, he, early on, decided to make his for me, and I still have a number of his gifts, including a tiki with two glass eyes, a jutting nose, and a dirty necklace string. He also made me a braided leather cord to hang a whistle on, if I was ever lucky enough to get one; best of all, in our last summer, he made me a leather case for my Barlow penknife and a piece of wood with I LOVE YOU carved on it and surrounded with hearts and flowers.

For me, my friendship with Johnny B. was something of a revelation, for in the world outside of Wynakee all my friends then were girls, and if it hadn't been for Johnny B., and a few of the other boys I knew at camp, I might have become a teenager without realizing that the best boys are *just like us.* They are sensitive to physical environments, and they like solitude and company both, and while they have bunk beds and fire poles, they don't live in a constant state of emergency. In fact, they cry sometimes when they are moved, and they like sitting on rocks and daydreaming, and they love Camp Wynakee, in all its parts, if they are lucky enough to get there.

Four

I WAS A WREN when Johnny B. was a Crow, and I had a Wren friend named Sarah Jacobsen, a shy girl who had shoulder-length brown hair with a bit of natural curl to it. Although she didn't fuss over it, her hair always looked brushed. This fact amazed me, since I always had, for Wynakee, a "camp cut." Sarah and I slept together in the biggest room of the Wren's Nest, which was the one with the hanging bay window. The second year that I was a Wren, I managed to push my bed right into the bay so that I could look down each night at sleeping Wynakee. And the bay, as a hanging bay, really felt rather like a ship about to cut loose and set sail across the compound. There was nothing underneath it but air. Nothing underneath *me* but air. Certainly that was almost as good as a treehouse.

Sarah thought so too, and she used to sit on my bed in the evening brushing her hair but mostly brushing the hair on her dolls; whereas I had brought Ruff-ruff to camp – and Ruff-ruff, as a pajama pup, wasn't even a stuffed animal, but had a zip going up his stomach – Sarah had brought three china-headed dolls. She had an extra set of dresses for each one, and lots of accessories like combs and Band-Aids, and she never, during the whole summer, took the dolls out of the Wren's Nest. In the Wren's Nest, she asserted, they were "safe," and they would not have to put up with any crude remarks from people who didn't know just how sensitive could be a doll's inner feelings. While it was Sarah herself, of course, who was thus made safe, since only we other Wrens knew about her attachment, we didn't point this out to her, and were relatively indulgent, even those of us who didn't like dolls. We liked Sarah, after all, and as for her dolls, well, all right. We didn't regard them as a capital crime.

So Sarah was shy, and liked dolls, and had long brown hair that curled, and was in every way that showed completely unlike me, but we had one common interest, which was the trapdoor in the room across the hall. We were both absolutely fascinated with it. It was a real trapdoor, which had presumably been put there as a fire escape from the servant's quarters, should the kitchen stoves ever start a fire, and it had a flat ring that fell down into an indentation in the wood, an indentation lined with a saucer of brass. It was heavy, as we had discovered by lifting it one day, and there was a ladder that ran down from it into the back of the Whatsit beneath. Somehow the trapdoor, and the ladder and the Whatsit below it, all had a dark and frightening appeal, and though we were glad it was not in *our* room, but in the one across the hall, it seemed clearly the Wren equivalent of the fire pole. It was a unique way of descending from a higher place to a lower one and though at first Sarah didn't want to do it, eventually I persuaded her that we really must go down it one night while the other Wrens were sleeping.

I guess Sarah and I were friends because I brought a touch of wildness to her life, and because she brought some tameness to mine. If I had not known Sarah Jacobsen, I might have always doubted that there was in the world such a thing as an honest-to-god-motherly-little-girl. But Sarah truly loved to take care of people and more than once took care of me, when I had cut my foot and didn't want to go to the infirmary. At seven, or whatever she was then, Sarah would run off to the bathroom with her toothbrush glass and her washcloth in her hand. She would fill the glass to the brim with water from the cold tap, then hurry back to apply the washcloth to my hurt foot, after which she would get out the Band-Aids that were actually for her dolls, and sacrifice one whole Band- Aid to my cut. And this was a Band-Aid with stars and flowers on it, one she would not be able to replace until she went back to her parents' home in the fall. But she didn't care. She might even cry a little, which I had not. Sarah, of course, cried pretty easily.

At the time, at least, it seemed to me "of course," but what I found remarkable about Sarah's crying was that she didn't weep and wail and sob and get puffy red eyes, as I did when I cried. No, she cried discreetly, with muffled whimpering noises, and with tears that didn't seem to pile up in her eyes but rolled down her cheeks in polite progression. At night, especially the first week of camp, I could sometimes hear this whimpering coming from her bed, which was next to mine both of my Wren summers. I would sympathize, since I liked her – though I also thought she was quite crazy. Once you had found your way to Wynakee, why on earth would you want to go elsewhere? But Sarah cried from homesickness, she cried when she felt she had failed at something, she cried when she was afraid and when she felt sorry for someone. It therefore seems quite remarkable to me that she agreed to go with me through the trapdoor into the darkness.

But I convinced her that she wanted to do this, that there was nothing she wanted to do more, by pointing out that two of the rabbits in the Whatsit had recently had babies, and that we could touch those babies at night, when no one was there to stop us; I did not want to touch them myself, as they were hairless and barely mobile, but I knew that Sarah would want to, and in this I was quite correct, as it turned out. One night we got our flashlights and took them under the covers with us, and waited until the breathing of the others indicated they were sleeping. Then, wearing only our pajamas, we crept quietly across the narrow hallway and into the room that held the trapdoor, which we kneeled in front of. Placing our fingers into the flat brass ring, we tugged it up and then pulled hard and harder, until the neat square of wood, very thick, released itself suddenly into our hands.

We peered down. It was dark underneath us and the smell of earth was rising, along with the smell of toads and frogs and rabbits and fungus and grasshoppers and long-dead butterflies. And suddenly I felt vertigo, a real conviction that I was falling into that blackness and that suddenly ominous odor. Somehow I had to get my legs onto the ladder and make my feet descend it to the ground, which might not even be there, so changed did Wynakee suddenly seem to me. I turned on my flashlight and saw something dimly. My batteries were already fading. I saw the ground, and the ladder against the back wall, almost inaccessible.

However, I had proposed this, and it was simply not possible for me to cancel it, so I threw my legs toward the ladder, somehow leaving my flashlight behind. Then I felt my way rung by rung down toward the earth. After a minute, Sarah backed down after me. We stood on the floor of the Whatsit and felt the raw earth beneath us, and we heard the caged animals in the darkness. Though the Wren's Nest was just above us, it seemed a place long ago and far away, which we had been deeply foolish ever to think of leaving. Sarah, at that point, started crying, and that was lucky, because I immediately felt a little stronger, and actually opened the cage of one of the rabbits and showed it to Sarah. Sarah stopped crying just long enough to reach in and touch the mother and several of her babies, while the mother quivered with annoyance and I stood well back from the whole encounter. Then, when Sarah started crying again, we both went to the foot of the ladder and she went up first, with me right on her heels.

In the room with the hanging bay window, we climbed into our beds, and Sarah, sniffling, comforted her dolls and told them that they would never need to worry, they could stay right here in their beds forever. I took Ruff-ruff, my pajama pup, and zipped and unzipped him, thinking how brave Wynakee could make a timid girl like Sarah. It was something about the place. Even the scary parts, like the trapdoor, weren't all that scary when you actually went through them. Before I went to sleep, I propped myself up on my elbows and looked down on the peaceful sleeping courtyard. In the light of a half moon I could see not only the compound, but the dark rim of the mountains far beyond it. And just above the stables and the tack room, there was a pasture where some horses were now sleeping. It looked like a fine cambric handkerchief that had been laid on the hillside to dry there.

Five

THE TRAPDOOR was an exception to the rule, for I generally thought of the main house as the center of Wynakee's most *civilized* activities: besides the Wienekes' private quarters, and the apartment for Aunt Helen's parents, whom we called Grandma and Grandpa, it housed the camp post office, the camp store, the infirmary, and, above all, the library. While we were not allowed into the Wienekes' quarters, as even Aunt Helen and Uncle Kuhrt occasionally needed some solitude, the back room of those quarters had been converted into a library that opened out onto a large porch with marble flooring. And although when I was at camp, I hardly did any reading, I used to love to go and sit in the library anyway. The room was open to any camper at all hours of the day and it had several big and overstuffed comfortable chairs in it. Into these you could draw your bare feet, and then curl up in perfect comfort, maybe looking through a book, or maybe not. The library was always warm, since it had an enormous fieldstone fireplace, and on chilly days a fire was always lighted.

The porch on the other hand, which could be reached through the library's glass doors, was always cool even on the hottest of days, and a collection of white wicker furniture was arranged there on the white Vermont marble – rocking chairs and benches, tables and plant-stands, and lots of straight-backed chairs. All these latter faced the same way, like a motley collection of theatre chairs, and the porch pillars in front of them were the proscenium, while the stage itself was the lawn, or Lawn, as we all thought of it, a great flat expanse of closely cropped grass. This lawn led right to the pond where we all learned to swim – blue-lipped, like any Vermont swimmers – but you couldn't see the pond from where you sat upon the porch, since there was a trench at the lawn's far end in case the pond should flood. When we ran from the Wren's Nest down toward the water, we would gather speed as we approached this trench – and then pelt down into it, and up the other side, trying not to lose any of the speed we had gathered. On the lawn itself, croquet wickets were sometimes set up, and it was also on this lawn that the flag would be planted during the evenings when the whole camp played Capture the Flag.

To one side of the lawn was a thing they called a wading pool, which was supposed to be especially for the small; in reality, it was a fountain rarely permitted to fount, as that great gush of water spinning skywards would have been an enormous temptation for children. And indeed, one of the few. times it was on, I remember lying facedown across it, so that the water pummeled my stomach almost painfully.

But sitting on the porch, one mostly didn't look at the wading pool, or at the strip of woods that lay beyond it and next to the river; one mostly looked at the lilacs that ran down the other side, or at the climbing foothills behind them. The grass was cut more than weekly, so there was usually a smell of fresh cut grass, and children would sit, if they could, with the soles of their feet flat on the marble floor, letting the cold seep gradually up their legs until at last it reached, in the most peaceful possible manner, their faces. If their legs were too short to reach the ground, they would compete for one of the rocking chairs, which allowed their feet to slap down at least every few seconds. I myself didn't like rocking chairs, but enjoyed the slap of other people's feet, while I thrust mine into the great porch fern-bank. It was ferns that were Camp Wynakee's most persistent, unchanging plant – though there were flowers, too, of course: lilies, poppies, wild roses. But in the two-month-long, endless, and too-soon-ended summer, the flowers would bloom and then be gone again, while the ferns endured around the porch, around the wheelhouse, banked by many stone walls. There was amazing variety: Christmas fern, lady fern, maidenhair fern, wood fern, ostrich fern, silvery glade fern. Each was different, each smelled slightly acrid. Sitting on the porch, I would often pick one, and then turn it over to study the hundreds of tiny black dots under the fronds, the spore packets which were arranged utterly symmetrically. It puzzled me, that organized underbelly, that hidden reproductive arrangement, and I would run my hands over it like someone trying to learn Braille.

Sitting on the porch, one often sat with Grandma and Grandpa, whose apartment was just above it, accessible by both an inner and an outer staircase; I don't know what they had done before they retired, but they were sweet, simple people with gentle smiles and good hearts, and Grandma helped out in the Arts and Crafts room, while Grandpa was an assistant at the woodworking shop. Grandpa would also teach all comers, boys and girls both, to whittle wood, which he did quite expertly, using a small blunt knife. Grandma taught girls to sew, both by hand and using a pedal sewing machine – I know this by rumor, since I avoided the sewing lessons as one avoids vipers. On the whole, of Grandma and Grandpa, I liked Grandpa better, because he seemed less guilty about doing nothing, and might sit rocking on the porch for several hours in sequence. His eyes had a milky look to them, and I think now that he must have had cataracts, because he walked slowly, and held his knife close to his chest, and sometimes felt the chair seat behind him with two smooth hands before he ventured to sit down.

Or perhaps I liked Grandpa better simply because I saw him less often; in addition to her work in the Arts and Crafts room Grandma was the postmistress and storekeeper, and in that double capacity she had dealings with me several times a day, when she opened the store-post office for half an hour after lunch and half an hour after supper. This place was small but magnificent; at the front, there was a glass case with a curved glass top, and in this case there was candy, toothpaste, soap, pens and pencils, and Wynakee stationery, and, whether I needed it or not, I was always buying this latter, for I felt that it was almost breathtaking. The paper was cotton rag, and there were several sizes for notes, and business envelopes as well as standard ones. The green Wynakee logo was a CW under a horseshoe, and under that a sketch of the sun rising behind the mountains. When I was at Wynakee I absolutely refused to write on anything less, and as stamps, too, could be purchased at the Wynakee post office, I would place my order with Grandma and then carry my haul back to my bunk with me, where I could admire in more leisure that beautiful paper. Sometimes I even wrote letters on it, though since we were required to do so anyway on Sundays, I generally figured that Sunday would be time enough, and I put the Wynakee notepaper carefully away in the top tray of my trunk, along with both business and standard size envelopes. If I was feeling particularly ambitious, I might stick stamps on the blank envelopes, as a kind of propitiation – quite a pleasant activity – and when I ran my eyes over all those stamped envelopes, I felt that most of the work was now completed. All that remained was a kind of mopping-up operation.

I would also receive mail from Grandma, who had access to a set of real post office boxes, retrieved from some old Vermont country store, and by the second day of camp, I knew at a glance where my own box was located, and since my name was Arthur, it was always in the top row. Sometimes it was the very first box, which made it hard for me to understand why Grandma would have to put on her half glasses to peer toward the place where I had a letter waiting; the thrill of getting mail while at camp never paled in my five years at Wynakee, though I rarely got letters from anyone but my mother. My father, in New Jersey, would write once a week, and my brother, at a camp in Maine, maybe twice a summer, but my mother, who was twenty minutes away, wrote me as often as if I had been in the Air Force, and although most of us at Wynakee were appalled when our parents actually showed up, getting letters from them was a very different matter. No one ever really thought about getting mail until after lunch was over, and then it would suddenly become, for all of us, all-important; thanks to my mother, more often than not Grandma was able to hand me an envelope. Then I would simply bask in a kind of associative glow as I walked slowly, with the others, back to Rest Hour; the associative glow was between me and the still-closed envelope I carried, which meant that I was loved in that other world I would someday have to return to.

All things considered, however, the main house, for all its civilized pleasures, was neither my favorite part of Wynakee the place, nor its most representative; it was necessary that it be there to move out from, but moving out from it was quickly in order, since there wasn't actually a whole lot that you could *do* there. I myself had a fondness for converting work places to play places, and thus I was a regular visitor to the woodsheds, to the garages, and also to the hay barn. In the woodsheds, with their great stacks of dry maple, I felt, as I've said, provident, proud of my Yankee canniness, able to predict bad weather, and also to forestall it. The stacks of cut and split cordwood, which I had had absolutely nothing to do with gathering, still connected me with the whole tradition of husbandry, and some of the wood was aged to a dryness that would send it up in a white flame of crackling. I also liked the woodsheds because there were often young animals there, and you could study them as you climbed on the stacks of wood; a mother cat had carefully tucked her kittens out of sight behind some kindling, a mother dog had her puppies on a splendid bed of wood chips. The conjunction of firewood and these litters suggested that even animals had methods of economy, and they, too, knew that it was best to think ahead; taken as a whole, the woodsheds always suggested to me, pleasantly but surely, that bounty comes from using carefully those things that come to you free.

Because Wynakee was not only a summer camp, but also a working farm – at least insofar as the Wienekes raised and sold Morgan horses – one of the barns on the old estate was still just that, a barn, and it was there that the hay for the horses was kept. In August of every summer, haying would take place, and while the rest of the camp went about its regular business, Seth and Uncle Kuhrt and a few boys hired from Danby or from Pawlet would spend ten-hour days in Wynakee's hayfields. By the time breakfast was over, they would already be at work, Seth driving the tractor, Uncle Kuhrt directing operations, while first the field was cut, and then after the hay was sufficiently dried, it was baled. The cutting and drying were very pleasant, seeming to pervade the whole camp with the industrious sound of the tractor and the hay-cutter, but the baling was an absolute delight – and if you could, and you were a camper, you would take time off from whatever you were doing to watch it. There was one hayfield which lay between Owl's Head and the Mettawee River, and I ran through this field every morning barefoot; after haying, the running was harder, for the stubble of the hay hurt the bare feet a lot more than the mere cold dew had.

The other hayfields were harder to get to, being above the stables to the north, but if you climbed into the treehouse you could see them, and wherever you were watching from, the astonishment of seeing the loose hay lifted from the ground, turned into a bale, and then dropped again was always the same. Nowadays, haying is so efficient that the hay is baled and placed in the hay wagon all in one swift and unromantic motion; but then, you got to watch while an entire field was littered with bales which would later have to be collected. Gradually, as the hours wore on and the baler moved up and down the rows with its great roll of twisted twine getting smaller and smaller, the field the bales lay in was transformed into a painting, a living painting with centuries of canvas behind it. In the landscapes of the Old Masters, and at Wynakee as well, this created the most fascinating study of shapes, the most delightful play of colors. The still-green beneath the straw-yellow, the dark brown beside the still green, and on top, the toasty square, the golden.

After the hay bales had been gathered by those young men from Pawlet or Danby, who followed behind the hay wagon and heaved the bales up over their shoulders, the hay was transferred through a high window into the barn where it would be kept, and where there had been only a little hay all summer. After haying, when the barn was full, it was an exciting place to play, since if you climbed all the way to the rafters, there was a considerable distance to be brave in. Johnny B. didn't like to climb hay, so I usually climbed it with Jack, my mumblety-peg partner, tackling the side of the wall of hay bales as if it were the side of a mountain. There were plenty of handholds – the twine – and plenty of footholds where the bales were uneven, but still, about halfway up we decided we wouldn't look down anymore; at the top we suddenly lurched forward, launching ourselves through space, and coming to a stop facedown on the topmost bales. These would give just a little beneath us, and as solidly as the hay had been packed, there was still a sense that it was somehow slightly tippy, so we would turn over on our backs, prop our shoulder blades on a convenient bale, and then link our hands behind our heads until it was time to leave.

Another place that not all campers visited, but which I myself found quite alluring, was Seth's combination garage/machine shop. Really, we weren't supposed to go there, but Seth would allow those campers to watch him who would be silent when he told them to, and who would refrain from sudden movements. Before I got to know him, I felt very shy around his arm, his missing arm, that is to say – or rather, the remaining half of the arm which was half missing – and though it was said that he'd lost it in the war, I found this hard to believe. I thought it more probable that he had lost it in a farm accident. I say this because I simply could not imagine that he could have gotten so good at what he did *after* he lost most of his arm below the elbow. It seemed much more likely that he had already been an expert mechanic and farmer before he lost a hand and five fingers. During the day, except when he was smoking, he was constantly at work – in the fields, in the shops, in the woodsheds and haybarn – using his stump with more panache than most people use their hands, and giving hard labor the look of something easy. The elbow joint remained, and about four inches of the arm below, and thus he could press with it, hold with it, and exert pressure, and within the crook of his elbow he could hold his pipe while he tamped it – or hold his knife or any of a number of other tools.

Seth's stump looked like the end of an elephant's snout, quivery, with two lips of skin nosing down; it appeared to be very soft, even delicate, like the spot on a baby's head, or the underside of a toad, or a scrap of flesh-colored velvet. Seth had no prosthetic, and I am sure had never had one, as he evinced no interest at all in such a thing. He was Seth, and Seth was one-handed, and had evolved every coping mechanism that he needed to run a tractor, drive a rivet or change a spark plug.

While he was working in the machine shop he would sweep the stump dramatically through the air, and then hold or pin or push with it while he adjusted a carburetor. The machine shop was not organized neatly, as the other shops at Wynakee were, but Seth always seemed to know just where to find what he needed. From a perfect jumble on his work bench, or a bunch of parts in a corner, or a sack full of something that was resting in a bin, he would extract the correct object, transfer it to the crook of his elbow and then, presto, it was already in place. On the tractor he looked positively jaunty, taking his hand off the wheel to change gears, steadying the wheel with great suavity with his stump.

I know it is a statement of the obvious to say that handicapped people can be more competent than their wholer siblings, but to me, as a child, Seth and his workshop were a revelation; maybe we who had two whole arms could even get as good as Seth at mending and changing and carrying and building. One day when I was a little sick and had been told to skip lunch as a consequence, I went to the dining room afterwards to get some broth, and there found Seth sitting at a table; this table was littered with brightly colored papers which Seth was rapidly folding, pinning, and then creasing. His stump was his tool for creasing, and after I got my broth, I carried it to a nearby table and watched Seth make a windmill, a rooster, a battleship, a salt cellar, and a pagoda. He explained that this folding was called origami, and after a while he invited me to try it, saying that everyone found the cake basket easy to manage, and giving me a perfect square of purple paper. Together, we discovered that I was not everyone, and that Seth's claim that origami required only patience was a fallacious one, that something more was needed – a cleverness of finger, a deftness of hand, a sense of geometric relationship. The paper was very fine, slick and pretty, and in gorgeous colors – reds and purples and oranges and all shades of blue and yellow – but after struggling with it for a while, and making a passable pig's foot, I decided that watching Seth work was more enjoyable.

Sitting there watching him, and with his stump in the air right beside me, I found myself asking him if, just once, I might touch it, and when he agreed, I reached out and stroked those lips of skin, and immediately became dreadfully embarrassed. Not, I think, because the stump end was phallic, but because it was the softest piece of flesh I had ever come into contact with, and I blushed to the roots of my hair as I realized that anything that soft must be commensurately vulnerable and tender. To cover my embarrassment, I asked him if it hurt, and he said matter-of-factly, "Sure. It always hurts. But in the part that's missing. " He explained that he had a phantom arm, and that sometimes it itched and drove him crazy, and sometimes it even got chilly when it was cold out. He also told me that in the morning when he first woke up he sometimes had to shake the phantom arm to get the blood moving; I was amazed, but this didn't lessen my respect for what he could do, or the way that he came to me to symbolize the possible. His unlikely profession, maintained in the face of such odds, his artistry with paper and all things physical, was like a simple image which I could not help but see thereafter, whenever I ran into something I thought too tough to handle.

And more than that, physicality itself was ennobled by Seth's half- arm, which belonged not just to him, but also to Wynakee, and which was housed in the very heart of one of the most beautiful buildings in camp, the barn with the dormers and the cupola. That building had its history, just as Seth had his arm's phantom, and the "main house," civilized as it was, would never have been possible had it not been for that barn and all the other workplaces that served it, and I knew that and honored it. Even more, I honored Seth when I was using a chisel in the woodworking shop or bemused once again by the challenge of a horse's bridle. I liked to hope that one day soon, I would find my own phantom arm, just as I had, somehow, found Dorset Hollow.

Six

IN A MEMORY FEAST like this one, you can't just skip

places, because if you do, you may find that they aren't there when you need to go back to them again. So there are a few other spots I want to visit in order to be sure that I am really back at Wynakee, and ready to start the round of daily and weekly activities. I will go out into the courtyard, and walk past the Crow's Nest and Seth's apartment, also the shower room and the machine shop and the woodworking shop. The hay barn is on the far side of these, but I will walk past it now to the other barn, more commonly called The Barn, around which was centered much of the social life of Camp Wynakee. The Barn held not only the dining room, where we ate three times a day – except on Sunday nights when there was a cookout by the river before Council Fire – but it also held the Hayloft Theatre, where I find it so easy to picture Aunt Helen, and where we put on plays almost every Friday. We also had Battle of the Sexes there, a summer-long contest involving games of skill and chance; for some reason the girls invariably won it. The boys had a desperate, already-defeated attitude from the first move in this lengthy game, and they would make the mistakes always made when hysteria undermines confidence.

With my affection for hay and my relish for acting, which I first discovered at Camp Wynakee, the Hayloft Theatre was to me a radiant place, dark as it was, and difficult as it could be to get to. In the bosky shadows at the rear, a steep and winding stair led down from the Hayloft to the kitchen, but though flats and canvas, costumes and makeup found their way up to the theatre that way, I never did. The path I took was the ladder to the loft, straight from the floorboards of the barn, and just a little to the left of the large double doors that had been constructed to lead into the closed dining room. This ladder had no sides, it was just rungs made of boards that had been nailed to runners nailed to the wall, and whenever I climbed it, hand over hand, it seemed to me like a ladder to the stars. In fact, whenever we sang "Jacob's Ladder" in Sunday meeting, which we did as a round, cabin to cabin, this was the ladder that I saw in my mind's eye, every rung higher, higher. And though it had been long since hay was stored there – at least seven or eight years since the loft had been commandeered – the hay smell still lingered, like photoelectricity, heat lightning on the black curtain of the mind.

The Hayloft Theatre had no windows, and thus the natural lighting, such as it was, was of the pellucid kind; it came in through cracks in the barn siding, filtered up from the lobby, and streamed in from the window in the farthest gable wall. The light carried dust motes in its beams, and it had a delicacy that didn't work well for theatre, so we had artificial lights on our little stage, can lights mounted on the roof joists above our heads. The roof joists were low and closed around the stage like ribs, so as a consequence the lights, low, could get very, very hot. When I was on stage in the Hayloft Theatre, under those lights and with the roof joists beside me, it felt to me as if I were standing in the belly of a wooden whale, or in the stomach of a ship that had been upended; arc or whale, Jonah, Jacob, or Noah, the Hayloft Theatre had a feeling about it that was Biblical. This feeling enhanced the grand seriousness of the dramas we enacted on it, many of which were tales of foreign places; there were plays set in China, for which we had a real gong mounted on a platform that had to be climbed for the gong to be rung. There were also plays featuring pirates, for which we had a canvas backdrop picturing the blue ocean and in the distance a tall-masted ship. We had plays that took place in the African veldt, for which the major prop was dried grasses, and plays set in the American Midwest, which seemed as foreign as Africa. Many of our plays were set in the nineteenth century, since we all loved to wear spats and ankle-length gowns, but however far away in time and space the play was set, the Hayloft Theatre, a simple hayloft, appeared effortlessly to command it.

Although the loft, now hayless, still smelled like a barn, below it the dining room certainly did not; there the barn had been totally reconstructed, so that the dining room and the kitchen behind it were really, when you considered it, the only modern places in the whole camp. New pine floors had been laid on the old floorboard, and lacquered to a splendid finish, and new pine walls had been put up and lacquered a good deal less, so that they had a soft and comforting sheen; in these walls were many, many windows, which flooded our meals and our converse with light. We had simple, glossy tables with sturdy square legs, and comfortable, curved-back chairs at every seat, and there were three antique sideboards which stood against the walls and held all the china and cutlery and napkins. These the CITs – the Counselors in Training, poor souls whom the rest of us pitied, though not because of this – had to unload before each meal as they set the tables, so that when we came in to our meals everything was neatly laid out, eight to a table.

To the sides of the dining room, accessible to everyone, and visited regularly by almost everyone at every meal, were the bug-juice and milk dispensers, gleaming brushed stainless steel, large and square, with stainless steel balls underneath. Nothing in the world made you feel quite as power-crazed as these dispensers, which had rubber hoses protruding from their innards; when you pulled up on the ball, and milk or bug-juice was released through the hose, you felt that omnipotence could take you no farther. I liked to watch my fellow campers when they went to these machines, see the feeling of satisfaction that spread across their faces; I also liked to peer back into the kitchen, where the cook could be seen behind a half-wall, and where the Wynakee dishwashers seemed as exotic as men in the Foreign Legion. After the meal was over, and the plates and cutlery had been collected, one camper from each table would volunteer to carry back the tray, to have the thrill of being bossed around rudely by these boys not much older than they were.

Behind the Barn was a classic barnyard, held in the embrace of two stone walls that went out at angles toward the east and west, and on the hillside above it were the tack room and the stables, where, all too often after a fine meal in the dining room, I had to climb in order to have my riding lessons. To me, the wheelhouse and the stables lay at the opposite ends of Wynakee's balance, because at the wheelhouse, all was sane and predictable and philosophic, while at the stables, all was unpredictable, even chaotic; an air of wildness seemed to rule them even more than it ruled the Crow's Nest. With its leather saddles and bridles, its wool blankets and pads, its cotton ropes, and the smell of wax and grease, leather and saddle soap, the tack room was orderly enough, and had an inviting and even comforting feel to it; beware, though, lest you be seduced by this into thinking yourself bold and warlike, accoutered with the soul of a Roman soldier about to embark for Gaul. No, this bold, warlike feeling would fade the minute you entered the paddock, or the stables with their generous, numerous box stalls. Morgans, in the great scheme of the horse world are, as I understand it, extremely gentle, and even amiable beasts – recommended as perfect for young children, on whose feet they were supposed *not* to regularly step, as they regularly stepped upon mine but amiable or not, they had huge teeth, and were by turns fierce and sudden, gentle and snuffly. While I went to the stables when I had to for my lessons, I otherwise gave them a wide berth. Some campers practically lived in the stables, often going after dinner to see a favorite horse and bring the animal a carrot; I much preferred to climb the hill that ran to the north and east, the hill that led to the deep upper woods and mountains.

Here, on the slopes, was the old springhouse, with the great flat rocks on which dairymaids had once placed vats of butter, pails of milk, and maybe even cheeses covered with cheese cloth to keep the flies off. Although many years ago, the spring had stopped its bubbling, the springhouse was still a sweet little building, and cool – or maybe I just imagined so – and an absolutely perfect place to go to sit in the door, on the doorstoop, because from the doorstoop you could see the whole valley, and the flanks of the mountain on the opposite side, and the dead-end road that led to the boys' cabins, and the pond and the river, often glittering now in the evening sunlight.

The Mettawee River had its headwaters high up in the Green Mountains and was called by local Vermonters a creek or stream, but to me and all the other campers it was always "the river" and visiting it was an activity in and of itself. "Do you want to go down to the river?" we would say, or, "Hey, are you going to the river?" or, "Let's not tell anyone we're going to the river," if you wanted to be there alone. And there were a number of different ways of going to the river, depending on whether you wanted to be wet, dry, high, or low.

The first way of "going to" the Mettawee River was to sit on one of the bridges that spanned it, one of them to the north of the wheelhouse and one of them to the south, both built on logs laid across the river's banks. The logs still had patches of bark, but in places they were a smooth, smooth gray, and across their tops rough-planed boards had been laid horizontally and then nailed with enormous metal spikes. These bridges were not merely walking bridges – they could and did take cars and trucks, which arrived on the Upper Hollow Road with goods or food – but though they were wide enough for a pickup truck, they were not a single inch wider, and they had no handrails on either side. When a vehicle crossed one, it would make a tremendous thumping, as the limber boards bent and sprang back, and after several summers and growing caution, the southern bridge was chained off, so that vehicles could only use the northern one.

Still, the northern one, next to the wheelhouse, remained the most popular bridge for sitting, for it was woodsier and more protected from the sight of the main house, and if we were going to the river to sit on the bridge, we would sling our legs over the downriver side, feeling the splintery wood against our bare thighs and knees. Then, having prepared beforehand with a good supply of stones, we would drop these stones the eight feet from bridge to water. This was a good kind of river visiting to do if you wanted to talk, since it didn't detract very much from an ongoing conversation; in fact, it actually enhanced it, with ready-made responses of stone, and the river registering surprise through its smallest splashes. But I myself generally preferred the other way of "going to the river," which was where you climbed down the steep embankment to get right in it.

On sunny days, the Mettawee always sparkled, and the rocks threw shadows on its bottom; this water was clean and absolutely clear, and it had the cold sparkle of a fine champagne without bubbles, flowing over colored rocks that had been smoothed by eons of running water. These colored pebbles and multicolored rocks created a genuine tapestry. They also proved irresistible, and time and again we would find the prettiest pebbles, with the most magnificent colors, and assemble a collection of them by the side of the river; there, we would lay them out flat on one of the large rocks or even boulders which also lay within the Mettawee's banks, and there we would watch them dry and fade. It was odd that they could not keep their color once they had been removed from the water where they lived, but it was always so, that in the dry air apathy ruled them, so we would take these ghosts and throw them back into the river, and watch them regain their colors of deep green, crimson, and russet. Some children took the stones away with them, and lacquered them in the Arts and Crafts room with shellac, but though they thus regained their color, they lost all their delicacy, and tempted as I sometimes was to do this with a particularly beautiful rock, I knew that it was a temptation I shouldn't give in to.

I was drawn to the river while I was at Wynakee, and spent a lot of time sitting on its banks, dipping my feet in it, selecting its rocks and replacing them. I also was committed to a water-hole that some friends and I built every summer, and into which we could actually climb and get wet up to our heads. Constructing it necessitated some major excavations, and also the building of some walls, and while each winter our work would be scorned by the frosts, when the next summer came around there was always some trace of where it had been for us to start with. Sometimes after swimming briefly in our hole, we would walk all the way from it to the spillway, the only group-set rule being that we had to stay in the river the whole time and not take the easy route, by rock-hopping.

The spillway, which was the dam that had helped create the pond, was a source of fascination almost equal to the water-wheel, since it was always overflowing at the beginning of the season, and had always slowed to a trickle by the end of it. The pond was not just river-fed, though the river provided much of its water, but also spring-fed, which you could feel when you were swimming, since the spring water where it entered the slightly warmer water of the surrounding pond was colder than anything but ice itself. If it hadn't been for these springs, probably by the end of the season there would have been nothing at all coming over the spillway – but luckily there was, and the Mettawee River always flowed, even though it would get a bit languid. And when we reached the spillway from the river, we could sit at its very bottom, letting the water rush down its side and onto our backs, and if it was coming fierce and fast enough, it would pound our shoulders like a massage. Some brave campers might even ride down the spill when it was flowing.

In its way, the pond above the spillway was almost as

nice as the river, though of course it was more static, cold and dark; it was in this pond that I learned to swim and developed a lifelong affection for water that somehow was never transferred to any kind of swimming pool. Yet, oddly enough, there was always a moment as I went into the pond when I felt viscerally afraid – the water was so *very* dark, and it was so *very* deep and cold. I had to get in and knew I would be happy when I had, but there was always that moment on the brink when it was frightening, and then the fear would be fought off and I would swim across the pond from end to end, cold as only children who swim in Vermont's spring-fed ponds have any notion of ever being for fun. In fact, the cold of the pond was so intense that, upon first impact, it would sometimes literally knock the air right out of your lungs; you would jump in and then surface as soon as possible, with a kind of dying / gurgle / scream, and want to rush immediately for the bank and scrub down with a good terry-cloth towel. "Stay in, stay in," Karl Wieneke would say sternly, he on whom all the girls had a crush, and though the boys might disobey, the girls, crush-ridden, could not, and we would paddle frantically, trying to warm up, until we found that we were somehow at once both warm and numb.

Some not terribly imaginative parents, who entirely missed the point of Wynakee, thought it was a pity that Wynakee lacked a lake such as other, cruder camps had, but what they failed to understand was that we had everything we needed. All was in balance. The whole world was ours, though not ours alone, because within the great Wynakee – its estate and farms, its river and pond, its woods and fields and pastures – there were inhabitants other than ourselves, animals both wild and tame, both visible and too small to ever catch a glimpse of. There were the dogs and cats who had their litters in the woodsheds, and were protective of their young when they were just delivered, snarling at us humans, or hissing or baring their teeth, and then as time went on generously sharing their babies; there were the horses who, though domesticated, didn't much like human beings, and appeared to have contingency plans of their own. There were the frogs and toads and fishes, the snakes and slugs and tadpoles, who had a subculture of the slippery and the slimy, and who were also absolute experts at hiding in broad sight, underneath grass clumps, in watery dens, or in tree boles. Also there were deer and coyotes, bears and bobcats somewhere in the mountains, but though we kept a fervent watch for these larger wild relatives, they disdained ever actually to be seen. There were other animals, though, like squirrels, groundhogs, crows and blue jays, with whom we had an easy, mingling kind of intercourse.

And there were also the praying mantises, with their extreme condescension, the grasshoppers with their enthusiasm for whatever was going down; there were spiders, whom we had an innate respect for, so clever, calm, and wise did they seem, and many of whom actually moved into our Whatsit. The butterflies, in many colors, lived for one thing and one thing only, the moment when they poised above the stamen, their wings folded ecstatically in half. In the woods we sensed small creatures – the mice and voles and chipmunks – who were frightened by everything, and perhaps had good reason to be. In the fields we saw wild rabbits nibbling in the dew of early morning, and then tucking their ears down and bounding quickly away, and because of their extreme shyness, we sometimes gave way to our impulse to tease them, though by the time we did, they were generally long gone, and only their tracks were there in the dew. The shadows of the trout darting beneath embankments, the calls of the great horned owls at night, all this was evidence that for every place we loved at Wynakee, there was an animal who loved it too.

Well, that was Wynakee, my outer body, the place in the hollow of the Vermont hills where I began my journey toward a world that was only occasionally its true reflection, and where I carved a wooden plaque, chiseling each deeply runneled letter from a motto I took from a sampler hung in the library. There I saw it during our Sunday meetings, above the fireplace where all could see it and where I read

That which is beneath us
That which is around us
That which is above us
Let us love

while we sang hymns chosen by Aunt Helen for just one theme, a reverence for the natural world and harmony between humans and the earth we lived on.

Every Sunday the whole camp would gather in the library with its cool waxed floors, its comfortable chairs and its walls of books, where Seth had stacked the firewood upright in large baskets, and fresh wildflowers had been placed on the mantelpiece by the Wrens. Every Sunday morning started the same way, the whole camp in its very best clothing – the little girls in short starched dresses with puffy sleeves, the little boys in suits with knee pants, some of the older girls wearing dresses that had crinolines and the older boys in suits of midnight blue – and everyone was clean from the Saturday showers and baths. Everyone had glossy, shining hair.

As soon as we were all gathered, the whole camp would rise to its feet and sing what I supposed was our unofficial camp hymn, the deep deep voices of the older boys booming, as they had just discovered their real vocal cords, hidden all these years under some silly squeaky things. The little girls' voices were sweet and high, and all the tones of our voices blended together to create one lovely note as we sang, once a week, the one hymn I still really love.

God who touchest earth with beauty make me lovely, too
With thy spirit recreate me, make my heart anew.
Like the springs and running waters make me crystal pure
Like the rocks of towering grandeur make me strong and sure.
Like the dancing waves in sunlight make me glad and free
Like the straightness of the pine tree, let me upright be
Like the arching of the heavens, lift my thoughts above
Turn my dreams to noble actions, ministries of love.
God who touchest earth with beauty make me lovely, too
With thy spirit recreate me, make my heart anew.

And looking around at all of us, the rocks of the fireplace, the wildflowers in the vases, the mountains and the river and the trees through the newly polished windows, I had no doubt that God had succeeded. A god who was incarnate, a god embodied; as I saw it, God was Camp Wynakee.

NOT TO A BUGLE

Seven

OUR DAY at Wynakee began at 7:00 We awakened, not to the sound of a bugler blowing his tune, but to the chimes of a great brass bell ringing and ringing in waves of deep sound across the meadow and the woods, and I would lie in my bed at Owl's Head, all three of my wool army blankets tucked around me against the chill of a Vermont summer morning, and slowly come to consciousness with a pleasant mix of feelings – the wish to sleep longer, anticipation of the new day, and warmth toward the bell which was like Wynakee's speaking voice. My sheets were good rough cotton, and the pillow was a large one filled with feathers, and it seemed to me as I lay there, the air chilly on my face, that no one could possibly enjoy sleep so much as I. The whole bed was warm with my body, and the cot was so firm and comfortable, and the blankets were so dark, protectively dark, and yet there was that bell mildly ringing. Unlike a bugle, which is demanding, assertive, even cranky, a bell has tones which are warm and random; they vary with the weather, and the force of the ring, and even with the mood of the ringer. So, though all bells have just one note, they strike it in a hundred ways, while a bugle, playing many notes, seems to strike just one. Wynakee's bell rang eight times a day and each time it rang it sounded a little different; now I listened to the bell, which I never tired of hearing, and which said to me not just "Listen," but "I hear you."

As a self-appointed Owl leader, it was necessary for me to set a good example in the morning, which I did by ripping back my covers and leaping to the floor, and then racing toward my trunk and flinging it open. While other girls had other methods, I had found that mine worked for me, and had selected today's clothes, from underpants to socks, the night before, and put them into the top tray in the order in which they would be called for. While some girls were still cautiously crawling out of their bunks – trying to leave their tucked-in covers intact so they wouldn't have to remake them – I was tearing off my pajamas and putting on my clothes so as to leave plenty of time for the masterpiece of my bunk making. Even at camp, in the communal life we led, there were some girls who seemed numbed by modesty and would attempt to dress and undress under a tent made out of a nightgown, but we others found this absurd, and absurdly time-consuming – and anyway, we were tough, we were bold, we were Owls.

We had inspection of quarters about 7:40 – our counselors came around and glanced briefly at our beds and trunks – and this was a big event in the day for someone like me who saw herself as a leader and, besides, wanted to win Best Owl. I would tuck in my blankets until they were taut, almost elastic, really, and the top blanket created its own plane, one that floated above the slight sag of the mattress and even made the sides of the mattress slightly bowed. The pillow I would drop several times onto my trunk until it had been fluffed out as fully as it could be fluffed.

Once I had put it in place on the bed, I would tug the ends of the pillow case out flat, and smooth the top of it with the palms of my hands. I had hospital corners, of course, and my extra blanket was folded so masterfully that no edges crossed any other edges, but were all precisely aligned, and the folded blanket itself was aligned precisely with the bottom of the bed. As for the trunk, the socks were in bundles. Everything else was in tall stacks, except for my pens and pencils, which were lined up facing bedwards, side by side by side. But since the counselors after a while knew that my trunk was always neat in the mornings, there were inspections when they didn't bother even to raise its lid.

While such mornings were disappointing, of course, at least they were quickly done, and it was on to the flag raising, which was at 7:55; just before that time, the great bell would ring again, though not as long as it had for reveille. Then it was time to run out the front door of Owl's Head, pound on the marble stoop, dash through the orchard and run across the road, and then simply hurtle down through the wet meadow toward the center of camp and across the Mettawee River. I always took this run barefoot, and in fact went barefoot all day, in keeping with my desire to be tough; only for riding would I put on shoes, or in the evening when it got quite cold, or when I was in a play, and had to. At the beginning of the summer this was painful, but by the end of the summer I had a crust on the soles of my feet so thick it took several months to peel off. When it finally did get loosened, sometime just before Thanksgiving, it was only after it had first cracked, and then softened, and it came off in big chunks, which I tried to delay by not picking at them, because as long as I had the crusts on the soles of my feet I had something of Wynakee.

The flagpole stood in the middle of the field that was between the main house and the river – the field where we also played baseball on occasion, and where we had the Fourth of July celebration, and cookouts before Council Fire on Sundays; it was a sociable and even patriotic kind of field. In the morning I took my place in the circle which had formed by now around the flag, and while some unlucky campers were honored by getting to raise the flag – it was too early for that for me – the rest of us would mutter the Pledge of Allegiance, hands on our hearts. We never listened to our own words, except for the very last phrase – and justice for all! – which, to us, meant *breakfast.*

Only somehow we didn't quite believe the promise contained in that phrase, and getting to the dining room first seemed likely to be important, so after the pledge there was quite a stampede up to The Barn, where breakfast was announced with a smaller bell, this one hanging from a bracket on the wall of the lobby. The meal bell was the frequent focus of unwavering, dedicated attention, since although there were some sane campers who knew that there was enough food for everyone, the rest of us would stare at the bell and its pull cord until one of the counselors got near enough to ring it, at which point we would be off toward the doors of the dining room like scattershot. We burst from the lobby through the double doors, and, as we could sit wherever we wanted, we tried to get a seat at a table ruled by our favorite counselor; or, failing that, a table that contained at least one special friend; or, failing that, a table right next to the milk dispensers. Of course, there was no running allowed in the dining room, and Uncle Kuhrt was always there to see to this, but there was some rather rapid walking, as I remember.

There was something utterly electrifying about breakfast,

when the whole day was still stretched before us, because although the noises were pleasant at all the meals – the ringing of the stainless steel pitchers being set down hard beneath the juice and milk dispensers while the rubber nozzle was unhooked, directed into the pitcher, and turned on, also the scraping sound of wood on wood as chairs were pushed back or pulled forward, the occasional banging from the kitchen as a pot was moved, the clatter of dishes piling up in front of the dishwashers, and the buzz of talk rising and falling in mysterious waves around the room – the sound of breakfast included a low harmonic that couldn't quite be heard by ear but was there every single morning.

The reason was that this was a day during which anything might happen, and yet which could be counted on to be much the same as the day before, a day that contained in advance the dual pleasures of predictability and the possibility of amazing surprise. During breakfast there was always the chance, for instance, that a camping trip would be announced, or the date of the annual swimming demonstration set; there was always the chance that some of us would be going to a play at the Dorset Playhouse, or that there would be a special trip in the afternoon to the old marble quarry. Best of all, there was the chance that today would be Klondike Day – yes, *today*, not tomorrow. At least until breakfast was over, there was always the chance that this would be the best day out of the whole summer, that Karl would leave, just to burst back in through the double doors, dressed in overalls and carrying a prospector's bag and shouting, "There's gold in these green mountains!"

But even if no such thing happened, and it appeared that a normal day was coming, we had the particular pleasure of the specific-yet-to-be-made-real, and at the end of breakfast, when the dishwashers were just starting to wash the pots and the frying pans, Aunt Helen would stand to ring a little iron triangle Then we would all fall silent while the day's announcements were made to the assembly, but the low harmonic of anticipation didn't disappear, and even after the announcements were over, there was still that hum of pleasure, as the day was poised, and lit, and fired out of the early morning.

The morning was generally spent in instruction in creative activities – at the woodworking shop, the Whatsit, the Arts and Crafts room, or the Indian Lore cabin – and also, occasionally, in repairing the longhouses, working on every summer's major camp project, a totem pole, or for those of us interested, rehearsing the play for Friday. Each morning every camper also had a swimming lesson, which was the only real scheduled event in most peoples' mornings – expert riders, I believe, also had riding lessons then – and to swimming, in your own skill level, you were expected to be on time. Otherwise, the morning was quite unstructured.

Of all the ways in which Wynakee differed from most other summer camps we knew about, where the unisex children were likely to wear blue uniforms and to live in identical "cabins," the looseness of Wynakee's scheduling was one of its most striking Usually, no one was rushing you along to something else. Some children moved every morning to all the creative activities. Others would stay from 9:30 to 12:00 working on a single woodworking project. One followed one's heart and one's mood, and to an obsessive like myself, these were the ideal things to be following.

But mornings always included swimming, and my mixed feelings about that cold dark pond. When I was a Wren, I couldn't swim yet at all. After breakfast I would run up to the Wren's Nest, through the breezeway, the screen door, the mud room, and then up the stairs to my bed by the hanging bay window where I would put on a swimsuit made of pure cotton. It was pink, or blue, and had ruffles along the bottom and a full-length zipper up the back, and as it clutched my body, the metal zipper was always fearfully cold, so the trip from the Wren's Nest down the long lawn to the pond always left me shivering. My little towel, just a thin bath towel, was wrapped tightly around my shoulders, but no matter how tightly I tugged it, the effect was always the same – it served merely to remind me of how very chilly I felt, not just my torso but my arms and legs and neck and feet. There *was* a certain distraction in wrapping the towel around me, because if I pulled it tightly enough it abraded my skin, and the pain took my mind off the chill a little, though the dew was still very wet, and there was a breeze – and anyway, the pond was waiting.

As a beginning swimmer of seven I got special attention from Karl, the swimming instructor, and one of my favorite people at camp. Karl was an extrovert, a jock, a tease, and a sweetheart – not an intellectual of any kind, but certainly not a person whom you would think dumb. He was just a whole lot more interested in the concrete than in the abstract – although, to my amazement, I discovered that his college major was English, and not "gym" – and he had blond hair, blue eyes, and a large, muscular body, with hands that were broad, with spatulate fingers. Good working hands, and they belonged on his good working body. He wore white socks and loafers, knee-length shorts, and shortsleeved polo shirts before these were universally popular. He was quite handsome, very Germanic, with eyebrows so blond they were almost white, and not bushy, but set close to his eyes, above which they veed in the middle. His nose was broad and rather large, but long enough so it wasn't thick, and he had a broad jaw, and full, generous lips. He looked quite different from his parents, and from his brother, Kuhrt Jr., who had dark hair and fine fingers, suitable for a surgeon. But when Karl smiled, his smile was total; it really lit up his whole face, and also added a special vee to the cant of his eyebrows, which gave him a special Karl look.

This look made all the female hearts at Wynakee, or all those that I ever knew about, melt; all girls, from the five-year-old infants to the full-grown counselors, had a special feeling for Karl. At the pond, during free swimming, which took place in the afternoon, Karl always had two or three clustered around him, several of them hanging on his arm, and I mean that quite literally, for in order to show off his strength, Karl would present his right bicep, then straighten up, holding his bent arm rigid, so that a girl of nine or ten might be lifted up into the air, clutching, shrieking, and giggling until the combination grew too much for her, and she fell off. I always wished to be one of these girls, but I was far too physically shy, so I never became one of Karl's water groupies But I certainly didn't condemn them for their constant hysterical flirtations. Indeed, I envied them with my whole heart.

Karl was in charge of all the waterfront activities, as well as the Mohawk cabin, which he ruled with a light hand, and he was also the head of the Dog Soldiers at the Indian Council Fires and a team leader in just about all of our group games; it was his easy, friendly sexiness that set the camp's libidinal tone. Teasing and flirting were fine if they were unthreatening. He always had not just water-groupies but actual girlfriends chosen from among the camp's female counselors, and it was the talk of the camp when Karl took a night off and took a girlfriend out to dinner and a movie. The next morning they would both look tired, and Sandy might be yawning at breakfast and Karl might – the implications were staggering! – actually go to the kitchen to get Sandy a cup of coffee, which he would set down before her on the table.

But Karl's real girlfriends seemed hardly more important to him than his play ones, the ones who dangled from his biceps, because, unlike the rest of his family, he didn't seem to take things very seriously, and that was one of the things that made him so attractive. And it was in this spirit of lightness that he never let any girls get too involved with him, too crushed by their own crushes. He was fair to all, and would send one away when she had, in his opinion, had enough. Another would move in immediately to take her place, and there were some girls so eager to have him touch them that they would regularly pretend to drown, for the pleasure of being handled by Karl when he leapt into the pond and swam to their sides. He knew well enough, of course, that these girls were not really drowning, but he was good-natured enough to play along with them, and maybe twice a week we got to see Karl saving another life, which was genuinely impressive. He blew his whistle. Everyone out! He tore off his sweatshirt and threw his towel aside. His arms stretched right above his head, he didn't bother with the diving board, but precipitated directly into the pond from the embankment. Then, with a powerful crawl of seven or eight strokes, he would be at the bobbing girl's happy side, and, expertly turning her over, he would drag her in to the shallows, and then unceremoniously leave her to get out.

So, if Uncle Kuhrt was our coach, and Aunt Helen was our casting director, then their son Karl was our lifeguard in more than the literal sense; he made even the most awkward girls feel graceful, even the shyest boys feel bold, and even the most inept swimmers feel that they were growing more competent. When he was the team leader of a game, or of one of our Evening Activities, he made sure that everyone on his team participated. His sunniness acted as an important counterweight for the more somber personalities of his parents – Karl, after all, was young himself, and he didn't expect much of youth but good health and good fun and good times whenever possible, and when he flexed his great muscles or jumped into the pond, first beating on his chest like Tarzan, he somehow did it not for himself, but for all of us.

So when I was a beginning swimmer, and for the rest of my swimming career at Wynakee, one of the things I liked best about swimming lessons was Karl, who, with the beginners, climbed into the water where we were all lined up in the shallows, and then moved from child to child, both boys and girls, making sure we were holding our noses. He demonstrated the proper crouch, with the feet firmly on the bottom, and the arm not holding the nose floating on the water in front of us. Then he got out, stood on the bank and called out "Duck!", until all of us bobbed our heads and held them for a minute under the water.

Our buoyancy was amazing, and no matter how hard we tried, we found it could be difficult to stay submerged for long. Some children would pop from the water still holding their breath with no problem, though most made explosive noises as they exhaled and surfaced simultaneously. After we were accustomed to this bobbing, Karl came back in the water and lifted us off our feet, then set us afloat on our stomachs, and, walking behind us, steered us. This was fun. A little chest wall of water preceded us, which sometimes lapped up and got into our mouths, at which we screamed in mock terror, sputtering and gurgling, and Karl lifted us right out and tossed us into the air.

I don't know what the approved method is with beginning swimmers nowadays, but Karl's methods worked amazingly well. Even the most timid children were swimming within the first few weeks of camp, as we moved from bobbing to stomach steering to the dog paddle, in which we were encouraged to actually act like dogs – to pant and bark, to wag imaginary tails, and to say "Woof woof!" In our delight at being dogs, we wiggled our rear ends like crazy and madly flapped our hands as if we were beating soup, and entirely failed to realize when, at some point during this process, we started swimming, striking out, barking, into deep waters. Karl, wise teacher that he was, didn't point out to us until we were ashore again that it had happened, since otherwise, like the characters in cartoons who discover that they are sitting on nothing but air, we might have panicked and sunk, instead of safely paddling our way back to the place where we had started. However, once this had happened at least a couple of times, Karl pointed it out while it was still in progress, and we tentatively reached our feet down toward the bottom of the pond, only to discover that we were supported by nothing but water.

Once I knew how to swim, I felt that swimming was my special secret. This may be hard to explain, since I was surrounded by other swimmers, many of them better than 1, and all of them clearly possessed of this special secret, this personal power. And yes, it was true, I might not be the strongest swimmer at camp, with too much body fat to move really fast, and also with little sense of rhythm, but to me that was not the point; swimming was not *athletic*, and a purely athletic conception of it was almost useless. What was wonderful about swimming was the way it allowed you to think, or rather, the way it allowed you not to; you never really chose the moment you went into the water, and, once in, you never really chose what to do next. In all this, your body made the choices for you. Now was the time for a duck dive; now was the time for a somersault; now it was time to swim ten strokes underwater. Swimming was the best kind of meditation, meditation you didn't even know you were practicing, and my special secret was that Zen, that dreaming-thought – made-real now. As summer went on, I found lessons themselves unsatisfying, as they were organized in linear time and separated mind and body, and the pond was the pond of union, all-time, no-time, and time without tomorrow.

Eight

AFTER THE SWIMMING LESSON was over, we ran blue-lipped back to our cabins and pulled off our icy cotton suits and rubbed ourselves furiously with our towels until our bodies started to glow and sensation returned to our fingers. We lingered over getting dressed again, hanging up our wet suits with exaggerated care – at Owl's Head on a line strung in the orchard – and then if we could, sat in the sun for a while, feeling the morning warmth pour over us, and glad that the hardest jump of the day was done.

Now was the moment to go on to creative activities, but occasionally – very occasionally – we did something else; one day when I was an Owl, my friend Wendy Runyon and I sacrificed an entire morning and walked all the way up Hollow End Road to short-sheet the Mohawks' beds. Wendy, who came to camp after Sarah Jacobsen had left, was the closest thing to a best friend I had as an Owl, and Wendy was a hell raiser; her idea of an adventure was certainly not climbing through a trapdoor to pet baby rabbits. Her idea of an adventure was hiding vital pieces of someone's laundry, or turning the house water off at the main tap in the basement, and then watching the counselors run around in a panic, or, one of her favorites, securing some Netop's bra, and then slipping it to the boys to run up the flagpole. Because she was not *really* my best friend, I didn't have to feel personally responsible for the misery that might result from Wendy's sense of humor, and while I didn't actually approve of them, I did feel that the activities she engaged in were those of which you could say, "Well, somebody had to do it."

Like Sarah, Wendy had brown hair, though hers was straight and lanky, and she used to wear it pulled back with an old-fashioned cloth headband. She had these in all colors, from aqua blue to neon pink, and she also had some of the plastic kind with large teeth in them. Her face was a little bit comical, since she had lips that were larger than you might have expected, and eyes that were spaced more widely apart, and these combined to give her an expression of surprise which easily became an expression of guilt; Wendy always got into trouble, even when she was innocent.

On the day that we decided we would short-sheet the Mohawks' beds – quite a task, since there were ten of them – we waited until the other Owls had departed for the main camp, and then walked quickly down the road past Netop. It was a beautiful morning, and as we walked by the wheelhouse, up the river, and then skirted the pond by a detour through the woods, we were wearing moccasins, as befitted a real expedition, though we took them off again when we reemerged onto the road. That road was pleasantly cool, hard-packed dirt that it was, and it held rocks and pebbles, like raisins in a pancake; these we kicked with our feet, selecting one each which we could kick ahead of us all the way to the Mohawk, and then the Mettawee cabins. Mohawk was a low-slung, long red clapboard house set in a field, but very near the river; Mettawee was an equally long and low-slung house but it was gray, and surrounded by tall trees. I found the idea of living in either of these houses – which were about as much at the bottom of the Hollow as you could get – rather unnerving, as if the houses, and the boys who lived in them in summer, were the very sediment of the land itself. Or rather, I felt that if *I* lived there, *I* would feel something like sediment, like that which was left when lighter things had drifted away, and I was happier than ever, upon seeing the boys' cabins, that I was an Owl, in my farmhouse on the hill.

But I found Mettawee, the oldest boys' cabin, an absolute wonder of order, swept and dusted, not a speck of dirt upon the floor, and with the bunks in their serried rows like rows of corn in midsummer, before it has gotten tall and out of control. Mettawee was very much like Owl's Head, and utterly unlike Netop, its female equivalent, and this puzzled me a lot, and suggested some fundamental difference between the respective developments of boys and girls. Now I am certain that the extraordinary order we found in the Mettawee cabin was merely the influence of Jo-John, then the Mettawee's chief counselor, and a man of truly remarkable presence who directed the whole Camp Wynakee Indian Lore program.

Still, Wendy and I were both stunned by the unexpected good sense of the older boys, which we had investigated out of the sheerest curiosity, and as we made our way several hundred yards further up the road to Mohawk, we were a little depressed by this evidence of hidden male equality. Our depression was quickly lifted, however, when we entered Mohawk itself, and let the screen door bang to on its springs behind us. The place was an absolute mess, and it wasn't just that the floor was unswept, it was that these boys had junk we would never acquire in an entire lifetime. The windowsills were dusty, the towels in the bathroom were unfolded, and the beds were disheveled, quite unconquered; ah, the discovery that the Mohawks, who were our own age both mentally and physically, were so much our spiritual inferiors was absolutely delightful. So we went to work with a will, ripping apart the beds and remaking them, with great relish tearing the blankets right off until they landed on the floor, and then whipping off the top sheet, which also landed on the floor. The sheet that was left was then folded back upon itself. In this state, it looked like a large white pocket lying on the top half of the now-bared ticking of the mattress, and when we put the blankets back on, tucking them in with hospital corners, the sheet was then folded back on them. This was short-sheeting.

In about half an hour, we had ten short-sheeted beds, and also ten sheets that we had to hide, so we stood and took five extra minutes holding these ten sheets between us, and then folding them in half, in half, in half and in half. Now we had a neat pile of ten sheets we had to get rid of, and, in a hurry since the morning was wearing on, we decided that we would simply stick them in the back of the downstairs closet, which looked as if it hadn't been opened in many years. The sneakers that lay at the bottom might actually have had mold growing on them, though we preferred not to bend closely enough to see, and as for the garments that hung on hooks, well, one could see at a glance that they had been put there *last* summer, not this one. So we placed the ten sheets on the floor and went outside, well pleased with our work and anticipating the incredible scene at nine-thirty or so that night, when all of the Mohawks at once crawled exhausted into their beds, only to have their toes hit a wall of cotton.

We knew, from personal experience, that the feeling is almost terrifying, that the whole world seems to shift in a moment to something strange, and that the first terror is followed by the certainty that your feet have merely somehow gotten tangled in what must be – must be! – merely a bit of hem. Kicking our rocks in front of us back down the road, Wendy and I speculated on whether any of the boys would actually tear their sheets in frustration at this sudden wall of cotton, and we chortled with delight at the simultaneous accomplishment of having spied upon the boys and also annoyed them.

In the event, however, all of our labor was wasted, for when Rest Hour came and the Mohawks returned to their home, the first thing they did, apparently, was to march straight to the closet where we had placed, or "hidden," the ten neatly folded sheets. Appearances to the contrary, this closet, as it turned out, was the very hub and center of Mohawk life, and at any time when the cabin was inhabited, not an hour was allowed to pass without the closet being opened and consulted. As the boys told us later, that closet was a kind of oracle, and they were its propitiating attendants; so they all remade their beds during Rest Hour without ever experiencing that frustration, that bewilderment, or that great aggravation. They also told us afterwards – somehow they knew we were the short-sheet perpetrators – that they would have figured out what had been done before bedtime in any case, as the minute they came into their cabin, they had sensed that something was wrong. The beds, after all, had actually been *made.*

Nine

THE SHORT-SHEETING episode was quite unusual, however, and most mornings after swimming we proceeded with our normal day, which is to say, with creative activities, which fell into the categories of Indian Lore, Arts and Crafts, the Whatsit, Woodworking, or Plays. If I had gotten really chilled at swimming, Plays were always nice, as they had a way of warming me up immediately – the Hayloft Theatre, being essentially windowless, and above the heated space of the dining room, was always pleasantly warm; I would never have called it, as an adult might, stuffy. No, to me, although it was a closed space, a musty space, in some ways a box, it rang with magnetic currents that were always pleasantly enclosing, and I was glad that I had discovered this my very first summer at Wynakee when Aunt Helen had picked me out to play a part in a puppet play.

And not just any part, but the part of the puppet hero, Casper, which flattered me immensely, since at seven I still could not read, and Casper had more lines than anyone else in the drama; after hearing my lines once, though, I generally had them memorized. This puppet play was a long and picaresque tale about the adventures of a normal boy, Casper, and the utterly abnormal people and situations that he discovered as he wandered the wide world in search of adventure. All the other children in the play – those who played the odd and the eccentric, the witch woman, the juggler, the deaf mute, the mad scientist, the giant – were older than I by some years and took up a lot of space behind the puppet stage, and so no doubt Aunt Helen had wanted a Casper as small as possible. Casper was on stage almost continuously throughout the play, and that meant that he was scrunched below eye-level of the stage; *I* was scrunched there, that is to say, arm extended, and speaking in my low, low voice, as my hand took its journeys through space.

And what a wonder it was, the way that Casper would react, his fear at the spells of the witch woman, his fascination with the mad scientist – and the way that, small as he was, he contained a fair amount of brain and could do whatever he liked with that lumbering hulk of a giant. I would feel him moving about, reacting somewhere up above me, and I would hear his voice inhabiting my mouth, and it really seemed to me that, although he was not myself, I *knew* him. Every time we put on the play – and we took it on the road, putting it on once in Bennington and once at a church in Manchester – I would get more confident about Casper and improvise lines for him more freely, and I could hear startled laughter mixed in with the applause. This was, obviously delightful, but because it was not *I* who was on the stage, I could take pride in whatever my character Casper was doing, and I would beam as if he were my child, and I merely a proud mother, scrunched up behind the puppet stage, invisible.

That was my only puppet play at Wynakee, though; once I discovered real acting, I never looked back at that puppet kind. Whatever the play, I was always there for tryouts, and always got cast, which was not hard, because Aunt Helen generally tried to cast everyone. But while some children were relegated to the very back of the stage, to parts with no speeches, to be a kind of forest, Aunt Helen knew she could count on me to take the plays seriously, and that in fact I played my parts as if I were on trial for my life. It wasn't that the plays weren't fun, because they were, particularly the wearing of the costumes, and when I was in costume, and it was hanging heavily on my shoulders, I would feel it as a cue card to my very sinews.

But there was that moment, too, which always occurred before my entrance, when I stood in the wings and felt unadulterated terror – when my heart was pounding, and the lights were bright, and I was sure I was going to fail. No matter how many times I had made a successful entrance, this terror never abated. I always felt like Anne Boleyn walking to the block, her hair pulled back on her head to expose the soft flesh beneath it, or Joan of Arc as she was taken to the square, or an unfortunate pirate, still on deck, but with the plank there before him. Would my tongue cleave to the roof of my mouth? Would I be turned to stone? At the very least, would I trip on a nail as I went on? These questions always arose, but at last I would move forward, and the world would thrum like a hummingbird until the first line was safely spoken.

During rehearsals, of course, which was what we had when I went to the Hayloft Theatre in the morning, my hair still wet from my lesson in the pond, I might giggle on the stage, or even have a tremendous bout of laughing, so tremendous that once or twice I actually wet my pants. There was Jack, my mumblety-peg partner, pretending to be a lover – a French lover in the court of Louis XIV – and when he said, "But Madame, my heart dieth," and his voice cracked in the middle of it, what could I do but actually roll on the splintery floorboards? Or there was Wendy, with her hair pulled back even more tightly than usual, as she prepared to play a Japanese geisha; watching her mince prissily across the stage, with her feet shuffling as they moved, was enough to bring down the entire cast. But during a performance at the Hayloft Theatre I never laughed, never giggled, never smiled, for to break character during a performance was the only great sin, and in this serious business of acting, when one was on trial for one's life, it was one's whole character that stood at risk. A play was such an opportunity that to misuse it or take it lightly seemed to be throwing away a chance to become more than you had been before – because when you were cast in a play you actually became someone else, not just while the play was on, but for the rest of your entire life.

That is to say, to be in a play meant feeling like someone else, meant thinking like someone else, meant *understanding* someone else, and if, in the normal course of events, this was often hard or impossible, it was magically easy when you were on the stage.

And the moments of the exits, when you stormed or swept back into the wings and hid behind the painted backdrops in the musty dark, those moments always felt like triumphs, partly because you hadn't been struck dumb, but more important, because you had enlarged your understanding. You had, if only for a little while, been another person in the eyes of a great company, and that had riveted the otherness to your own soul – so that from now until the day you died, you would never forget what it felt like to have been a pirate with blood lust in his heart. You would never forget what it was like to have been a fragile young maiden, or a greedy king, or an old woman whose last child had just died in a bloody war; no, forever and forever, after that one brief moment in the lights and with the whole camp watching, you would remember. Now, you knew what it was to be a Japanese samurai warrior whose code in life revolved around death and honor; now, you knew what it was to be a spoiled Southern belle whose only thought was to indulge herself, never others.

In real life, empathy tended to be painful, since generally I could best imagine what someone else was feeling only if that person had been hurt. But on stage, empathy was exhilarating, as I got to try out every emotion, and every perspective in this hay-sweet place. Although the faces that I put on were faces that someone else had written, or someone else had thought of, and that someone else had dressed, those faces were never Aunt Helen's, or Gilbert and Sullivan's, or anyone else's; those faces were *mine*, faces I hadn't known I had. All the evil, all the generosity, all the heartbreak of human life was in those faces which I made on that small stage, and once I had uncovered them, there they were always. What an amazement, how many different people one person could have inside her.

&

IF WE HAD rehearsal after swimming, it generally took about an hour, which left time for just one other activity before lunch, and after the intensity of Drama, I would move either to Arts and Crafts or to Woodworking, rather than the more emotionally draining Indian Lore or Whatsit. One emotionally draining activity was enough for any morning, and Indian Lore was something I approached with tremendous focus; Nature, which was the Whatsit, was more relaxed, but as it had many animals, it too required a fair degree of emotional interaction. So I would move, if possible, to Woodworking, which was something I always enjoyed, though I was certainly not a much better tool user than an athlete, and whenever I was working with tools, whether in the woodworking shop or somewhere else, I was always supremely conscious of my hands. They were mine, and if they were mine, I was in charge of them, and it was up to me to tell them what to do, and that blessed unselfconsciousness that surrounded me when I was in the water certainly did not surround me when I walked into the woodworking shop. But I loved the shop's environment anyway.

At one end of the shop, chisels were arrayed, each inserted, blade-down, in a board that had been drilled with holes for them; on the wall above the chisels the wooden mallets hung, some small, some large, each for different tasks. The files and rasps were also on pegboards, as were the hacksaws, the keyhole saws, and the ripsaws, but there was a special bench where Kuhrt Jr. kept the planers – the grooving planer, the jack plane, the scraper – and also sandpapers of all kinds in huge stacks at the back along the wall. There were also knives, and adzes, and small hatchets, too; in fact everything that a real carpenter might be in need of. Kuhrt Jr., Karl's brother, who was studying to be a surgeon, could probably be thanked for this amazing extravagance.

Kuhrt Jr. took after his father in more than just his name. He resembled him physically, although his face was broader. And he, too, was fairly reticent, which made me feel that the profession he had chosen was appropriate. While his father, reticent though he was, needed of necessity to speak to his athletes, Kuhrt Jr.. would rarely need to speak to his patients. They would be unconscious, after all, when he was most intimately involved with them; this was my own fancy, however, and no one else's. Though without question Kuhrt's brother Karl was the more popular of the two men – "popular" being a word that even boy campers used in those days – Kuhrt was well-respected, and was always listened to and obeyed, and I forgave him his reticence because he so clearly loved Wynakee. He could often be seen sitting by himself on a fence, or on a hill or a rock, just looking out over the world, with the sun on his face, and his fine hands idle, as if he were dreaming – dreaming, perhaps, just as I did, of staying at Wynakee forever.

This created, without question, a splendid atmosphere for woodworking, an atmosphere of silence and relaxed dedication to one's work, and for those children who were good with their hands, Kuhrt Jr. took any amount of trouble to show them how to saw, how to chisel, how to plane. Some of these children carved heads there in the woodworking shop, where Jo-John was also often at work, and some of them made beautiful maple salad bowls for their mothers, and even matching maple forks and spoons to serve from them. I myself found the hardwoods – the cherry and maple and beech – absolutely impossible to work with right from the start, so I got to work instead with pine, birch, and oak, which was considered rather a soft hardwood. I made things like letter openers, so thick that they couldn't conceivably have opened a letter in any place but Brobdingnag; spoons as big as my fist that would hold no more than a teaspoon, and a breadboard, tiny, and so soft that my mother thoroughly destroyed it just chopping parsley. But this tendency toward thick, soft artifacts really didn't embarrass me, though others were polishing their maple salad bowls with the finest grade of sandpaper, and waxing them when they were done, so that they absolutely shone, and could have been displayed in Dorset, on sale at Peltier's general store. There was a sign on the wall of the shop which read "He who works with his hands is a laborer. He who works with his hands and head is a craftsman. But he who works with his hands, and his head, and also his heart, is an artist," and while I aspired to at least reach the first level, it was clear to me from the start that anything more was forever beyond me.

It wasn't my projects, anyway, that made me love the wood-working shop; it wasn't even the trust that the Wienekes showed in giving us real tools. It was the wood itself, the blocks and boards stacked in the rafters, the logs piled in the corners, and the fine pieces that lay on the bench. I loved the sawdust floating through the air, catching the sunlight on its tiny, moving planes; I loved the long, sensuous curls of the fresh chiseled wood. I loved the sawdust and shavings on the floor, which was swept only when they got too deep. You could shuffle through this stuff as if through autumn leaves.

And hooray for this wood! all your senses would say. Smell this wood! See this wood! It was a kind of solid water, or a non-edible bread, and it had nourished other living things first when it was a tree, throwing shade, drawing moisture, or holding and weaving the wind. Next, it had nourished as log, either rotting and becoming forest, or carved into totem pole, or sent to the sawmill to be sliced into lumber. Now, it nourished still, as board, with its textures and its patterns; it nourished as wood chip, as sawdust, as wall or floor. Do with it what you wanted, and wood it would remain. There was no form in which it lost its spirit.

The Arts and Crafts room, on the other hand, held no such magic for me. It was a place of pragmatism, and to my mind, a good deal of silliness. Some mornings, silliness was what I wanted, though, and by silliness I meant a mind-set that regarded products as more important than the process that brought them into being. I enjoyed making things in the Arts and Crafts room, but I also always sensed their artifice, and if they came out successfully in the end, it was only because each project's most crucial characteristic was that it took absolutely no artistic talent. Granted, for those who had some instincts, there were sketch pads and pencils and chalk, and campers could take these outside and work with them as they wanted, but for the rest of us, the majority, the sketch pads and pencils were left on the shelves, and we were given tasks that had some chance of success. We made driftwood animals, for example, and geometric mobiles from straw; we made nut figures or ornaments, working with corncobs and pinecones. Native materials, which we ourselves gathered, were incorporated into many projects, and I am happy to say we never worked with raffia. But after we'd gathered the straw, or the nuts, or the pinecones, we had no instinctive ideas about what to do with them, and so there was guidance – too much guidance, in my opinion. I didn't *want* to paste beans, of no matter how many different colors, onto cardboard until they looked like a flower; I didn't *want* to make a doll out of a corncob and some corn leaves. I didn't want to make a pinecone figure, with a pinecone head, and bean eyes. I most especially didn't want to do cross-stitching.

No, my favorite activity in Arts and Crafts – besides mobiles, which were rather fun – and indeed the only project I ever did there that I actually got lost in, was the making of marbled paper, which was used, after it was dry, to cover boxes and notebooks and cups and jars and even pencils. To make marbled paper you needed a large basin, which would be filled almost to the brim with water, and you also needed thick sheets of paper that wouldn't easily dissolve. Most of all, you needed oil paints to float on the surface of the water, and a good big corner of the room to work in. We who were making marbled paper that morning would sit behind the basin filled with water, and the oil paints would be lined up on a nearby table, in bowls, with small ladles in each. Tiny ladles. Quite enchanting. When it was my turn to work, I would usually choose the red ladle to begin with, pouring a small amount of paint onto the water's surface. The oil was strangely excited atop water, and it would swirl and dance, like pictures of galaxies forming, so that I got excited, too, and sometimes added green after red, only to have the red and the green combine to make brown and brown only. Another day, after the red, I would sensibly add some orange, and this worked far better. I would set crosscurrents moving in the water until there were curves and whorls and patterns that rivaled, as I saw it, the creation of the universe.

Only when the paper, having been poised above the basin, was lowered upon the paint and water, though, could you really get an idea of what that creation might have looked like, as the marbling found its way onto the paper. The now wet and heavy paper would be lifted carefully, usually with some help from Grandma, and set on a long counter to one side of the room, where it would dry in a day or two and be ready for the next stage in the process, which was the cutting and then the gluing onto containers. I liked this stage, cutting and shaping, almost as much as I liked the other, watching the oil paints run wildly across the water – and it was the combination of the two things, the free form and the controlled receptacle, that gave marbled paper its real fascination. Over the years I gave my mother so many small boxes for holding pins and other detritus that she ceased to find any use for them, and stacked them in a row on a bookshelf, as if they were objets d'art, which to me they were. How I admired them! But I didn't keep a single one, since in the making of any objects, whether in the Woodworking shop, at Indian Lore, or in the Arts and Crafts room, the greatest pleasure always came from giving them away. Yes, it was always to my mother I gave them, but that was not really the point; the point was that however soft, thick, unartistic, or repetitive, these works of my own hands came to me as gifts, and gifts needed, by their nature, to be circulated.

Ten

IF I HAD NOT had play practice on that particular morning, and therefore had not already been beleaguered by my own feelings, I would go to neither Woodworking nor Arts and Crafts, however, but would choose either Indian Lore or the Whatsit. The Whatsit had few planned or programmed activities, and almost no projects or artifacts; it was looking and studying, and collecting, and hurting nothing. The Whatsit had rabbits and guinea pigs in cages, which we respectively fed and watched and fed and held; it had fish in aquariums, and snakes in glass boxes, and caterpillars in various cardboard containers. Microscopes and magnifying glasses were available so you could observe things closely, and children brought in pond scum and salamanders and tadpoles. When ferns were ready to spore, we might knock the spores out onto paper, and see the spore pattern for weeks, until time and wind erased it. In the Whatsit, spiders were allowed to build webs, and we could climb up on stools and watch them as they bundled up a fly, or mended a hole with their amazing spinnerets.

Sometimes there were field mice, which no one was allowed to touch, as we were given to understand that field mice were like baby rabbits, and that a single contact with a human hand would give them a heart attack. But if we wanted to we could touch the box turtle, which was one of my favorite creatures, and whose habits with food I found vastly amusing. A counselor would bring him his meal – usually a worm, I think – and put it down in the corner of his cage for him to feast on, but James, the turtle, was not like us children. He would not just dash over and seize it. No, his approach to the whole enterprise was a good deal more circuitous. First, he would stay very still, until the huge hand of the counselor, that terrible monster, had definitely returned to wherever it came from. Then he would raise his head, and, taking those lurching, mincing steps, he would approach the food very, very slowly. All the time, he kept raising his head, up and up and up and up, on that extensible neck that seemed to have no limits, and when he was inches away from the worm, his head was finally fully aloft, and he cocked it sideways, and looked down the side of his face at it. He stood thus for what seemed to me like minutes, staring at the food with interest, and looking utterly comical, a minute monster from the deep, but a very cautious one indeed, one who was not about to take any chances. Finally, he was satisfied that all was as it should be. Then he would release his neck and strike, pinching the worm between his jaws and raising his head again, looking surprised. Eventually, he began to eat, with a thoughtful, cowlike expression. He did this every day, and then retracted and went to sleep.

Sometimes at Camp Wynakee wild animals might be orphaned, and the babies brought first to the Whatsit. We had a fawn one year, and another year a woodchuck, both of which were raised to be released again into the woods they had come from, when fall came. Of course we all adored the fawn, which had a special pen constructed for it, and we would sit and watch it, doing little else all morning. Indeed, the nice thing about the Whatsit was that you didn't have to do anything while you were there. You could just take an animal out into the sun and oversee it while it breathed. We had one guinea pig with a splotchy white face, and shaped a bit like a pear, who, unlike most guinea pigs, did not always lie down and curl in his feet. Even when he had settled in, he would stand on his forefeet as a dog might, those tiny white feet spread as if to support great weight. This was everyone's favorite guinea pig, since he had a real personality, his ears sticking out to the side, his eyes nervous but friendly. I'm afraid that in his case, there may eventually have been death from overpetting, which was the one real danger most Wynakee animals ever faced.

My own favorite animals at Wynakee were the hound dog and her puppies, but I have to say that the spiders came a close second; I liked to watch the rabbits, but I never felt that I could trust them, and I was always, actually, quite scared of them. We had three kinds of rabbits at Wynakee, standard chinchilla, Dutch blues, and angoras, and though they were all very different in appearance, they were not different in their behaviors; to me it was clear that all rabbits from the smallest to the largest disliked people.

What particularly fascinated me about rabbits was the way they jumped, and also their eyes and teeth, though not necessarily in that order – because although their lidless eyes were striking, their teeth were really their most amazing feature, with that split in the middle of the upper lip. The chisellike front teeth were rather like the teeth of beavers, but rabbits also had an *extra pair* of small teeth behind the large and prominent front ones, yet with all those teeth – and all those incisors – they were said to eat nothing but the leaves of plants, and I have to admit that with all the time I spent watching them, I never saw them eat anything else. They were given carrots, and loved them. They were given lettuce and they loved that. But they were never given a worm, as was James, and I always wondered what they would do with it if they were offered a small portion of meat. I personally thought that they would happily devour it. To me, the rabbit came to symbolize not meekness, not fear, but cleverness, cleverness in hiding some of their deepest, darkest feelings, and since this was not possible for me, except when I was on stage, I found the rabbits foreign, enviable and frightening.

As I say, there seemed no question that they simply didn't like human beings – the way they just lay there all the time and stared at you! – and they seemed to feel also that they were prisoners, unlike other animals, who didn't seem to mind their cages. Since their eyes were set so far back, they could only look at you with one eye at a time, and the effect was pretty disconcerting, particularly as they simultaneously wiggled their noses, with their acute sense of smell, and seemed to find your smell pretty disgusting. And one eye was, after all, plenty to see right through to your black heart.

Spiders, on the other hand, were wonderful, deeply understandable and therefore easy to love. My favorite habit of theirs was the habit of spinning a dragline, not just occasionally, but whenever they moved from one part of the Whatsit to another, since if a spider was crawling up the wall, and I climbed up on a stool to watch it, I would find that it was prepared for this eventuality. Just in case, it had been spinning a dragline, and – just like a climber with chocks and pitons – attached the line at regular intervals to the wall as it climbed, so that when my face was suddenly beside it, and maybe my fingers were getting too close, it would have its own safety line all ready to use to escape me. But unlike a human climber, whose rope was of a certain fixed length, the spider could spin more line for herself as it was needed. In fact, wherever she was, she already had plenty of rope, and could always get right to the ground in a heartbeat.

Then, too, when spiders caught prey, they wouldn't just

sit down and eat it, the way other animals did – even the turtle, really – but would prepare their food for eating, very much in the manner of humans, who are also fastidious about food. The spiders would swathe a fly in bands of silk before they settled down to suck out its fluids, and while the sucking hardly reflected well upon their human counterparts, the swathing did seem reminiscent, for example, of the waxed paper one wrapped around one's sandwich, or the way one might split and lick an Oreo cookie. Be Prepared – by way of the silk dragline. Wrap Your Food Before You Eat It. And, the third rule we shared with spiders, Build A Nice Place To Live In. To watch a spider building its web was to watch a consummate artist, far beyond the level of laborer or craftsman. I never actually saw the whole process, but I knew that the web started with a foundation line, or with a spider climbing to a high place that she thought might be a bug flyway, and then secreting a light silken line, which would hang beneath her in the air until a light breeze picked it up and blew the end across to a twig or leaf or board. The end would become entangled, and then the spider would climb across it, adding more silk to the line as she traveled. From this small beginning, the whole web would be spun, and it would mix the sticky and the smooth, the warp and the weft, just like any weaving.

Eleven

WHILE I loved the Whatsit for its animals, and the woodworking shop for its wood, my feelings toward Indian Lore were complex beyond easy description. To me, going to work at Indian Lore was both wonderful and very sad, and there were some days when I simply didn't feel up to it. Not just in the Indian Lore cabin, but in the entire Indian Lore program – which included the carving of the totem poles, the building of wickiups, Council Fire with its stories and Indian games – I felt more than anywhere else at camp a sense that summer was fleeting, and that time was moving, always moving, around me. This was, I imagine looking back at it, because I was well aware that the Indians had lived out of doors not just in the summer, but all the time, in every season, and they had known things I myself could never know, things that not even Jo-John could teach me. They had known how to hunt, tan hides, grow corn, start a fire with a flint, and make arrows, but most of all, they had known where they belonged, not just here (where now there was Wynakee), but across the continent and, in a large sense, across the universe. And it was in this fact, and in the Indian Lore program which tried to evoke it, that Wynakee's deepest mood was set for me from the beginning – a mood that wove through Wynakee's days like flowers in the meadow grass, or like the colored stones beneath the river. Indian Lore was not, as it was at some camps, set aside just for special times – though there were times when it was emphasized more strongly – and it was not, as at some camps, confined to a single place, though of course the Council Circle in the woods was the heart of it. No, it existed everywhere, and it was imbued in everything, like an odor of woodsmoke that had been absorbed forever; if you followed your nose, you would find it, and for me "it" became an aspiration, the aspiration to actually be an Indian.

I suppose not all campers felt this way, but from the moment I first saw the log for the totem pole which lay every summer next to the woodworking shop in the courtyard, and learned that the whole camp would carve it, until it became that summer's gift and emblem, I was a fanatic about Indian Lore, feeling that here, in the totem pole, the totem, was the perfect symbol of Wynakee's unspoken ethic. We would all do our own part, but the totem pole, in the end, would be one thing, and it would stay with the camp forever; when finished it was to stand behind the members of the Wayaka Huya, the Indian Honor Society, made up of those campers who were considered among the best of us. Moreover, I could not help feeling that the Indians – from what I then knew of them – had been better than white people in many ways that mattered, and that it was a pity that hard as I might try, I would always suffer from the sheer handicap of having been born blond, blue-eyed, and even freckled. It was bad enough that I wasn't an Indian, but that I didn't even look like an Indian! I would have forsaken my own heritage in a second if I could have become even a half-breed, and of course, as in most such matters I had little identification with the female half of the equation, and wanted to be a brave, preferably the son of a famous chieftain. This was not a frivolous wish, in the sense that it was superficial or passing – it was a genuine ambition, and therefore, in a real sense, tragic – and while I have relinquished the ambition since, I never did at Wynakee, where I had my own personal Indian to emulate and study.

At least, I believed Jo-John was an Indian. I think now that maybe he was not – not biologically – though I have no way of verifying the truth of the matter. In appearance, he was dark and lean, with the kind of muscular arms in which the biceps are no more important than the shoulders. He had long, beautiful hands, which he could hold flat upon a file to steady it while the tips of his fingers rode just above, in the air, like balances. The trunk of his body was smaller even than Uncle Kuhrt's; compared with Karl, or even Kuhrt Jr., Jo-John was almost adolescent in his general construction. If you saw him from the back you might notice most the bagginess of his pants – the way his buttocks couldn't quite fill them – and he had dark hair, almost black, that he wore very, very short. His complexion was dark, and his eyes were dark, and he rarely smiled.

I would say that Jo-John *never* smiled, if I could believe that to be the case – everyone must smile sometimes, or so I imagine – but some people's faces are so expressive that everything they feel passes across their countenances like wind rippling water. To me, it seemed that Jo- John's was just the opposite, and that his face might have been one of his own carvings, crafted like an Indian mask, finished and done with. He apparently liked the result, and saw no need to change it, so that if he looked up from a project he was at work on, his eyebrows might rise, very slightly, but as he looked back down again they would sink, and you would wonder if you had just imagined it. If he was working on the totem pole, and had come to a difficult cut, you never could have told it from watching his face, not even intently. His tongue didn't protrude, his teeth didn't clench, and his eyes didn't narrow At most, his lips might part, slightly.

And as Jo-John's eyes were more than dark, they were black, although one assumes they must have had pupils, the pupils were generally lost somewhere in the iris, so that you got the strong impression of an undifferentiated eye, and that eye was very clear and far-seeing; Jo- John brought a high seriousness to everything he touched, which was most of what went on within Camp Wynakee. Still, when Jo-John had feelings, they were expressed most openly in his eyes, and in the lids, and in the tiny muscles around them; if he was angry, it was his eyes which kindled, if he was happy, his eyes which smiled, and if he was sad, his eyes which welled with sorrow. But Jo-John's heart was not really in expression, nor in its sibling, demonstration; it was in creation, and all his energy went into one thing. He gathered that energy and used it like a blowtorch, an artist with wood, metal, and leather, feathers and quills, beads and bones. He was a most unusual counselor, since he didn't act upon children, and he hardly interacted with them, either. He acted upon things, and the children could be there. Or then again, they could not. He was universally admired.

It wasn't that Jo-John didn't teach – he did, mostly by example – and it wasn't that he didn't talk – he did, in short sentences – it was that his love was of transformation, and not the transformation of human beings, but the transformation of the physical universe. Revealing the head inside a block of wood, revealing the totem at the top of a tree trunk, revealing the war bonnet that lay beneath a pile of leather and feathers, this was what he was meant to do – and he wasn't a purist about tradition, though he was a purist about both methodology and artifact. He mixed his own paints when he needed them, he gathered his own birch bark for the wickiups, and he studied many books, which he kept in the Indian Lore cabin; always he insisted upon authentic patterns and designs, always on equally authentic procedures.

For example, one summer when a snapping turtle was discovered in the pond before camp started, and it was removed and killed, Jo-John asked if he could have it for a rattle, and for weeks after we arrived that season, this dead snapping turtle lay by the Indian Lore cabin, its insides rotting in the sun because, according to Jo-John, the turtle could not be cut open. The insides, once they were rotted, could be scraped out through the mouth, and water could be poured down the amazingly long neck to hasten and aid the process, but only after weeks of natural putrefaction could this be done, and that putrefaction took place in the full smell of everyone who went anywhere near it. Given Aunt Helen's belief that soap bars transmitted germs, I find this quite amazing, and I may be lengthening the rotting time as I remember it, but there is no doubt that at least for some days, we who were going to Indian Lore to make our projects, skirted a rank, rotting snapping turtle corpse. Eventually that summer the snapping turtle was cleaned, but it took another year before it was dry enough for Jo-John's liking, and it was only the following summer that this rattle of Jo-John's was finished, and pebbles introduced to the turtle's shell through its neck and mouth.

After that, it was, as it turned out, one of Wynakee's most important ceremonial tools – created, as it had been, out of joint suffering – and when Jo-John shook it at our Council Fire, those of us who had been with it from the beginning felt that we understood what this fierce rattle symbolized. In his beautiful, feathered, war bonnet, with feathered bands upon his ankles, Jo-John would crouch and leap and the spirit of the snapping turtle was with him as he leapt, giving him its strength.

I guess that Jo-John was probably the first man I ever loved, and I think that love is the proper word for it; I did not have a crush on him, as I did (as we all did) on Karl Wieneke. I was not particularly taken with his body. It was his spirit I was drawn to; he seemed to me unique, a soul without whom the world itself would have been impoverished. When he told an Indian legend, the fires burning beside him, the night enfolding the circle of the Council, he stretched his arms up skywards, embracing the living circle, and all the other circles which lay beyond it. Like a walker from another time, he had the longer vision, and his respect for the natural universe was contagious; there are people, few and far between, who are in touch, who have never been cut off, and Jo-John's art was, I think now, just an expression of his inner completeness. Jo-John made us all humble, aware of our own limitations, and yet he was one of the least arrogant people who has ever lived. His body, he seemed to feel, was a vessel for the greater spirit, and from my first summer at Wynakee, my largest hope was to be considered worthy of *anything* by Jo-John.

The rumor was that Jo-John was part Seneca, and as a result I wanted to be a Seneca, though I would have settled for being a Mohawk, an Oneida, an Onandagua, a Cayuga or a Tuscarora; the Iroquois had originally lived all over New York State, with many of them on the Hudson River, just two hours west of us. There, as elsewhere, they had been, as I discovered later, both very political and very bloodthirsty, but this was not discussed at Wynakee, and I knew nothing about it; at Wynakee, the best of Indian culture had been selected from the various Indian traditions.

The eclectic quality of our program was nowhere so clearly demonstrated as in and around the Indian Council Ring itself. This Ring lay about a half mile down the valley from the central compound, in the opposite direction from the Mohawk and Mettawee cabins. Here the woods were still wild, having never been cleared or harvested, and here there were paths that had been made by Wynakee campers, and marked with white stones that these same campers, myself among them, had drawn from the waters of the nearby Mettawee. The paths, several paths, led most crucially to the Council Ring, a great circle of sawdust strewn on the forest's floor, and behind which were set the totem poles, and also the split-log benches on which the Wayaka Huya sat during Council Fires. The paths led also, however, to the teepees, and to the wickiups, and also to the Iroquois longhouses – and that's what I mean by eclectic, because in this one or two acres, we had Indian cultures that had spanned the continent.

When the Iroquois were building them, longhouses were commonly set in the open, forming small villages in the middle of great fields, and they were fifty feet or so long, so I suppose that authenticity had in this case given way to what was possible at Wynakee. Our longhouses, in the woods, were perhaps twenty feet long by ten feet wide, and not all that high; they were built of wooden poles which had a certain degree of flexibility to them, and which were lashed together with rope and then covered with bark. They were rectangular, with gable roofs – more poles lashed and rigged like trusses – and they had only one entrance, curtained by canvas rather than bearskin robes. When you were inside one you found it quite dark, and if a fire was lit, very smoky. But there was something quite charming about the way the sunlight filtered down through the trees, and then through the interstices in the bark, and on Cabin Nights, occasionally the Owls would decide as a group that what we wanted to do was to sleep out in a longhouse. One summer when I was helping to replace some of the bark – the longhouses were semipermanent structures – one of my Owl friends, a rather scholarly girl named Karin, told me something she had learned in school about Iroquois divorce. I don't know if this is true, but according to Karin, when an Iroquois woman no longer wanted to be married, all she had to do to get rid of her husband was to throw his moccasins out the door into the night. After that, I broadened my ideas. While I still would have preferred, all things considered, to be an Indian brave, well, perhaps being an Indian woman would have been all right too. It sounded as if the balance of power between the sexes had not been all that bad. I wondered if it could be *any* pair of moccasins.

But on a typical Wynakee morning "going to Indian Lore" meant going to the Indian Lore cabin, and here, when you came right down to it, much of the activity was beadwork, since this was a task even the most inept or unmotivated could grasp. There were various sizes of looms available, whole tubs of multicolored beads, and lots of heavenly-smelling beeswax; to make either an armband or a headband, you would first string your loom with thread and then tighten the threads with two lug nuts at the ends. Next, you would take that sweet beeswax, and rub and rub until the threads were coated. Then you would try to work out some kind of design in advance. Some campers opted for eagles, and some of them did bears, and some did flowers, or stars, or even fish swimming, but as my criterion for art was *not too representational*, I always chose to do geometric designs.

We didn't just do beadwork in the Indian Lore cabin,

however; we worked with a number of natural materials as well, and some were the very same materials that might be found in the Arts and Crafts room, not too far away. But while the Arts and Crafts program turned these materials into something unnatural and useless – who wanted a woman made of straw and twigs? – the Indian Lore program turned them into things that could be worn or drummed or carried, and this made a tremendous difference to us all. Then, too, this was "Lore" – not Arts and Crafts, a collection of oddments, but a body of knowledge, seamless, broad, and deep, and if it was hard at every moment to see just how what you were working on was "lore," well, the word was there to remind you. Beyond that, in the Indian Lore cabin, many of our materials were animal, and not, as in Arts and Crafts, solely derived from plants; here we had fur, and hair, and porcupine quills, leather and turtles' shells, and feathers, and we even had skulls and bones.

So although, on a given morning, I might be working as usual on my loom, carefully stringing beads and then fitting them across my headband, I was always very aware that there were other people around me, doing things that were far more important. Jo-John himself would be over in one corner, working on a new war bonnet or a leather-fringed jacket; there was a Crow making a gourd rattle, a Netop working on a bone necklace; a Dog Soldier working on a fringed leather loincloth. A new member of the Wayaka Huya was working on her Wayaka Huya costume, an entire dress, with two armbands and a feather anklet, and I watched her with reverence, for what she was now doing was what I wanted someday to do, above all else. Only the Wayaka Huya could go to Sunday Council Fires dressed like Indians from head to toe. Only the Wayaka Huya could sit on those split-log benches, facing the camp, and right next to Jo-John. But most important, really, only the Wayaka Huya, chosen as they had been to receive such a special honor, could go through the secret initiation rites, and afterwards, serve as acolytes to Jo-John, and to the Indian gods. So for me, an hour at Indian Lore was always rather intense. I *might* be Wayaka Huya someday.

But also, I might not, when you came to think of it.

Twelve

AT 12:00 EVERY day, our morning was at an end, and we had half an hour of free time before lunch. Some campers returned to their cabins then, but most of us hung around the courtyard, talking to people we hadn't seen all morning. If we were blessed with fine weather, we leaned our backs against a building and stretched our bare legs out into the sun, or we walked up past The Barn and lay in the grass looking at the sky, not getting *too* far from the food smells now wafting from the kitchen door. We might play jacks on the flat piece of concrete which had been poured in front of the shop, or mumblety-peg on the grass road between the barn and The Barn. I don't know why I was good at mumblety-peg, but I was, and I found it exciting to spin my Barlow and then see it land, point down – *thwuck*! – in the ground. The Vermont day was just reaching its height, and it was wonderfully warm but not hot, with the air perfumed with grass smells and flower smells and leaf smells, mostly, and there might be a small gusty breeze which would nudge the leaves of the maples so that they shook with pleasure at the glorious noontime.

If it was raining instead of fine, huddled in our plastic ponchos, we would run at 12:00 right into The Barn, and there, smelling of wet hair and wet clothes and wet leather, cram – all sixty of us – into the lobby, part of which was officially called the "Rec Hall." This Rec Hall was really only a corner of The Barn with some chairs in it, and also board games and several packs of cards; these were used by only a few of the campers, some of whom actually had such a fondness for cards or chess that they would play them even on sunny days. To the rest of us, however, the Rec Hall was just a place to sit, steaming, on rainy days, waiting for lunch, and since we couldn't smell the good food smells as we would have had we been outside, our mood there tended to be less peaceful and more ravenous. Indeed, half an hour in the sun, lying against a building or playing mumblety-peg, was measured on a different clock entirely from half an hour waiting in The Barn; on rainy days, by the time the gong rang, we were all deeply impatient, even a little irritable, with the pangs of growing hunger.

The noon meal at Wynakee was called Dinner, and Dinner indeed it was. The main meal of the day, it was the one that was most furiously consumed and also, by a logical extension, the one that left us most completely exhausted, and in genuine need of the Rest Hour scheduled to follow it. In fact, long before Dinner was over, when we had gulped our way through the first two-thirds of it and were now just filling in the stomach corners, a feeling of satiety began to overtake all of us, and the electrifying quality that had endured through breakfast was quite gone. The day was now almost half over, and certain things had been made plain.

Not only was it certain, as it had been for hours, that this was *not* Klondike Day and would not be, it was also certain, as it had not really yet been at breakfast, that the rain would last all afternoon. Also, in Arts and Crafts, you had finished your straw mobile, and so that was one thing done, though since it was damp the straw was damp, and therefore, hanging in the breezeway or not, it had a limper appearance than you had intended. Tonight, there would probably be an indoor activity, so you could give up your hopes of Capture the Flag, and all this made Dinner, after the first frenzy of consumption, a meal that was rather calm. Or, if it was sunny, and indeed quite perfect, certain things had also been made plain. There was absolutely no question, for example, that, unfortunately, this afternoon's physical activity would be volleyball. Again, you had finished your mobile, though this time it looked jaunty, since the straw was dry and the breeze was brisk, and after lunch you might wander by, perhaps with a friend from Owl's Head, and just casually point it out with a careless hand. And since it was so sunny, and it had been two whole weeks, there was a good chance that tonight *would* be Capture the Flag. But in either case, the low harmonic of mystery that had ruled the substratum of sound at breakfast was gone at Dinner, replaced with simple noise.

Announcements were again made after the meal was finished, and after the announcements we were all released, and for a half hour the post office and store were open, Grandma presiding, so some of us would walk over to pay a visit there every day. Before Grandma arrived, I would peer through the window, cupping my hands around my eyes to cut the glare, and trying my best to see whether or not there was a white slash across the brown box that was marked with my last name. Rarely could I do so, because of the angle of the door, and I would have to wait for Grandma's often slow arrival, and her equally slow unlocking of the door, which would involve locating the key in a pocket of her apron. If there was a letter, I took it unopened to my bunk at Owl's Head, perhaps with some stationery which I had taken the opportunity to purchase; I and some friends would walk as slowly as possible to the bridge and then dawdle up with amazing foot-dragging through the meadow.

Rest Hour was really a whole hour, and you could read or write during this sixty minutes – thus I saved reading my letters until the hour had truly begun – but talking was absolutely forbidden, and many campers, even the older ones, actually went to sleep stretched out on their wool blankets and feather pillows. I used to go to sleep quite regularly as a Wren, but as an Owl I felt that I really shouldn't, and by resisting sleep, I would get sleepier and sleepier until at the very last instant I would actually lose consciousness. Then, of course, the bell would ring, and I would wake up from those few minutes of sleep feeling genuinely grumpy at being awakened so soon. This was supposed to be Rest Hour! What were they trying to do to us?! Why, for heaven's sake, couldn't they let us get some *rest*!?

So in the event, Rest Hour, which beforehand always loomed so large, was always shorter than any of us had expected, and when the great bell rang at 2:30, whether I'd been asleep or not, it was an effort to get going. There was something very comfortable about Owl's Head, and it occurred to me that it would be rather pleasant if I could just spend the whole afternoon there, idling; this was due to the fact that almost every single day of camp, what came after Rest Hour was Physical Activity. And while you were often allowed to choose your own activity, that was only within the limits of what was available. Some days, unfortunately, there wasn't much choice. Whatever you did, it was bound to have a ball in it.

God, how they made me nervous, those games like volleyball and baseball, and even lawn tennis and croquet; if a ball was involved in it anywhere, then a game, to me, was hell. I hated balls, all balls, with a mighty passion. There was a reason for this hatred, which was that wherever I wanted a ball to go, and whatever level of gentle or violent persuasion I might apply to it, the ball always defiantly managed to go elsewhere and disappear. It might disappear into the woods, or into the river, or the meadow grass, or, more usually, into the hands of someone bigger than myself; this person would then proceed to carry it somewhere far off, without any protest from the now acquiescent object. That in itself was all right – the disappearance of the ball – but its reappearance could unfortunately always be counted on, and it would always reappear right at my feet, just as I was finally starting to relax again. Whether the ball was large and squishy, small and hard, I regarded it, after all this, as a loathsome artifact, and wondered why it had ever been invented, and what indeed, anyone could see in it – so round, so slippery, so bouncy, and so intractable.

The only good thing that could possibly be said for the ball sports at Camp Wynakee was that we played on teams of mixed age and sex, and therefore I felt I had an excuse for being a black hole on the playing field. At school, back in New York, we played on teams composed of people who were the same age and the same sex as ourselves, and therefore there was no clear reason why I could not or should not manage to be as good at a ball sport as everyone else. In New York I was a klutz; but at Wynakee I was still a little girl, and had the potential someday to become something better, so while I hated balls, I didn't hate my fellow players, but felt instead a distinct fondness for them. I felt this particularly for the big boys, since it was not only they who accomplished most of what got accomplished on the field, but they, too, who regarded the small girls like me with the greatest kindness. When I got a hit in volleyball, and it actually went over the net – an occurrence as rare as a harvest moon – I could count on a boy or two to pound me, and maybe even shout, "Good going, Arthur!," and until I went to sleep that night I would remain in a glow. So although my feeling toward the ball was always the same, ball sports weren't a total loss. And I had a marginal talent for baseball. In baseball, as long as I held the bat low, and bunted very cautiously, I actually had moments of something like elation as I raced toward the haven of first base, thinking always that yes, I would *get* there! before the ball disappeared into a mighty mitt.

&

LUCKILY, HOWEVER, there were two Physical Activities at Wynakee that did not involve, in any way, shape, or form, balls, and these were riflery and archery, where concentration and discipline mattered, and agility and quick reflexes were not so important. If I had the choice, I went to riflery, which was easier than archery, and anyway, guns I intuitively understood. Some girls were scared of them, or pretended to be, and would screw up their faces when riflery was mentioned. But we didn't much care for those girls, and were glad to leave them behind. Then, with Uncle Kuhrt, we shooters would go to the equipment room to pick up our rifles and our boxes of bullets and the targets, and then together we would carry all this down across the bridge and into the meadow which lay between the camp and the Indian Council Ring.

Basically, this spot had been chosen as the range because there was an excellent hill there to act as a bullet stop; bales of straw were stored under tarps, and extra tarps stored there as well, for us to spread out on the grass and lie, kneel, or stand on while we shot. When we first got to the rifle range, we all laid down our targets and guns and helped to establish the range, and then, depending on how many of us there were, we might all either get into place immediately, or be divided, by Uncle Kuhrt, into two shifts.

Being on the second shift had its pleasures. We would sit behind the first shift, now in place, and as it was a sunny day today, by definition, we would close our eyes and relax in the sunshine, with the marvelous sound of the bullets pinging their way through the air – acting, in their way, as secondary soporifics. But there was no fear or dread of the moment when Uncle

Kuhrt called, "Next shift!" and the campers who had been shooting took the bolts right out of their guns, and then left the bolts by the rifles, which were pointing toward the targets, and away from us who were now walking toward them.

My favorite position was prone, though sitting was also all right; standing, at my age, tended to be very wearying, since a target rifle is heavy, being designed for the utmost possible accuracy, unlike a hunting rifle, which is always a compromise. So even lying prone, the gun barrel propped on my forearms, which in turn were propped on my elbows, and with the help of a leather support strap, I could only shoot for about fifteen minutes before my arms started to tremble, and I had to move back to watching and listening while my arms recovered. Otherwise, my shots would have started to go completely wild, and Uncle Kuhrt would have stepped in and lifted the rifle away from me, setting it down so that I could remove the bolt; later I would recover and go back for another round, probably sitting, with one knee flat, the other knee vertical.

Whether prone, or sitting, or standing, though, the pleasure in shooting was always the same; the way the whole world just faded all around you, and what was left was merely a sight, and beyond it a black circle on a target; you yourself were just an instrument for uniting them. You would let your body relax, and you would close one eye, but not tightly, and you would allow the gun in your arms to wander, knowing that at a certain moment it would suddenly be *there*, the place from which to fire it, and that when it arrived there, fire it you would. There was no rush to the process, though, and as you lifted the single bullet, placed it into the barrel, and then snicked the bolt on it, you knew that *you* were in control this time, not some slippery ball that would not cooperate. There was a Cheshire cat feeling of complete satisfaction.

I loved archery, too, though it was far harder than riflery; bullets were just bullets, each one identical, but arrows had individual personalities, and some had dull points, and many had feathers that had been torn or nicked. Because they were made of wood, there was a living quality to their actions; every time you drew a bow you were aware of the arrow's wood spirit; I myself was often surprised both by the erratic progress of my arrows and by the sharp pain of the bowstring as it twanged upon my cheek.

Unlike rifles, bows were light – a twenty-five-pound bow (which took twenty-five pounds of pressure to draw) weighed about eight ounces – and in archery you always stood with your legs spread well apart and the quiver of arrows hanging across your back. When you got into place about fifty feet from the target, you would first fling the quiver into place, and then string your bow, bending it by bracing the bottom against your right instep, then pushing down with all your might upon the top. The string was already attached to the bottom, but now had to be slipped over the top, where there was a neat girdle cut out of the wood to hold it, and when you had managed this and released the pressure the string would hold the bow taut. What a pleasure, the way this always happened.

After the bow was strung, it was time to put on the finger guard, which folded sweetly and curiously over the hand; in a way, the finger guard was like a miniature triple quiver, with my fingers the arrows that this quiver had been made for. Once my fingers were inserted into the leather guard, and the palm guard covered my palm, I always felt just a little different about my capacities; the strange glove made me aware of my hand, and what a miraculous thing it was. It made me feel jaunty and confident I could hit any bull's-eye.

I rarely did, however, because the wind was blowing suddenly, as I reached back over my shoulder and extracted the first arrow, then fit it onto the bowstring, feeling the feathers in front of my fingers, and drawing them back so that they rested just beside my jawbone; I felt the wind whispering around me as I studied the point of the arrow to make sure that it was perfectly straight, perfectly situated. And the feeling in my chest as it was opened to the whole world, the bow, the string, and the arrow forcing my shoulders far back. It was wonderful. Deep breaths. Deep concentration. Now, the release of the arrow, which rode the wind, and landed in the embankment ten feet from the target, point down, tail feathers quivering. Another arrow, another draw, another deep concentration, and this time the arrow would hit the target; another miss, when I slammed my cheek with the bowstring; but now, and this was the wonder and joy of archery, I could sense even as I drew that *this* was the arrow, and I would watch as it warbled its way toward the center of the target. When this happened, then at least for another arrow, which I would draw from my quiver with special self-consciousness, it would be easy to fantasize about my career as an archer in the merry woods of England. Ah, yes, before I'd become a mere girl, with short legs, and for heaven's sake, freckles, I'd been with Robin Hood. What a pity I'd forgotten everything I'd learned from him.

&

PHYSICAL ACTIVITY, of whatever kind, was from 2:30 to 3:45, and it was always followed by free swimming, which I always went to; the day was now at its warmest, and I was thoroughly heated even from archery and riflery, so I would go back with the others to my cabin to change into my swimsuit, which was hanging, dry now, on the clothesline behind Owl's Head. Carelessly leaving my clothes in a pile on the floor by my bunk, I would run down the road to the pond barefoot, towel flapping in the wind behind me. My haste to get to swimming generally resulted in an awkward situation, as I was invariably the first swimmer to arrive, and I would have to wait by the pond's edge for someone to show up who could be my "buddy" in the free swim to come. I would stand by the Buddy Board, a large piece of shellacked plywood, which contained upper arm-sized rubber rings in sets of two, and pick out my favorite set, which hung under the number 7 and had little metal 7 tags to match.

But that didn't get me very far. No, it was no problem to lift down the rings. Far more of a problem was finding a buddy. Since I didn't care who I got in the way of a partner, I had a well-deserved reputation for being indiscriminate. For many Wynakee campers, the issue of who you buddied with was finally more important than the issue of whether you went swimming; buddying, for these children, was the biggest social event of the day. For me, things were far otherwise. I would have buddied with Quasimodo if there had been a reasonable likelihood that this would have given me ten extra minutes of swimming, but sometimes I had to wait through an agonizing series of arrivals, some of them "waiting for their buddy," some of them "not having decided yet whether to swim." It was at this time, more than any other, that I found my own species a mystery, and alternated between philosophical speculation and choleric despair, until at last someone showed up who agreed to take the other 7 ring, and I could plunge with joy into the cold dark pond.

I always started with a cannonball, right off the edge of the platform, and then I clambered up the ladder immediately to do a second one and a third; by the third, I was thoroughly warmed, by the climbing as much as by the cannonballs, and now I could stay in the water for an entire hour. This prospect was total bliss, and although every fifteen minutes Karl would blow his whistle and say, "Buddy up!," at which we were all required to locate our buddies, clasp hands, and raise them out of the water, this didn't seriously interrupt my pleasure. In fact, whenever the call "Buddy up!" went out, I had generally lost my buddy about as completely as one could – perhaps another reason why I was not a popular buddy – and it took me a minute's frantic search to locate the other half of my ring unit, who might well be on the other side of the pond. With enormous splashing and frenzy, I made my way over to him or her, along with the other buddies who were doing the same sort of thing, and the rest of the camp waited impatiently, treading water, their hands clasped righteously in the air. Almost the instant my buddy and I had finally been reunited, Karl, who had been counting pairs all along, blew his whistle, and we released our hands and swam off, until the next fifteen-minute call, when we were again separated by a pond's length, and the whole process had to be repeated.

It seems incredible, with a system so well regulated, that there were occasions, and not all that rare, when swimmers actually misplaced their buddies for good. Swimmers would often leave without informing their other half, and even walk away still wearing their rubber rings, and when the whistle blew, someone was really missing, and no amount of splashing around could find him. At that point, Karl would insist that everyone get out of the water, presumably so that he could check the pond for bodies, even though someone would say, "I *think* I saw him leave," or "Didn't she have to go up to the stables?" or "I know he said he was going to stop early." Standing in the wind, often with my teeth chattering, my lips blue, and my fingers wrinkled, I still yearned to get back into the pond, and would contribute my bit to the fact search, crossing my arms on my chest and chattering my teeth harder to feel the interesting vibration in my jaw.

Thirteen

AT LAST though, Karl shrugged his shoulders and let everyone back into the pond, except for the unfortunate buddy of the missing person; *he* was sent off to locate his erstwhile friend, and to drag him back to the pond to prove that he was among the living. After the hour was quite up, and most of the swimmers had departed, we few who were left would be called out of the water, and even then, though we had all changed buddies at least once, if not twice, it seemed to us that we were being forced to emerge too soon. But being the last one out of the pond did have one downside, which was that it gave me little time to prepare for the next event of the day; by the time I got back to the cabin, most of the other Owls were already changed, and quite warm and dry and lying on their bunks. And I was in a rush, because quite soon now, at 5:30, the flag was going to be lowered, and we would have Personal Inspection and Lost and Found, and given the time, there was no way that I could take a nice hot bath. I would have to run for the flagpole still blue from the pond.

For some campers, the double event of Personal Inspection and Lost and Found stood in relation to their lives as Physical Activity did to mine. It was the low point of their day, and these campers straggled to the flagpole, late every single day. At 5:30, the bell was rung, and we all gathered in a circle around the flag, which was lowered again by some specially honored campers, and after they had folded it into a triangle and presented it to Aunt Helen for safekeeping, it was time for Uncle Kuhrt to make his rounds. We held our hands out in front of us, and then turned them over once, as Uncle Kuhrt passed, so that he could scrutinize both our palms and our fingernails. He would also examine the face, the neck and the ears, and the knees if they were plainly visible. He was never fierce with the girls, but with the boys – particularly the poor Crows – he was sometimes merciless, actually yanking a dirty ear or arm. I myself never had to worry, because while I took no time with grooming, my hour in the pond had pretty much scoured me clean, and this was pleasant. The real purpose of Physical Inspection was supposedly to spot a rash or infection the very day that it appeared, but Uncle Kuhrt, it seemed to me, sometimes forgot this basic fact, and got quite exercised about dirt behind the ears.

After Physical Inspection was over, and the regular culprits had been discovered and exposed, it was time for Lost and Found, which could be an awkward routine, even for those who weren't implicated, but who had to stand by and watch while items were displayed which were sometimes intensely personal. One of Uncle Kuhrt's pet peeves was children who didn't keep track of their clothing, but simply left it lying around wherever it fell, and just as people regularly lost their buddies, they also regularly lost the equally improbable – their underwear. Which, invariably, Uncle Kuhrt came upon.

Other things, too, were regularly lost – towels, shoes and socks, raincoats, my hateful cap – but underwear cropped up with amazing frequency, and often went missing, week after week, from the same bewildered children, who had to come forward abashedly to make their claim. None of us liked to probe this coincidence too deeply – and indeed, it remains a mystery to this day – but for the underwear losers Lost and Found was agony, and for the rest of us merely painful, as Uncle Kuhrt would hold up the lost items one by one, reading the names he found on their name tags. For some reason, the little boys were again the usual culprits, and as a result, they won the pity of all and sundry. I presume this sex-linked tendency was a cultural phenomenon, but even to this day, it seems to me more like a secondary sex characteristic.

Of course, occasional female underwear also appeared in Lost and Found, generally not underpants, but what was then always called a brassiere, and Uncle Kuhrt would bark out the owner's name more gruffly even than usual, and hold the offending object out sternly in his hand. For the older boys among us, this might have been a golden opportunity, but Uncle Kuhrt saw that it was not, glowering at them menacingly, silencing them with his glance, so that they actually looked at the ground, or at their shoes, or at something in the far distance.

When Personal Inspection and Lost and Found were accomplished for another day, we were off almost immediately for supper. Sometimes we waited five minutes, sometimes we waited fifteen, depending on how long the preceding ceremonies had taken. But in either case, it seemed a short while until supper, no matter how hungry we might be, because now was the time of day when we *wanted* things to go slowly, when we wanted to prolong the ending of the day. From now on, there could be few surprises waiting ahead, and what surprises there were were bound to be pleasant ones; we wanted to savor the evening ahead, as for many campers and not just for me, "Evening Activity" was the uncontested high point of the day. Whereas all day we had been divided into parts, each part functioning somewhat separately, at Evening Activity we all came together.

So at supper there was relative calm. Supper was a definite preliminary to what would follow it – a kind of aperitif of the spirit – and at supper, in anticipation of the coming cool, many people were already wearing sweaters, or sometimes their Camp Wynakee sweatshirts. Unlike the Wynakee T-shirts, which had just the camp name on them, the sweatshirts also had numbers, boxed in a rectangle on dark green, and these numbers were like the numbers on football jerseys, only smaller. Sixty-one might be your number, or thirty-eight, or seventeen. Whatever it was, it made your sweatshirt unique, since only one of every number was ever issued. As I looked around the dining hall at supper, I might see ten or eleven Camp Wynakee sweatshirts, each one an individual badge of honor, each one enclosing a different and numbered part of camp. My number was eighty-nine and even if I left Camp Wynakee someday, no one else would ever have it. My number was even more exciting to me than the name tag inside the sweatshirt. My name had always been mine. My number had context.

Supper was over at about 6:30, and though some of the older campers lingered and drank coffee, we younger ones burst through the screen doors as soon as we reasonably could, since the store was open only briefly after supper. During this time we could buy – but only with the permission of our parents – either five or ten cents worth of candy, and many parents took the opportunity to devise schedules so creative that they seriously stymied poor Grandma. There were campers, for example, who were allowed to buy candy just one night a week, on Wednesdays, say, or Fridays; other campers who could have five cents worth of penny candy every night, *or* one Sugar Daddy every week *and* one night of sour balls.

As for me, I was allowed to buy as much candy as I wanted, but I always bought just five cents worth, and I always bought the same thing, although the store sold chocolate drops, and licorice, and gumdrops and Tootsie Rolls and Sugar Babies. But while all these candies, in their way, tasted *better* than my choice, I always bought root beer barrels because this was Camp Wynakee, and in much the same way that I wanted special camp clothes, I also wanted to have special camp candy. I didn't want anything in my mouth that might remind me with its flavor of other times, of days in Pleasantville, New York, or at the farm in Rupert, Vermont, and I would run to the store after supper to buy my special Wynakee-only candy, glad that I had remembered to find my moccasins in the brief interval between free swim and the flag lowering. Pulling open the door into that silent, cool little room, where Grandma was now standing behind the counter with her half-glasses on, I stood in line calmly until I could say, "Five root beer barrels, please, Grandma," and she placed them on the counter one by one and marked them on a paper. Every evening it was the same, and every evening I put four of them into my pocket, and then unwrapped the fifth while I pushed the door open toward the birches, and then walked onto the greensward, where, leaning my back against a tree, I put the clear crinkly paper into my pocket.

Then, and only then, was it time to put the candy into my mouth, and I didn't bite or chew it, but just let it lie there melting; this time after supper and before Evening Activity was a time I hoped would dissolve as slowly as the root beer barrel. By now, the shadows of evening were starting to lengthen, the sun was moving toward its bed behind the mountains, and the light was slanting in a strange arresting way, while the grass held, already, a hint of coming chilliness. This was the time at Wynakee when I most realized that camp was all too fleeting, and that I had, unfortunately, a future, and not just an indefinite present, much as I would have liked things to be otherwise. Down at the Forest Garden, a place where I built twig fences, and other campers transplanted ferns or moss and watered them, there was a totem that Jo-John had carved some summer before I arrived, a large and beautiful hardwood head. This head, which was called Eekanyw, had a long, protuberant nose that ran right down the face from the space between the eyebrows to the lips; the nose was the largest feature of the face, which also had a wide mouth, but which had gentle, widely spaced, farseeing eyes. Eekanyw's nose was a wish-nose, and whenever you walked into the Forest Garden, you rubbed the nose as you passed it on your way elsewhere, but you could also make a special trip to Eekanyw and address the totem in perfect privacy.

So some evenings, as the root beer barrel melted, and the shadows grew long and arresting, I walked down across the lawn to the Forest Garden and stood before Eekanyw, who rested on a half-log set on end, put my hand to his nose, and rubbed and rubbed and rubbed it. While I didn't really believe in magic, or rather, believed in just the everyday kind – the kind that had allowed Camp Wynakee to come into being to begin with – I tried hard to believe that if I really rubbed (that is, rubbed very hard), the wish I made on Eekanyw would actually come true. The wish was simple, to stay at Wynakee forever, and if intensity of desire had counted, Eekanyvv would have granted my wish, I am almost certain; and even if I didn't actually visit him, on any given evening, I made the wish, somehow, and on something. I might visit the filly and the colt, and stroke their noses, oh so slowly, or I might walk up to the springhouse which lay above the stables, and look down at the roofs of Wynakee stretched below me in the valley. Here was Wynakee the place, its sounds and smells and shapes, its sun sinking toward its forests and its river running seawards; everything changing in the light, everything just as always, everything just exactly as I loved and needed it.

When the first root beer barrel was gone, and the other four had followed it, it was time to gather for this night's Evening Activity, and I joined some of my friends who were now hanging around the courtyard waiting for the bell to ring its great announcement. We had been told at dinner what the evening activity would be, and were therefore looking forward to it with an appropriate degree of pleasure; the Evening Activities were so various that they constitute a subject in and of themselves and never really became in any way typical. We had square dances; we had social dances; we had hayrides, late and by moonlight; we had dramatics in the Hayloft Theatre; we had folk singing nights in the library; we had, of course, our Sunday night Council Fires, which were always preceded by a riverside cookout. We had Battle of the Sexes, we had Kick the Can and Capture the Flag; we had a wonderful game called Messengers and Interceptors. Whatever we did, we did as a whole camp, as one family, and a family it was: there were rivalries, there were special friendships, there were people one admired from afar, there were big brothers and big sisters who took care of their younger siblings. And when we were together in the evenings there was remarkable all-camp harmony, so that even competitions brought us closer together.

The best Evening Activities, in the opinion of all, were not the ones that emphasized our differences, but the ones that seemed instead to almost totally erase them, to make us a group mind sharing a single imagination. When, in the evening, we played Capture the Flag, or Messengers and Interceptors, or went on an all-camp hayride on the high-piled hay wagon, we were questing after glory in the company of our fellows, and we all returned to Wynakee from the same imaginary kingdom. Evening fell early, and by 8:45 we were normally gathered for dispersal again into our separate cabins, but if we had an Evening Activity that had a definite goal and ending, then it might be almost dark by the time we were finished. The bell would ring at last, its long peals echoing in the growing darkness, and we would gather, not at the flagpole, but on the greensward by the birch trees in front of the Wienekes' worn white marble doorstep.

There we came together in a circle, but a tight circle this time, and we crossed arms and held hands with the people to either side of us; in this circle, in the dusk, we sang two songs, one after the other, the Wynakee camp song, and afterwards, taps. Taps was like taps anywhere, somewhat sad and somewhat soothing, and with its pro forma sudden intrusion of God, but the Wynakee camp song had been written not by a grown-up, but by a camper, and not on assignment. Though the camper was no longer among us, we all knew of her and the legend of how she had given this song to Uncle Kuhrt and Aunt Helen at the final banquet, and had thus left behind her the gift of her own wonder at what she had had, which we still had, and hoped to have forever.

Dark green mountains all around us,
A little village safe and sound,
The waterwheel goes round and round,
Camp Wynakee, that's where we're found.

The sun comes up with a burning glow,
Up with the flag and to breakfast we go,
We'll always remember the friends that we know,
Camp Wynakee, we love you so.

Day goes by and the night comes round,
We say goodnight to our little town,
The campers form a circle round,
And say goodnight to the friends we've found.

Good night, Aunt Helen and Uncle Kuhrt,
Forest green and water dark,
Good night until the morning starts,
Camp Wynakee, you've won our hearts

As I stood in the circle in the growing dusk, my arms crossed in front of my heart, my hands clasped tightly in the hands of the campers next to me, I sang as loudly as I could without losing the melody, and around me I could sense that others were singing that way also.

When the final words of taps had been uttered and had dispersed, we too dispersed to our separate cabins, and we did so slowly, with no running and little talking, as the final shades of night drew down around the Hollow. By 8:30 or so, on a typical night, we were up at Owl's Head changing into our flannel pajamas, and, in my case, choosing clothes to wear on the morning that would follow. At 9:00 the last bell rang, when it was quite dark outside but for the moon, and the counselors tucked us into our beds and turned off the light; I lay in my bunk staring out of the window and listening to the soft breathing of the other Owls, who fell asleep, it seemed, almost immediately. I never really wanted to go to sleep myself, preferring to lie awake in the darkness, listening to the silence and smelling the sweet air through the open window – but it was never long, after such a day, before sleep would overtake me. And I would let it. I could count on the morning bell. "Listen. I hear you."

GOLD IN THESE GREEN MOUNTAINS

Fourteen

NOT EVERY DAY at Wynakee was that soothingly predictable. There were a number of special events in the Wynakee calendar, and they were so interesting and exciting that each year we envied the new campers who would be experiencing them that summer for the first time. But we who were "old campers" had our own kind of pleasure in knowing in advance what these events would be like, and at least we were prepared, before we even got to Dorset Hollow, for the first one – the Fourth of July Tournament.

Since this generally occurred no more than ten days after we all arrived at camp, the whole beginning of each summer revolved around Fourth of July preparations, which threw each cabin into frenzied agitation. I am sure that there must have been normal daily activities during those six, seven, eight, or nine days that led up to the great event, but I really cannot remember this; what I remember about that first week of camp was the creative fervor into which the whole of Wynakee was catapulted. Because in the time before the tournament – at which parents would appear, as well as special guests invited in from Dorset – each cabin was expected to choose a theme for this year's Fourth, and then prepare a float, a skit, and a song. Once the Owls had all arrived, our bunks were made and our trunks in place – and the same was true for the Crows, the Wrens, the Mohawks, Mettawees and Netops – we would hold the first of several secret meetings, at which potential themes would be brooded upon.

During these meetings, as I recall, campers were posted guard so that no one from other cabins could eavesdrop at our windows, since – at first – we had the pleasant illusion that we were such brilliant tacticians and strategists, when it came to themes, that ours would be wanted by everyone. What if we, the Owls, picked the theme of Dogpatch, and then the Mohawks went and took that theme also? We would almost certainly lose the prize for originality, and even though that was, in a way, the booby prize, we didn't want to risk a single honor.

Our theme was *wonderful.* Or would be, if we ever found it.

Not that we really wanted to be picky, but most of the suggestions, as they were made, sounded so intensely stupid that it was hard to keep from chortling, with the consequence that as the secret meetings went on, fewer and fewer people dared to speak, and even the counselors, whom we had been counting on, became tongue-tied. So we would soften our rigid stance, and this time all suggestions, no matter how poor, would be given the most respectful consideration; perhaps we could all dress like insects, and pretend that we were a swarm. Well, yes, that was always a possibility. Or maybe we should be different kinds of rocks, igneous, sedimentary, and metamorphic. Well, yes, yes, we *could* be rocks this year. By the third secret meeting, however, with the days passing around us, there was no more time for such pathetic absurdity.

No, we *had* to pick a theme, and we had to do it now, and so came the desperate decision to choose one, *any* one, *something*; all that was needed was costumes and a float and a song and of course a skit, and how hard could that be, that theme, really? Inevitably, we would retrace our steps back to our first meeting, and we would pull out the very first thing that had been proposed then. It had been hooted down with universal scorn while we still thought that such creative people as ourselves would certainly come up with something better. Now, we could all see the good of it. Yes, we would choose and decide, be bold, and although immediately upon choosing we all had a deep and sinking feeling, by now there might be only four days left until the Tournament. Four days was simply not enough time to indulge in doubts any longer, it was sufficient only for papier-mâché, costumes, and rehearsals, rehearsals, rehearsals; there was no going back. The counselors would organize us ruthlessly: someone to design the float, many to build it, someone to write a song. The counselors to amend it. By the time the Fourth rolled around, whatever the results of their labor, each cabin had been through purgatory, and had triumphantly emerged from it.

For our parade, and our songs and skits and floats, we had a real audience, since this was a day when the parents who lived near enough to camp were invited to come, and it was the first time since these parents had dropped them off that the Wienekes, who were strict about this, had allowed them to come near the children they had parted from. We liked having an audience, though frankly, we would have preferred one made up of more townspeople and fewer parents, since parents by now were nothing but a distraction, unnecessary in any sense. By now, even the newest of us loved our camp with a loyalty as fierce as rose thorns, so that when our parents showed up on the Fourth of July, they were lucky even to see us. A week before, a new camper had been crying, and his parents had come fully prepared to pack up the poor child and take him home; now, the poor child, when they at last recognized him, appeared to be dressed as a pirate from the Spanish Main, and would say nothing to his parents except through the dagger clamped between his teeth.

The Fourth of July Tournament began with an all-camp parade, in which each cabin, in costume, assembled around its float, and marched from the Barn down to the field by the river. This was the big moment when the floats, which had been kept – incredibly – secret, were revealed to us for the first time. Afterwards, they would be set aside while the other business of the day went on, but that astounding first appearance was never to be forgotten, not that day, not for the rest of time. One year the Mettawees constructed a two-car train, with an engine and a caboose, and you could hardly see the tractor and the flatbed wagon that it pulled, so mighty was the edifice of cardboard. Everything was squared off, and there were wheels painted on, and diamond-shaped windows, and even a cardboard cowcatcher; NYC had been drawn in a circle above it, and real steam came out of a hole at the top.

Another year the Mettawees (who usually won Best Float), built a Greenwich Village "beatnik pad," and it was almost as big as a real room in a real house, with one side cut away to reveal the boys inside it. These boys were dressed totally in black, and many of them wore berets from the Hayloft Theatre, and they were snapping their fingers, slumping, and looking very very languid, as their pad was drawn by in front of the crowd of spectators. In the corner there was a water-cooler entirely filled with liquid, and the cooler bore a hand-labeled sign which read HEROIN; while we watched in utter amazement, a boy or two sauntered over and drew off a small paper cupful of this fluid.

But although the Mettawees could be expected always to have a good float, there were sometimes surprises, like the triumph of the Wrens one year when we did The Old Woman and her mighty Shoe. As might have been expected, when we won the coveted Float prize, there was a certain amount of grumbling among the older boys, who suspected that the male counselors had snuck around to help, but they hadn't, I can attest to it, since I was on the Shoe Crew, and we did it all by ourselves, with Aunt Helen's expert assistance. The Shoe was magnificent, big enough to hold four Wrens, two popping out of the top, at the ankle, two sticking their heads out near the severely folded-out tongue, and the laces were of real leather, being reins borrowed from several bridles. Aunt Helen, the Old Lady, had a mob cap on her head.

Generally, we all thought that the best floats were the ones which, like the Shoe, could *contain* some campers; getting inside a float was quite different from riding upon it, as when the Netops did Dogpatch Express and all rode on the dog cart. And so it was that the greatest Float triumph, during my years at Wynakee, was the giant Crow that the Crows constructed. Even I, a partisan Owl at the time, was stunned by this mighty Crow, fifteen feet high. Two campers stood inside its belly, and walked, with the bird atop them; all that showed was their legs and feet beneath it. They had the mouth controls in their hands, and they would shift them until the mouth opened wide, and then they would bray and screech. The mouth could open very wide – it was an amazing piece of work – and the wings were controlled by rods from outside; the two campers posted to each wing had obviously trained to work in unison, as the wings lifted and fell, lifted and fell, never out of synchronization. The Crow was papier-mâché on a chicken wire frame, painted black and with two inset eyes, and from a distance it looked so much like a live crow that it must have been Jo-John who designed it. Not only did the Crows win Best Float the year of the Crow, but the Crow was not destroyed, as were all the others. It was stored eventually in the cow barn, where the boys could visit it anytime, and marvel at their part in its construction.

After the parade of floats was over and the floats had been set aside, it was time to move on to the skits and songs, which were judged separately. Costumes also won a prize, since it was important in the great scheme of things that each cabin win at least one award for its efforts. As I've said, "Originality" was the booby prize a cabin got when the judges despaired of giving it anything more substantial; we Wrens got Originality when we were Smallest Bathing Beauties and wore our regular bathing suits with paper sashes – and that pretty much tells you everything about it. But as Owls, when we were *The Wind in the Willows*, and we acted out the scene where Toadie and Rat and Mole go out on the open road, we won both song and skit, which perhaps we deserved, since we had really practiced. It was odd, though, acting like that, in the sunshine in a grassy field, where your voice, which usually was piercingly strong even in this setting, now vanished in the dirt somewhere just past your toes, and everyone in the audience bellowed, inconsiderately, "We can't hear you!"

The audience of mostly parents was sitting on folded chairs, which had been rented, I presume, for just this occasion, and we were regularly entertained by a chair folding right up on a hapless parent, who would fall to the ground and find himself the sudden center of attention. The other parents, those on either side, who had been to a Fourth of July before, or had quickly sized up the situation when they got there, realized that only from one another were they likely to get any sympathy, and they would mutter comfort to the folded one, and then bellow again, "We can't hear you!" So we would raise our voices to the same piercing shriek we used when we were playing baseball and shouted "Go for home!," in part from simple frustration at the vagaries of sound, in part as punishment of our parents for wanting to hear us.

When the skits and songs were over – and though hard to be in, they were great fun to watch, since the unexpected could be counted on, as when a pirate's pants fell down to his ankles – an "unbiased" panel of judges, parents claiming children from each of the six cabins, would select the winners and award the prizes. Then we would all have lunch, which would be served on tables set up along the riverbank near the stone fireplace where each Sunday night if it was fair we would roast hot dogs and eat coleslaw; today, however, though we ate outside, there was no rest for the cook, who had prepared a sumptuous and varied cold buffet. As it was physically impossible for each and every child at Wynakee to avoid his or her own parents in the food line, although there was a great deal of jockeying for position as we all tried desperately to get away from them, in the end, the inevitable occurred, which was that our own parents found us. Then, for the next half-hour, we made our way with them through the line, found a place on the grass near the chairs to sit with them, and ate the elegant luncheon while staring at them numbly, and eating the food without really tasting it. Some children, of course, must have enjoyed eating with their parents, but most of us found ourselves in the awkward position of having absolutely nothing to say to them. We would ask politely how they'd been, what had been happening to them in our absence. But their answers might as well have been telegrams from the moon, so unimaginable was the world they described to us, and as for *us* – well, what could we say? Our parents couldn't conceive of how far from them we had traveled.

After lunch was finally over, there was the pie eating contest, for which few children had been self-controlled enough to starve themselves, and which the Wienekes apparently felt presented little risk to life or limb when it was held on a full-to-bursting stomach. The pie eating contest was voluntary, and I myself never took part in it, since I had an acute fear of looking ridiculous in front of other people; this fear was luckily not shared by all of my contemporaries, however, and many of them would line up eagerly next to the pies, hands clasped behind them. Then at the signal "Go!" they would bend over and bury their faces in a chocolate cream pie, or a lemon meringue pie or a coconut cream, and we who watched felt an odd sense of appreciation, that they were willing to do what we were not, as if it was a simple necessity that occasionally *someone* look very silly. No prizes were given for the pie eating contest – whoever won simply got the pie – but the huge round of applause we gave the winner, a goofy grin showing through the cream or meringue smeared on his face from the chin to the eyebrows, was prize enough for him.

Other games now followed, and they lasted most of the afternoon, in a Tournament of Games that began with a Tug-of-War and ended with baseball. The Tug-of-War was the first event in the summer-long Battle of the Sexes, which mostly took place on rainy evenings in the Hayloft Theatre. Its pie-covered faces washed and dried, the camp would be divided into boys and girls, and every year the boys would prepare for the Tug-of-War with a lengthy strategy session, huddling together well away from us, and discussing weight ratios and inertia and sudden force. Every year the girls, during this same interval, held no strategy sessions at all, just waited, slightly bored, until the boys were ready, and then, while the boys were getting themselves organized to put all their marvelous tactics into operation, we girls would just get on the rope, and start pulling, digging our heels in and leaning backwards. The rope, saved from year to year, was tied with big knots, and it was helpful if you were able to get right on top of a knot and embrace it, but even if you couldn't, you could get a fairly good grip, for the rope was huge, of thick and abrasive hemp, which smelled strongly of tar. This smell of tar perfumed the whole area, and after a minute was joined by the smell of sweat, and an absolute cacophony of boys grunting out orders and girls simply shrieking.

The organization that they insisted on was always the downfall of the boys. In fact, the Tug-of-War always followed an identical pattern. While the boys were still lining up their ranks, we girls had won a good foot and a half, and then when the boys noticed this, they decided to regroup, and in the process lost another twelve inches. We just threw ourselves ever more precipitously backwards, shrieking, "Come on, come on, come on!" until we had gained a third foot, a fourth and a fifth, and then dragged the flag over the finish line. Each year, at this satisfying moment, the same thing always happened: we released the rope, and the boys, thinking that they had *finally* gotten organized, dragged it mightily in the other direction, and right over their own finish line, imagining for some reason that this made them the winners. When it was announced that this was not the case, the boys looked physically stunned, then started arguing about why it had happened, and who, exactly, could be held responsible; we girls would be jumping about, still shrieking, and they would observe us gloomily, and disbelievingly, as if at some sleight of hand which too obviously involved mirrors. They never quite grasped that they had lost *again*, so conceptually impossible was such a phenomenon, and we had to rub it in very hard for them to begin to get it. Usually, we did this by shouting, without stopping for at least two minutes, "We won! We won! We WON! and so on, etc.

After the triumph of the Tug-of-War, the rest of the games were bound to be a letdown, and since participation was voluntary, I would not take part in all of them. I was no good at either the three-legged race or the potato-sack race, each o] which required a certain measure of patience, as did the egg and spoon race, which I had, many broken eggs ago, given up on. But I was always a very popular wheelbarrow, and several boys would contest the right to wheel me, since in this event no patience or holding back was needed; an all-out assault on the ground, with the arms, was all that was required. Actually, there were a number of different theories as to the most successful combinations of wheeler and barrow, with some of the older boys choosing to wheel other older boys on the theory that the longer arms and greater strength would generate additional speed, but often the older boys were too impatient with their fellows, and the barrows would end up with nose and mouth filled with dirt. In practice, what seemed to work best was big campers wheeling little ones, and after the Tug-of-War, the moment when I and my wheeler swarmed across the finish line was my favorite moment in any Fourth of July .

The various races ended, and the prizes awarded, the whole camp would settle in for baseball, in which the poor parents would at last be included – those who hadn't already left, as many did after the races, hastily gathering their things, kissing their offspring and taking off. Those who remained by 3:00 or so were invited to join in the game, and politely chosen first, before the campers. What this worked out to in practice was that the campers would do almost anything to avoid being chosen for the same team as their parents. Horrible facial grimaces to the two team captains, hand signals of a desperate nature; often the only recourse was to feign illness or exhaustion, and so many campers ended up doing this that the teams in the end might be composed mainly of parents. Few mothers, I am sorry to say, took part in the game in those days. So the fathers would get out there, hearty and apparently bluff, but many of them by now – with all the days' tensions – out for blood, and this was even more entertaining to the campers who sat cozily on the sidelines than had been the parents who had been folded up in the collapsing chairs. At 4:00, over or not, the game ended, and there was the signal for free swim, and with great relief we would say good-bye to our parents and see them securely locked into their cars – and then, as they drove away, we felt a belated burst of love, and waved madly after them, screaming, "Good-bye! Good-bye!" I suppose we felt safe enough in this gesture, since now we could relax for the rest of the summer. We were *not* going to be taken away, which was what we had really been afraid of.

As for the parents, by then, without question, they were overjoyed to be leaving, and probably repaired immediately to the nearest inn for an early cocktail.

Fifteen

BUT THEY WERE NOT to be let off so easily, those parents who lived nearby, for there were two other special events at which their presence was required, although, as these came later in the summer, the parents at least had the chance to recover from the Fourth of July before they were again summoned to Dorset Hollow. The ARC Swimming demonstration and Water Show and what was officially called "The Horsemanship Demonstration" had in common that they were composed of Wynakee campers exhibiting their new skills, but they were otherwise entirely different, for the swimming was fun for everyone, while the horse show was nothing less than agony.

We at Wynakee, by the way, would have none of this

"Horsemanship Demonstration"; we called it what it was. It was the big, the only, the All-Camp Horse Show. "All Camp" sounded impressive, like "All-County" or "All-State," and I'm sure it was the riding counselors themselves who gave it this appellation. I hey did so as they tried to make the event astonishing, both for the riders and for the nonriding campers, who would be, after all, the bulk of the audience. Yes, some parents did show up, but somehow by this point in the summer, a lot of parents were likely to have "important things" to do elsewhere.

Of course, those who lived very nearby, like mine, came, as did those who had children who Took Riding Seriously. The latter, actually, might not come, since having children who were horse-sick was a lot more difficult than having children who were homesick. Those children who Took Riding Seriously didn't long for their own *house*, they longed, by this point in the summer, for their own *horse* and they made their feelings known to their parents, should they be unwise enough to come near, so those with any kind of an excuse prudently remained elsewhere.

Thus the audience in the end consisted of about forty people, since upwards of half of the camp would be riding. Forty people was quite enough to watch you do something you didn't want to do if you did not Take Riding Seriously. Actually, I *did* take it seriously, the way you might take seriously an attack of measles, or any other disease that was unpleasant but not usually life-threatening. Despite the repeated assurances of Megan, the head riding counselor, I was afraid that, in my case, riding would actually be fatal. So I stood in opposition to those children who thought their lives would end if they were not given their own horse to take home with them. I was convinced that, slight as my contact might be with the enormous beasts, my life would end if I spent too much time near them.

This made the day of the Horse Show hard, for it was the day when my private affliction – fear of horses – might become, at any moment, public knowledge, and I knew that since I was a little girl, the affliction was particularly shameful. Little girls were supposed to love horses. Before I ever met a horse personally, I had heard that this was true, and that is why I had asked for riding lessons at Camp Wynakee; it was only in the course of my first riding lesson, when I was seven years old, that I became aware that a mistake had been made somewhere. I was a little girl, and this thing was a horse, and love at first sight was supposed to be a given. Why, then, did I feel raw fear, the first prolonged physical fear of my life? My head felt light. My heart was pounding. Even my mouth was burning.

I was, naturally, in a class for beginners, and there were maybe four or five other new riders; Megan and her assistant had saddled five gentle Morgans. Mine stood placidly by the fence post to which his bridle had been tethered, and I was introduced. "Elizabeth, this is Blackie."

While the other children rushed to their horses, cooing and gurgling and talking baby talk, I approached "my" horse, Blackie, and he got bigger. He was black, yes, and he was big. I had expected that he would be big. But could any horse be *that* black and *that* big, truly? His legs alone looked like tree trunks. His neck was the breadth of a boulder. I could see the tiny muscles rippling under his neck skin. He snorted in a treacherous fashion, as if he were engaged in plotting his strategy, which revolved around how most effectively to dislodge the young Elizabeth. His tail switched, brushing flies, but to me, it was evident that this was merely an outward expression of his inner elation at the plan he had concocted for this young rider standing next to him, should she be foolish enough to actually try and mount him. He would wait until I was up, and then he would simply start running. And while he was running forward, as fast as his legs would carry him, I would stay where I was, falling from the back of where I should have been to the ground way below me. Way way below me; where was the ground, anyway?

Even now, the smell of a horse will bring this moment back to me complete, the moment when I first learned the meaning of courage. It had nothing to do with real bravery, but everything to do with concealment, with pretending that you felt confident when inside, you were screaming. From the first time I got on a horse, I was terrified most of the time, and my favorite moment, from then to now, has always been when I got to climb down off of it. But so persuaded was I that admitting this would be shameful that I kept riding for my whole five years at camp.

Given what riding lessons cost – I do not know, but I do know that they cost extra – I am sure that my mother would have been amazed to discover that I thought of riding as a form of torture. I was thrown within my first month, and thrown once or twice a summer after that, and not only was this dangerous, and often painful, but I always took it quite personally. I would be sitting on this huge horse, trying to make myself as light as possible, and wishing that it were not necessary to remind the animal that I was upon it by pressing it with my knees or nudging it with my heels. And then the command would come to *trot* – or as the case might be, to *canter* – and I would do nothing but breathe a little faster, assuming that the horse probably knew best. The horse did. When he saw all the others trotting or cantering, he decided to simply go along with them, which was usually quite all right, but sometimes unfortunate, as occasionally I was unprepared for the sudden movement. So as the horse went forward, I went back, and I would not even have time to scream about it before I found myself once again with all the wind knocked out of me and an unexpectedly fine view of the blue sky.

It was with this background that I went into the All-Camp Horse Show, one of thirty or so young riders, wearing my jodhpurs and my white shirt and a borrowed black hat which was covered with velvet and had an elastic strap on it. Not everyone had real jodhpurs – jodhpurs were "optional," along with the musical instrument, the favorite game, and the cap – and I felt even more embarrassed about my fear because of them. I had been given *two* advantages in my relationship with horses. Not only was I a little girl, but I also had special trousers, and despite these assets, I still was afraid, though more determined than ever not to show it.

Actually, this determination was probably a disadvantage in itself, for there were generally two main types of camper-riders. There were those who liked horses, and somehow instinctively understood them, and who rode with style – no doubt as a consequence – and there were those who did not like horses, and did not pretend to understand them, and did not ride with any style whatsoever. They let their arms and legs flap anywhere, and their buttocks bounce high and wild. The flapping arms and legs were the outward and visible sign of an inward lack of connection, so it was probably a pity that I worked so obsessively on my seat, and could sometimes conceal what would otherwise have been obvious.

On the day of the All-Camp Horse Show, we who were riding went up to the stables right after breakfast to help groom the horses. Grooming I didn't mind, since the horses seemed actually to enjoy it, and made it as easy as possible on their personal attendants. When the grooming was over, though, it was time to saddle and bridle, and this was a far different story; even though I was too young to saddle, since the saddles were very heavy, I was considered old enough by then to bridle. And it was in the task of bridling that my inherent incapacities were revealed with sickening clarity, since those who loved to ride would hold the bridle in front of the horse and the horse would seem to just inhale it. Then it would chew contentedly on the metal bit that was now in its mouth while the other child proceeded to fasten straps under its chin and over its forehead.

When *I* held the bridle in front of the horse, however, the horse would turn its head away in irritation, and if I insisted, it would jerk its head back so that its nostrils pointed at the ceiling. This gave me an excellent view of the teeth, which like the rest of the horse were enormous, and though there was a space at the back of the mouth which was toothless, that space, where the bit might be fitted, seemed to me a lot like the joke about the Vermont farmer: a city slicker stops on a country road, and asks a farmer at his gate how to get where he is going, and the farmer, after great cogitation and drawing maps in the dirt at his feet, says, "Sorry, You can't get there from *here*, mister."

This was my normal experience with bridling, but on the day of the All-Camp Horse Show, I was in such a fever pitch of fear and determination that I would grasp the horse's head, stick my fingers into its mouth, and to my astonishment, feel that mouth open biddingly. The bridle would be in, the strap would be buckled, and it would be time to go change into my jodhpurs, as I gave the horse a pat and sauntered out of the stables on the verge of a five-hour spurt of self-confidence. This confidence lasted me from the time the bridle went into the mouth until I stood with my horse in the winner's circle – yes, the pathetic thing about this was that I inevitably won a ribbon, beating out children who were far more competent riders. I was usually in two classes, and sometimes in three, and it was a rare year when I didn't win two ribbons, which gave my parents and others the illusion that I actually had some skill and promise as a budding horsewoman. Heels *down*, stomach *in*, shoulders *back*, seat *steady*, hands *together* – it basically amounted to No Flapping – but the judges looked most for the placement of the elbows, or so I always suspected. To me, there seemed no question that it was the elbows that rose with the first stirrings of inward terror; they rose, I am quite convinced, because the natural instinct at the time was to grab for and cling to any passing tree branch.

On the day of the Horse Show, and that day alone, my shoulders might have been glued to my rib cage, and the funny thing was that when I had the right seat for long enough, I could sense the real pleasure of riding. On the day of the Horse Show, when the judges were calling, "Bring in your mounts," or "Canter," or "Circle," I had moments when I felt that the horse and I were one, and that the horse was almost an extension of my body. I wheeled on a dime, and got on the right diagonal without even needing to consider it; once I was the only person in my class who was cantering on the proper foreleg, and that year I consequently won the blue ribbon. The judge, in presenting it – the judges were strangers, riding counselors from other camps – said in a voice loud enough for my proud mother to hear, "This child is a natural rider," and Megan, my own riding teacher, managed to conceal her true feelings, as my horse, Stepper, accepted the honor.

&

THE ARC Swimming Demonstration and Water Show could not have been more different, and while I never won anything at it, nor wanted to, I liked it for that very reason a hundred times better, and also because, after the first year, my parents didn't attend it. To the spectators, it was boring – even watching the best swimmers was dull, and watching bad swimmers flounder was simply numbing – but to the people who got to swim, at least to the people like me, it was a very happy event. Basically, it was a chance to stay in the water longer than I was ever otherwise permitted to, until my lips and fingernails were deep blue, and my toes and fingers looked like prunes. Even the skin on my palms grew soft and porous. I achieved this fine effect by volunteering for everything, from being a Water Clown to being part of Neptune's Court, and also being in the boat races.

We had, I think, two kayaks and three metal Grumman canoes, and the first event, which was Water Safety, involved swamping them, and you didn't swamp them wearing swim suits, as if you just happened to be all prepared for your boat to sink – you swamped them wearing clothes. You wore long pants, and a long-sleeved shirt and even sneakers, and though you had your swimsuit on underneath all this, the whole point of boat swamping was to make it to shore without taking all of the clothes off. So we climbed into the canoes four of us to a canoe, and then paddled it out to the middle of the pond, where, by rocking from side to side, and then roooooooccccccckkkkkking and rooooooccccccckkkkkkking and roooooooocccccccckkkkkkking, we managed to get water pouring in over one gunnel. The instant it started to pour in, the canoe would tip even farther in the direction of the flow, and the force of our last roooccccckkkk took us that way also, so that the canoe tipped over, spilling the four of us into the water, while the canoe settled easily upside down and we grabbed it.

It was amazing how much our clothes weighed us down, and how cold and slippery the bottom of the Grumman was, so the next step in the process was to take off our sneakers, and, clutching the canoe with one hand, tie the laces together and sling them around one of the thwarts. Inevitably, someone would drop a set of sneakers to the bottom of the pond instead, and be of little further use in the boat activities as he peered down through the inky blackness, utterly distracted and wondering whether he would ever see his dear sneakers again. Usually, they would eventually be recovered, but the pond *was* very dark, and the fears of the bereft person were not utterly ill-founded; we others, though, having successfully fastened our own sneakers upon them, would cling to the thwarts beneath the overturned boat, where it was great fun to remain as long as possible.

Of course, the longer we remained there, the dimmer became our chances of making it to shore first among the three boats; boat swamping was technically a race, but as it happened, the three teams were rarely evenly matched, and so before the boats had even swamped, it had already become clear who was going to win. In some boats, the rocking just went on and on, with the timid participants never quite putting enough swing into their invitation to the water to join them. Another boat was *rock rock rock* and it was over, as the four dedicated swampers practically threw themselves right out of the canoe in their frenzy. So there, underneath the boat, it was fun to take a break and listen to your voice ringing like a steel ball in a pinball machine. You might whisper "Bbbbrrr, it's cold," and the word "cold" would bounce and bounce until, after a while, it settled.

At the end of this too-brief interval, you would all line up on one gunnel and fling the boat over until it flipped right side up into the water; and though it was still half-full of pond then, and riding very low as a consequence, it was still a little difficult to climb over the gunnel in the sight of all, with your extremely heavy pants and leaden shirt dragging you down. In fact, what you would have liked to make as a graceful spring actually turned into an ungainly seal-flop, but at least you *did* manage to get from the large pond of water into what had become a smaller one. All paddles, of course, were now long gone – indeed, that was part of the point – so you got on your knees in the water of the canoe, and then you all stuck your arms out sideways. Cupping your hands, you pushed and pushed at the water until you got the sluggish canoe slowly moving, and it was astonishing that you could propel yourself with just eight palm paddles, just six of these really enthusiastic. The other two belonged to the shoe-bereft camper, and he was reluctant because he was moving farther and farther away from his sneakers. He knew that as long as he was approximately above them, there was always the chance that they would return to him; if he deserted them, however, as he was now doing despite himself, they would feel, as he saw it, truly unwanted, and would probably sigh, and decide to drift away, following the spring currents to the sneaker graveyard.

Once you finally reached shore, you had to bail out your canoe until it was light enough to pull up and turn over; then you would turn it, dump the water, and place it bottom-side down again. Now you were done, and everyone should start clapping. They rarely did, though, as the whole camp had long since lost interest – for one thing, the winners had probably won ten minutes before – and most of the campers and their parents were talking and laughing, or whittling or reading, waiting for something else to happen. In fact, the only people watching now with what might be called full attention were the parents of the sneaker-dropping child, who saw all too clearly that in the afternoon to come they would be making an unscheduled trip to Purdy's, a Manchester shoe store.

The kayak races came next, and they were a lot more fun for the spectators, but for the participants they lacked something, which was water; as opposed to every other event of this day, they required you to stay dry. If you got wet, i.e., spilled, you were automatically disqualified. With only two kayaks, we had to have races against the clock, and that was also relatively disappointing, as you always felt, while paddling, swinging your double paddle *here*! and then *there*! that certainly you must be the person who was winning. *Whup*! you went, skidding to the left, and then *whup*! you skidded to the right, but the fact that you couldn't stay on course hardly seemed to matter, since you were moving so *very* fast – at least in your own opinion – that surely no amount of seesawing could slow you. For the kayak race, buoys were planted, and these were thus rather like barrel races, with the campers doing figure-eights across the pond. If you hit a buoy, or missed it, you had to go back and go around it, and that was indubitably a bad thing to have happen. Still, your speed was dizzying, almost enough so that it made up for the fact that during this event you couldn't get as wet as you would have liked. You did get wet, of course, from the waist up, if not from the action of your own paddles, then from the action of the only other kayak in the pond with you. And when the triumphant moment came when your time was read aloud by Karl, who was holding the stopwatch, you were always quite astounded to learn that with absolutely no trouble at all, you had achieved the distinction of paddling the slowest kayak.

But really, it didn't matter, because next came Neptune's Court, where you got to play a mermaid or a water nymph, and for this you could get quite wet again, and frolic until everyone was sick of you. Now came the real business of the day, which was sidestroke, crawl, backstroke, and breaststroke, and, for some campers, the butterfly and diving; everyone in his or her own class, and everyone moderately well-coordinated, though this certainly wasn't synchronized swimming. Those parents who were there now sat up and really took notice, for they were able to observe their own children's progress as swimmers, and while I never shone in these events, I glowed just from being in the water.

After the swimming demonstrations there were races – optional for everyone – and I always raced only in the breaststroke, impatient, even as I swam, for what I myself considered the most enchanting event of the whole ARC Swimming Demonstration. This was called Endurance, and it was the last event of the great watery day, taking place when most of the campers were bored, cold, and tired. But for those few of us who were not bored, it was wonderful to get back into the water and simply stay there for as long as possible. I truly loved Endurance, when I got to float on my back, and tread water, and float on my stomach, lifting my head regularly. About fifteen of us would enter the Endurance contest, and the purpose of the contest, as at a marathon dance, was to be the last one left in the water. I always knew as I went in that I would win, no question about it, because Endurance took no skill, no strength, no *noth-*

ing – all it took was a love of water and a willingness to hand yourself over to it fully, and to know that it would never trick or fail you. Also, Endurance turned what I wanted to do anyway into something prizeworthy and admirable, turned blind faith and absolute determination into virtues. Unfortunately, Karl had the power to call any child out of the water if in his judgment we looked too blue or kept sinking too quickly. And Karl always decided to pull me out before the end, not for sinking, of course, but for blueness. But it didn't really matter. *I* knew I could have stayed in longer. In my own opinion, in Endurance, I was always the real champion.

Sixteen

UNLIKE THESE other special events, the CIT Carnival, which fell in the middle of every summer, invited no guests, and was an internal affair entirely, and the reason for this seemed all too clear the first time I lived through it, for it was, in some ways, the dud in the pile of fireworks. The CITs were Counselors in Training, sixteen or seventeen years old, and if they were lucky, they would return the following summer as full-fledged counselors; at the moment, however, they occupied an uneasy position between childhood and adulthood, having responsibilities but very little power. The CITs at Wynakee were the people who set the tables, and they also helped out in the kitchen every few evenings. To them fell the unwanted task of peeling the potatoes, and they could often be seen behind The Barn, on its small greensward. There, contained by the two arms of a truncated stone wall, they sat on the grass, enormous kettles and equally enormous piles of tubers, some peeled and some unpeeled, before them. Sometimes, potato peelings adorned them.

These potato peelings, and the cutlery which they set out three times a day, gave us campers a pretty fair indication of the CITs' status; the CITs also cleaned up the game room regularly, putting all the games back into their boxes, and they shepherded the youngest campers to the shower room. While they attended Wynakee for free, we campers who observed all this had our doubts even before Carnival Day about whether being a CIT was worth it, since without question they must have felt a kinship with indentured servants. Someday, and not too long from now, they would be released from the articles which bound them – mainly to root vegetables and eating utensils – and they would be Camp Wynakee counselors, with full power and glory. But would it really be worth it?

Well, in the meantime they at least had the small consolation of getting to organize and mount the CIT Carnival, and to construct a House of Horrors, and a Feed the Dragon Game, and clown acts, and the ducking chair. We all knew in advance when the CIT Carnival would be held, since there was no way that the CITs could have pulled it off otherwise, and for days before the event, we were warned away from the buildings where special preparations were underway. But we didn't even try to peek, since we knew – we who were veteran campers – that whatever pleasure the Carnival might finally have for us would lie solely in the surprise of it – that, and the sympathetic relief we would feel for the CITs when the day and its attendant miseries were over. Somehow, it was clear to us that the Carnival was not really for us, but was more in the nature of an elaborate test for the Counselors in Training, a test disguised as a pleasant opportunity for its poor victims. Had the CITs been pigs, the test, disguised as pleasure, would have been along the lines of, "Let's attach wings to the pigs and see if they can fly!" Everyone but the pigs would have known perfectly well beforehand that the chances were exactly nil that the pigs would manage it. But the poor pigs, when their big day came, would inevitably be all excited as the wings were carefully attached, and they would crane their heads back over their shoulders, or, looking down at their chests, they would admire the colorful harness; shifting eagerly on their trotters, they would feel the catch of the wind as it stirred and ruffled all those bright feathers.

So when the CIT Carnival approached, the whole camp had an air of resignation – at least, the whole camp except for the CITs themselves. *They* were always determined that this year it would be different, that this year they were actually going to make it. Last year's Counselors in Training, what a sorry lot *they* had been, and as for the year before! Quite pathetic! No, it was no wonder that the CIT Carnivals had been such flops when they were run by those dismal incompetents. The illusion that things would be different in the fine year that was the present – CIT One, or the first year of the new calendar – persisted right up until the day, and for many of the CITs, well into the middle hours of the morning.

I suppose it should be admitted that I myself never much liked carnivals anyway, as they always lacked something that was to me rather important: a theme to move within, a point toward which events were heading, or, at the very least, some kind of logical progression. Whether at Wynakee or elsewhere, they lacked what you would call in a novel the plot, a causal relationship among the different events which contribute to the whole. The Fourth of July had a marvelous plot, as did the ARC Swimming Demonstration and the Horse Show – as did, above all others, Klondike Day. But a carnival lacks a plot entirely; one wanders from booth to booth, or ride to ride, or game to game, with no sense of direction. And there are so many decisions to make. Shall I now watch the clown act? Shall I pay extra to see the World's Largest Snake? But there is no governing principle to guide you when you come to make a choice, with the result that there is never any catharsis. If you pay to see that snake, much against your better judgment, you will see no evidence of reptilian life whatsoever, and the snake's keeper will inform you that just this minute the snake has crawled under a pile of shavings. So, in an effort to avert a similar disappointment, you give a miss to the world's smallest thoroughbred and try to shoot some cardboard ducks with a special rifle fastened to a post. By accident you hit three, and are presented with a rubber chicken.

No, I am not a carnival sort of person, so my perceptions here may be skewed, but I think that I was not the only Wynakee camper who felt that the CIT Carnival was an event to be not enjoyed but endured, an event for which Rest Hour would be an appropriate ending. What was painful about the morning was not *just* the fact that the ducking chair, which had been days in the building, inevitably failed to function, and the CIT who sat on it went time and again into the drink when no one of any size or description was anywhere near him. No, it was also painful when the biggest, toughest boy in camp *was* there, and hit the plate with a driving fastball; *then* the chair, which up until that time had been dropping when the CIT breathed in, stuck tight like an egg in a Coke bottle. It could also be counted on that the donkey featured in the donkey ride would, after a short saunter around the courtyard, lie down in it and go to sleep, as if he had been waiting the entire year for this day when he could rest up for the following summer; no amount of pleading, loud noises, or hauling, would rouse him. The CITs would bang blocks of wood right by the donkey's long ears, as if they were trying to wake someone from a coma; they would whistle and shout and stamp. The donkey slept right through it. He would wake up just in time for Rest Hour. As a kind of substitute for the donkey, the CITs would secure a horse, but horseback riding was bad enough under normal conditions. Under these conditions, it lacked any appeal at all – particularly when you had to ride around the slumbering donkey.

Oh, all sorts of things could be counted on to happen at the CIT Carnival. Several of the CITs, for example, always dressed up in clown suits, and then demonstrated their skill at juggling, which they had been practicing for weeks. Of course, they would drop every ball they tossed skywards. Or perhaps there might be a mime, in whiteface, and with a black suit on, and we would watch him with frank incredulity. Was he a spider crawling up a wall? Was he eating a meal of spaghetti? It was impossible to say, and we preferred not to know the answer.

The wise old camper would do just two things at the CIT Carnival – go to the cakewalk, and enter the House of Horrors. The first one was pretty dull, of course, but at least you got to eat cake, if you stayed on it long enough – which you did, since nothing else was beckoning. The music would play while you walked around the squares, and you could study the chocolate cake, which sat on a nearby table. The music would stop, and you would generally find yourself on one of the noncake squares. So what? Eventually the music would start again. In fact, if you were lucky, this might take most of the morning, and finally some chocolate cake would be proffered to you, and you would eat it very, very slowly. Then, at about eleven, you would walk up the hill and go toward the tack room, now the House of Horrors.

I suppose that part of the reason I found the House of Horrors so successful was that the tack room was always a little horrible anyway because of its association with horses. Once, the House of Horrors was constructed in the under-barn, which smelled of cow, and consequently was not as frightening; no, the tack room was surely a better place for it, since when you are wearing a big black blindfold, the smell of horses evokes not just personal but racial memories. You are a peasant, you suddenly feel, living in a grass hut, a nice quiet life upon the Asian steppes, and suddenly Attila the Hun and his vicious horsemasters come calling, and in a moment all is carnage and slaughter. Or you are a peasant again, this time living in England, and it is the fifteenth century, and you just finished gathering in your harvest when the lord of the manor arrives with his stallion and his minions, and in an instant, there goes most of your harvest. In blindfold-created darkness, in fact, the horse, along with its tackle, smells something like an instrument of oppression, and also smells truly mythical, an animal that can strike lightning with its hoof, and that on any ordinary paving stone. A cow, though, if one is a peasant (and even if one isn't) smells pleasantly reassuring and domestic. One thinks of byres and milk and cheese, and Sunday mornings, of Jerseys and Guernseys with their limpid eyes, of the sun just coming up and the plangent moos rising to heaven. Or, in a different mood, one thinks of the evening shadows growing long, and the gates about to be opened, and the barn door closed for the night, when all is safe and well again.

The stoop of the tack room was good white marble, as were the door stoops of most of Wynakee's buildings, and when you got to it you would sit, with your back to the closed door, feeling the cool marble on your thighs. The long morning on the cakewalk had come to an end, and you prepared for the reward that lay in store for you – the reward of feeling, if only for a short time, frightened; if you were very lucky, you might anticipate feeling totally and completely terrified. You would close your eyes and listen to the shrieks and shouts behind you – also the giggles and the thumps – and another camper would come up and sit on the stoop also, closing his eyes and listening with you. This would take some time, but eventually at the far end of the stables another door would burst open and campers would erupt, shouting and shaking their bodies like dogs shaking off water, proud of the invisible drops of fear on them.

Indeed, the second advantage to going to the House of Horrors last, when the CIT Carnival was almost over, was that by then it had had time to absorb some of the fear which had been sprinkled around it by previous campers. Not just at the far door, but at the near door as well – and certainly all through the building – there was the hushed sense of a place where awful things have happened; the House of Horrors, by late morning, had been well seasoned. So we four or five who were now waiting for the guides to put things back in order would get to our feet and stand on tiptoe, listening at the door; we thought we heard the floor creak. But the astonishing thing was that *no one was on it.*

Then it would be our turn, and the CITs would come and distribute to each of us a black blindfold, which we were on our honor to leave in place once it was on our eyes, and had been properly checked by a guide of horror. It is possible, of course, that some of the campers looked under their blindfolds from time to time, but if they did, they cheated no one but themselves, for the House of Horrors had no visual effects. It had mattresses laid on the floor, and planks balanced across two bricks, and bowls full of grapes and cooked spaghetti; it had sheets that had been shredded and then hung from a low beam, and it had a rope with a noose, a body under a sheet. We put on our own blindfolds and passed into the tack room, and there the story began. Each year different, each year the same, each year about courage in the face of death.

Oh, they didn't put it that way, those seventeen-year-old kids, as they led us from mattress to plank, but that was what it was about, and the more intensely you imagined it, the more acutely you suffered as a result. The plank laid on two bricks was not four inches from the floor, it spanned two buildings, each of them ninety stories high, and if you fell, that was it. Here was someone who had fallen. Just put out your hands and touch him. And we put our hands on a piece of raw meat. And the mattress wasn't a mattress, laid on a tack room floor, it was a tussock in the middle of a great swamp; if we fell to either side of it, our bodies would be sucked into the mire and we would never again be seen by living eyes. Here, put your hand out, and we touched a vat of mud, and when we drew our fingers back, the mud made sucking noises; after that, as we walked across the mattress, we felt it rock and buckle beneath our feet, felt the clumps of grass, smelled the poisonous gas that was rising.

And the shreds of sheets, of course, weren't cotton, slit and hung from a beam above our heads, they were the strands of the web of a giant spider, a spider as big as a bear cub, who liked to eat smaller kinds of children. If we listened, we could probably hear him scuttling. Off in a distant corner, someone or something would make noises that sounded like the footfalls of a huge arachnid. Eight legs, you could tell from listening. Two and two and two and two. And this arachnid, so said our guide, was quite invisible. As for the bowls of grapes and cooked spaghetti, they were the usual eyeballs and entrails; the body under the sheet would suddenly jerk. And the noose we brushed into accidentally, with no warning at all from our guides – we would discover it only when it had touched our necks.

The House of Horrors was, in its way, a supreme illusion, and thus was a true work of art, for it took us farther away from Wynakee than we would have believed possible in the space of just a fifteen-or-twenty-minute walk. Had we taken off our blindfolds, had we looked at the space around us, all we would have seen were the tack room and its props. And we knew that, and yet forgot it, in this world that was always waiting, this world of the imagination which lay beyond the door. I used to emerge into the sunlight still shivering with fear, taking off my blindfold only once I was outside, and then, like those before me, I would shake off the fear that had come upon me, all mixed with the smell of horses, until it was loosened, and then scattered, and then extinguished.

Seventeen

BUT IF THERE WAS one special event which was more significant than the rest, one day of the summer which the summer grew around, that day was Klondike Day, which anyone who had lived through could never possibly forget. In fact, although Klondike Day happened just once a year at Wynakee, and almost never occurred until after the end of July, it was a day that reached back like memory right to the day when you first arrived at camp, with your trunk full of new clothes and your duffel bag neatly packed. Your parents were bringing you to camp, and you had name tags on all your clothes, and you had ugly blankets, a musical instrument, and a horrid cap; you had, as well, a laundry bag in your trunk, which your parents thought was to hold your dirty clothes. If it had been just for dirty clothes, though, why would you have insisted that it be made of canvas or some other fabric that was very tough and strong? Why would you have demanded so vehemently that it be *big*, and that it have attached to it, not just a string, but a strap from which it could be hung? Your parents thought you eccentric, and they gave you the bag you wanted, never knowing that its real purpose was to harvest gold; yes, the gold that lay around Wynakee, that was in Wynakee's woods and fields and streams, the gold that would, just *one* day that summer, reveal itself.

And from the moment you got to Owl's Head and unpacked your duffel bag and trunk, hanging the laundry bag in the closet next to the bathroom, you never forgot for a moment when you were stuffing in dirty clothes that before the summer was over it would be aching with a greater crop. Someday, sooner or later (but probably in the first week of August), you would go as usual to breakfast in the Barn, and your feet would be cold from the dew, for you would be barefoot, as you always were, and you would be spooning a bit of oatmeal into your mouth. Then there would be a stir in the area near the double doors, and you would look up, a little bit curious, but never dreaming that this could be *it*, that Klondike Day might at last have really arrived, and even after those great doors opened and Karl Wieneke stepped inside, there was a moment when you couldn't believe your eyes. You looked back at Karl's usual table, and you saw that yes, he wasn't there, and that that man in the doorway, wearing great overalls and a felt hat, might, in fact, be Karl; but this man who had just entered was dirty, and he was holding aloft two great gold rocks and he was shouting something you couldn't at first understand. Perambulating around the dining room, carrying his rocks, thrusting them out for all to see and touch, he kept shouting and shouting, "Gold! I found gold! There's gold in these green mountains!" But by now, it was hard to hear him above the roar that was growing in the room, the shrieks and shouts that were rising from every open mouth. "Klondike Day! It's Klondike Day!"

And many hands reached out to touch the rocks of gold.

You, too, reached out as Karl passed, because by now you, too, believed that yes, this was Karl, and no, this wasn't Karl at all. This wasn't Karl the lifeguard, this wasn't Karl the team captain, this was Karl, the man who had found the mother lode. And as he walked by your table, his face smudged with dirt, his old hat lopsided on his head and his overalls worn and ragged, you just managed to reach out and touch the gold, and then to touch him, or rather the sleeve of his old blue button-down shirt. And in that touch, so brief and fleeting, the whole story was nonetheless made plain, the many years that this man had spent wandering through the hills, impoverished and lonely, living on coffee grounds and grits, and being called, by all who saw him, a vagrant or a loony. Oh, they had scoffed at him, those people, for wasting all his time, looking for something that simply could not exist; no one in their right mind could believe that there was gold in these green mountains. How *could* there be, when no one else had found it? But *he* had, Karl had done it, and those people who had said he was just a bum would have to admit now that they had been wrong about him, about everything.

By now my heart was beating so hard I could feel it in my chest, and the room around me looked unusually light, as my pupils dilated. I found it hard to breathe and impossible to eat, and the din around me was enormous. But no one stopped it, no one stopped the shouting, no one tried to curb the excitement, they just let it roll and roll like thunder on the mountains. They, too, the counselors and the Wienekes, had waited for this day, planning for it in many secret meetings. They had spent many hours in the cow barn, where we were not allowed to go, painting hundreds and hundreds of rocks a bright and shiny gold. They had repainted last year's rocks – all those that had been found – and they had gathered new rocks, as well, to add to the incredible bounty. And they had painted, too, the Klondike Stone, the biggest stone of all, so that it gleamed and shone like a beacon. Then, the night before, when all the campers were asleep, they had loaded all the rocks into the hay wagon, and while Uncle Kuhrt drove the wagon, they had tossed the gold over its sides into the grasses and woods that were at that time hidden by the darkness. Hundreds of rocks they had thrown, until their arms had been weary with throwing, and the black night had accepted them all and covered them. Last, they had placed the Klondike Stone, carefully lifting it out of the wagon and transporting it to a place of special magic.

And now on this day – this day out of all the year – they were not Camp Wynakee counselors at all. Some of them were bankers, and some of them were sheriffs and some of them were outlaws; Megan, my own riding counselor, normally staid in her drab clothes, would today be wearing a many-tiered ruffled dress and a satin petticoat. Today, Megan's hair would be up, pinned with a hundred pins so that when some came out it fell down sexily, languorously; today, she would wear real perfume, and she would give male campers a kiss on the cheek – for the proper price, which was one hundred spondoolees. And Jo-John, who said little anyway, was the banker for our small town, and he wore a green eyeshade and a white shirt with black garters on the sleeves, and he stood or sat by the assessor's scales, weighing each child's gold as it arrived, carried in a heavy-duty laundry bag. Jo-John the banker carefully lifted the bag onto the scale, adjusted the weights and measures, and then grudgingly took the money box down from a shelf behind him, and then gave the child back his empty laundry bag and some pretty paper spondoolees to recompense him for the loss of all that beautiful gold. Today, Kuhrt Jr. was the town doctor, and a busy man he would be, dealing with the gunshot wounds that were almost inevitable in such a setting – particularly as the Black Bart Gang, that notorious bunch of ruffians, was bound to hold up innocent prospectors going about their business. Karl would be Black Bart, transformed after the breakfast interlude into the nastiest outlaw on the planet, and Aunt Helen would be the Widow Thomas, Black Bart's unfortunate mother, who did not know how a son of hers could have gone to the bad like that.

Yes, no wonder the shouting wouldn't stop, because the counselors also were doing it and all pretense of eating the rest of breakfast was forgotten, until at last, after Karl had banged back out, there was relative silence, and Uncle Kuhrt stood up to read off the list of outlaws and sheriffs. To be chosen as an outlaw was considered a great honor, because only outlaws could be put in jail, the old spring-house; to be chosen as a sheriff was generally considered boring, because sheriffs never collected as much gold as other campers. But whether you wanted to be an outlaw, or whether you wanted to be a sheriff, or whether you wanted to be simply an ordinary prospector, mattered not at all to the omnipotent Uncle Kuhrt, who dispassionately read off the names, while the camp erupted. One year and one year only was I a ruffian.

I didn't like being a ruffian, and I wasn't particularly good at it, because contrarily, I discovered that, as an outlaw and a member of the Black Bart Gang, I actually had to be far more social, and sociable, than any ordinary prospector. And while I wasn't normally antisocial, at least not at Camp Wynakee, I rather resented having to take other people more seriously than gold on Klondike Day; being a thief, a member of the Black Bart Gang was not allowed to do his or her own prospecting, but had to remove other campers' gold from them at the point of a water gun. To me, this was not much fun, particularly since the other campers resented it, and since it put me at risk of having to spend ten minutes in jail; when I *did* spend ten minutes in jail because a sheriff had caught me stealing, it was the longest ten minutes of my life. So each year, after that one year, I listened with bated breath until Uncle Kuhrt was done, and I discovered that no, I was neither sheriff nor outlaw; I was again what I wanted most to be that day, which was an ordinary prospector, plainspoken and hardworking, frugal with money and good with a canvas laundry bag.

After breakfast was over, or the uneaten food had been cleared away, Aunt Helen rang the gong and released the campers to their cabins; on this one day out of the whole summer, Uncle Kuhrt didn't stop us when we ran for the door, bumping against chairs and tables. During the interval between breakfast and ten o'clock, when Klondike Day officially began, we campers would be in our cabins, getting dressed for the great day, taking our laundry bags into our hands and adjusting the straps on them; the counselors, though, would be working, transforming Wynakee's main compound into a mining town, as befitted the occasion. Since the compound, fronting as it did on its large gravel courtyard, and consisting as it did of workshops, carriage houses, and covered walks, bore, in any case, a remarkable resemblance to a western frontier town – at least, if you folded the main street of such a town into a square – this procedure consisted of labeling the various buildings with huge paper signs: BANK / SALOON / DOCTOR / CAFE / JAIL / HABERDASHER. One sign said HORSES TO RENT, BY THE HOUR. The letters on these signs were stenciled, and they were appropriate to their meaning, so that BANK was very plain, while SALOON was very fancy. DOCTOR, as I recall, had a mortar and pestle painted on it for those of us who had not had the opportunity to get a good education, and HORSES TO RENT, BY THE HOUR, had both a painted horse head and a clock on it. SALOON, of course, had a glass and a bottle of whiskey. And these signs absolutely transformed the buildings.

Inside, the buildings were transformed also, generally by some small detail: the woodworking shop became the bank purely by virtue of the assessor's scales; the shower room, the haberdasher's because towels and shirts lay on a table there; a carriage house, the smithy because there was a plow in it. The Whatsit, with all of its animals and plants still there, was the doctor's office, with some bottles of dried herbs added for the occasion; here Kuhrt Jr. reigned with a stethoscope, at least until he wanted a break, at which point the camp nurse would take over, telling us the doctor was out "on an emergency." A garage where a Model T was normally stored was emptied of vehicles and turned into the saloon, with the addition of a bar and some bar stools, one or two tables, and some cookies and pitchers of lemonade – and also, of course, and most especially, with the addition of Megan and some other female counselors, who were cancan girls, and would kick up their heels to prove it. To me, they looked absolutely radiant, with their ruffles and the ribbons in their hair, and how they must have looked to the Wynakee boys I can only imagine; but I know that a crowd of boys was always gathering, getting a glass of lemonade for ten spondoolees, a cruller for twenty spondoolees, and that kiss on the cheek for a hundred.

Some of the horses were saddled and bridled and tethered western-style to a hitching post that had been constructed in front of the birch trees near the Wienekes' veranda; they could be rented in increments of fifteen minutes, for a very reasonable price, and they were in constant demand from tired children Lunch that day was to be held not in the dining hall – well, of course not! – but in the field by the river, where we had cookouts, and you had to *buy* your lunch to get it, though naturally if a child couldn't afford it, he would be given the meal on genuine spondoolee -credit.

Credits could be run forward from one year to the next, but it must have been a lazy camper indeed who would have actually needed this service, because so much gold lay in the green mountains that there was never a camper who didn't find some, and didn't have the pleasure of dropping gold rocks into a canvas laundry bag. The weight of the rocks didn't really matter, since it was an open secret that when you dragged your bag to the bank, and Jo-John as banker set it on the scales, his green eyeshade making him look predatory, each rock, whatever it really weighed, was equal to about twenty spondoolees. You had to find five for a kiss, one for a cruller, and only half a rock for lemonade.

Since – at least in theory – there was plenty of gold for all, but gold, once found, didn't actually bring you untold riches, most of every camper's Klondike Day was spent roaming the woods and hills – an activity that we called "going prospecting." Returning campers, some dragging their bags, were asked where the best lodes were located, but they never told, just swaggered across the courtyard; as for me, I rarely had crullers, or lemonade, or horse rides, or anything else. I was too busy looking for the Klondike Stone.

The Klondike Stone. How to describe it, the meaning that it had to those of us, like me, who had been enthralled by it? How to somehow capture the glory that those two words contained, the promise they held of endless, wonderful tomorrows? Somewhere in the mountains, or in the woods, or the fields, or the river, there was a rock that was larger than all the rest of them, that was huge and heavy and every ounce of it enchanted, and if you found this one stone, this huge stone, then you had found the Holy Grail, the sacred treasure. It didn't need to be weighed at the assessor's shop, but could be exchanged at once for everything that you otherwise needed spondoolees to buy – its finder, if finder there was, could ride for hours at a time, drink endless glasses of lemonade, get kisses until his cheek was sore. But to those of us who sought it truly, all that was quite irrelevant to the main object of finding the Stone, which was that its finder was cleansed, remade, newly wrought. It seemed that only the pure in heart had ever found the Klondike Stone, the very boldest and the best, the kindest who walked among us, and just as being made a Wayaka Huya was an honorable thing, so being the finder of the Klondike Stone was something that honored the finder.

With the Wayaka Huya, however, a human agency was clearly involved in the choosing, and Jo-John and Karl, as well as the other members, made the selection of their own society's initiates. The finder of the Klondike Stone, though, was chosen by nobody, or rather by nothing embodied; he or she was selected by accident – if accident you wanted to call it. But to those of us at Wynakee, those of us who lived through this high mystery or sacrament, it was clear that the finding WAS no accident but the workings of fate itself. No one in the Black Bart Gang, in the whole history of Wynakee, had ever found or stolen the Klondike Stone, and many years it was not found at all, though almost every other piece of gold was, in the course of the day, recovered. In my five years at Wynakee, the Klondike Stone was found only two times, both times by people who were much admired. How this could be, I do not know. It was this fact, above all, though, which raised Klondike Day in my own heart from just another marvelous day to a holy ritual.

And the holy ritual was not merely the actual search for the Stone, it went far beyond such a simple interpretation; the holy ritual was the entire activity of honing the imagination until you could see, in one thing, everything. On the Fourth of July, imagination was important, but it was important in advance, and because it produced something; you might think of the cabin theme, you might help to write the song, but then what you had was a product. On the day of the Horse Show, the last thing you wanted was to utilize your imagination even slightly; as for the Swimming Demonstration, great fun though it was, no one could say it called for much of anything.

But Klondike Day! It was an entire story, and the story was as simple or as complex as you cared to make it; it had a marvelous cast of characters, and a profoundly classical plot, and of course, colorful details like the gang and the sheriffs. But mostly it had what I suppose you would call a theme that was *the* theme, the one and only. And the kind of thrill that I got in the House of Horrors' darkness, with my blindfold on and all my other senses working, was nothing to the thrill I got out in the Klondike Day sunlight when I was filled not with brave fear but with clean desire.

I played my role of bad guy or sheriff or ordinary prospector with absolute devotion, from the moment that breakfast was over until the Trial, when, as a coda to the day, all the members of the Black Bart Gang would be thrown into the pond with their clothes on. Because Klondike Day was my chance to be someone other than myself, *more* than myself, not just for a brief moment, but *all day long*, and to me when I was at Wynakee a day was like a lifetime – it *was* a lifetime. On Klondike Day I was no mere child, with nothing real or important to strive for, but a human being who knew the lure of the free life of the outlaw, who knew the responsibility of the law's defenders, and who knew, most of all, the long, hard climb that was the task of the ordinary prospector, a climb that might or might not – who knew? how to know? – be rewarded when it was all over.

Yes, the part of the ordinary prospector appealed to me as a child, as few other parts in life have done, or could do, and even thinking of it now I feel a thrill of genuine excitement as I prepare to go out into the mountains. My blue jeans are strapped to my waist with an old leather belt from the prop room, and I have borrowed a large chambray shirt from Jack, my mumblety-peg partner. In my pants is my Barlow penknife, fastened to a leather thong, in turn fastened to one of the blue jeans' belt loops. I have no cap, but I am wearing shoes, as befits a poor man who is nonetheless sensible – a poor man who has left his wife and family and traversed the raw country by stagecoach and has arrived in the mountains without any money. But I have the clothes I am standing in, and I have my red bandana, which will protect me from the dust of my soon-to-come prospecting, and I have the hands and feet I was born with, which will lead me, or not, to the Klondike Stone. I will gather other gold, of course, if I find it – pebbles and nuggets – and I will carry them down from the mountains, but even 1, an ordinary poor man, know that other gold is just gold, and that it is the Klondike Stone that I am seeking.

I could not figure out why other campers at Wynakee did not feel about this Stone the way that I did, why some of them were content to find just gold enough for their needs and then forget it. Other campers, at least half of them, were satisfied with their accomplishments if they had had a nice snack of lemonade and sugared crullers. But that left half who were like me, who had nothing on their minds from the moment that Karl burst into the dining room but the finding of the Klondike Stone, and I knew which of my fellow campers were part of this religious order almost by merely looking at them. Heading up into the hills again, having emptied my load of gold and gathered spondoolees enough to last forever, I might run into a friend who was heading the opposite way, and she might ask me where I was going. In character, I would nod my head and say gruffly, almost reluctantly, "I hear there's a stone. A big stone, they tell me," and the friend might say, "The Klondike Stone. Yes. I met a man who said he'd seen it." Or, if she were a different friend, she would say, "Oh, nobody finds the Klondike Stone!" And if she said the latter, I would know she was someone content with the sufficient. If she said the former, I would know that here was a kindred spirit, who wanted everything and believed in the impossible.

My day would be spent in the pastures, or at the Council Circle, or looking in the river, or walking in the hayfields behind the stables, and the afternoon would grow hot, and then it would grow cool again, and I would find gold, gold by the sackful. The day would grow old, and I would grow weary, and down in town the can can girls would be sitting on the barstools, and the saloon would be closing, and the horses unsaddled and unbridled, and led to water and then to their paddock. The day would grow old, and Klondike Day, except for the Trial, would by now be almost over, and still the Klondike Stone would be somewhere out here. Even though at the time I might be high in the hills, or down by the river with no one else near me, I knew that if the Klondike Stone had been found, I would have known of it, because the news would have come to me on the wind's telegraph.

No, it was still out there, and even now it could still be found, right up until the last minute, until Klondike Day was over, and I was going to keep looking, because no matter how little time remained, I still had time enough, just, to meet with it. To meet with it – that was what I wanted. Not even to carry it into town, not even to present it to Jo-John, but simply to meet with it, wherever it was, and look at it in the wild, to see if my eyes were dazzled by it. But I knew that wherever it was, even if it was right there in plain sight, I would not find it unless it chose to be discovered, because one year it had been left by The Barn, lying in some grass below the wall, and it was said that one camper had actually sat on it. And one year it had lain in the Mettawee, just below the waterwheel, where I myself must have looked directly at it. Merely looking for it was not enough. It had to *want you to find it.* I never found it. The Stone never revealed itself.

But although now Klondike Day was over, the bell was ringing and the Trial was to start, and I had to get to my feet and hoist my bag to my shoulder one last time, I was not really overly disheartened. I knew it would be another year before Karl burst again into the dining hall, carrying aloft those rocks, shouting, "There's gold in these green mountains!" but I knew that that day must come, and when it did I would be ready for it. And after the Trial was over, and Klondike Day was truly done, there was still something I could do for the rest of the summer. I could go to visit the place where the Klondike Stone had lain, and where I had not been able to find it. In the river by the waterwheel, in the grass by The Barn, or near a wickiup down by the Council Circle, I would sit close to where it had been, and marvel that this spot – of all others – was the very place where I had missed it. The river ran sparkling in the sunlight, the grass bent, brushed by the wind, the floor of the forest grew ever darker and richer; such an ordinary spot this was, this patch of grass, this bit of woods. So ordinary, so simple, and right there in front of me.

THE LONG TRAIL

Eighteen

THE ONLY OCCASIONS during the summer when I could bear to leave Camp Wynakee – except for an occasional swim in the Dorset Quarry – were the occasions when we got to go on hikes, or even better, on what we called "overnights"; we also referred to this as "tripping," short for "going on camping trips." If an overnight was in the works, I volunteered for it every time, even though it would mean traveling far from Wynakee's center. As I saw it, though I left the camp proper, I didn't really leave *Wynakee* if I remained in the natural world of woods and meadows. Leaving Wynakee in its largest sense, however, was something that I simply wouldn't do – not for anything – during the eight weeks when I was in residence there. At first this created some problems, since my mother and stepfather lived nearby, just twenty minutes away, on the top of Rupert Mountain.

And while my stepfather would have been content to drop me at camp during the last week of June and not see me again until the end of August, my mother was a mother, and in her way a particularly fond one, and she appeared to want to see me almost constantly. The first summer I was at camp, she kept suggesting that she and my stepfather take me away from Wynakee for a "special treat," as she put it. It took me the entire season to convince her that she could have suggested this until she collapsed, and I still wouldn't have gotten into the car to go anywhere, save perhaps at gunpoint.

After the first summer, though, things settled into a routine, with my mother and stepfather coming to visit me every Sunday. At about eleven o'clock in the morning, after Sunday service and before lunch, I could expect my stepfather to drive his Mercedes into the courtyard. There was no actual rule against this, though the Wienekes discouraged too much visiting and preferred to have parents come just on special occasions, but Aunt Helen sized my mother up early and saw that if she didn't let her come on Sundays, there was always a chance that she might appear another time, quite unexpectedly.

So when I woke up on Sunday mornings, looking forward to Council Fire that evening, to the cookout by the river, to the big noon dinner, even to morning service, I would also immediately be aware that this was the day when I would have to see my stepfather, although at least I would not have to leave Wynakee with him. Luckily, he never wanted to stay long, but even for the hour or so that he and my mother would be there, I would, I knew in advance, be at quite a loss, because I would have to entertain them, and since they came every single Sunday, varying the entertainments sufficiently could be difficult. For one thing, my mind always went blank when my stepfather asked the question, "So what did you learn this week?" just as he always asked at dinner after my day at school, "So what did you learn today?" and I would stare vaguely at the table, trying to summon up a single memory, a single thought, or a single impression of reality. "Math," I might finally say, during the school year, and my stepfather would appear to be satisfied with that, but a whole hour, on Sundays, at Wynakee! It needed to be planned for in advance. And I planned for it, every week, very carefully.

When my mother and stepfather first arrived, I would be waiting for them in the courtyard, and would, of course, run over and hug my mother tightly, while my stepfather stood by, waiting for this display of emotion, as he would put it, to be over and done with for the time. Then I would carefully peck his cheek, and ask them if they wanted to see the Wienekes, which they always did, which was always a relief, because it took at least ten minutes of the hour, and made only fifty minutes more to live through before I could wave them both good-bye. I watched from a distance while my mother and stepfather talked to Aunt Helen and Uncle Kuhrt; then it was time for the presentation of cheese. They always brought me cheese; they were not supposed to bring candy, and while many parents brought it to their children anyway, my stepfather thought cheese appropriate, and stopped his Mercedes at Peltier's in Dorset each Sunday to get a piece of it wrapped in waxed paper.

I would thank them both for the cheese, and then ask if we could take it up to Owl's Head, so that I wouldn't have to carry it around with me for the next hour; since my stepfather didn't like to walk, he sometimes insisted that we drive up in the Mercedes, which was diesel and had a smell that I feared and loathed. Just getting into that car for the two minutes that it would take to drive up to Owl's Head always brought me to the edge of a genuine anxiety attack – my breath would get short, my heart pound, and my head grow light with the fear that I was about to be kidnapped. I didn't think of the word "kidnapped," I just feared, with a gut-wrenching fear, that my stepfather would drive on past Owl's Head, and then down the Hollow, and that the car would be going so fast that I wouldn't be able to open the door and fling myself out, as I had seen people do in movies. So I would sit, scarcely daring to breathe, until the car pulled up at Owl's Head and then I would leap out and run into the house, where I put the cheese away. Although I really liked cheese, that piece of cheese in its brown paper seemed an awfully small reward for the terror of having lived through another two-minute Mercedes ride, and some weeks I could not bring myself to eat the cheese at all, and simply gave it away to my fellow Owls.

After the cheese incident, it was time for activities, and while my stepfather drove his car back to the compound, my mother and I walked, at my suggestion, down through the field, and the next half hour was entirely devoted to taking my mother and stepfather to see my projects, to showing off the animals, and, perhaps, to demonstrating new skills. If it had just been my mother who was visiting, I am sure that we would have sat in a field somewhere and talked, she telling me about her week and me telling her about mine, but since my stepfather was also with us, there was no possibility of that, and I think the wildly different motives with which these two had come was one of the things that made the visits so difficult.

My mother was always brimming with love, and appeared to believe that I would die of grief if a week went by without my seeing her; my stepfather knew that I would not die of grief if a week went by without my seeing him, which unfortunately made him even more sardonic than usual. And to have the two of them show up weekly, carrying on this unconscious tug-of-war between them – my mother seeming to think that it was worth it, my stepfather that it wasn't – never grew less disconcerting, putting me into a state of true alarm; I felt like an animal arrested by a set of headlights. As I grew older, I did my best to discourage my mother from coming, telling her one week that she should really skip the next one, but: "Of course we will come next week, dear! You mustn't ever doubt that."

There was one visit from my mother and stepfather which in its sheer agony stands out most clearly, and that was the Sunday of the solar eclipse, my third summer at Wynakee. The whole rest of the camp was going on a hike, climbing the mountain with bag lunches, to be able to watch the eclipse from the best possible vantage point, through exposed film with which everyone was to be specially provided. The day of the eclipse dawned warm and sunny, and when I woke up at Owl's Head I instantly remembered it, but for a wonder, didn't remember about the Sunday parental visit; I assume this was because the counselors had been talking of little else all week except for the great event which was to come, this partial solar eclipse and the great all-camp hike that would herald it. We would pack up the picnic lunches, and the strips of developed film, and, it was rumored, maybe even bottles of orange soda, and because the eclipse fell on a Sunday, we would not be having a Sunday service in the library, but instead would have a brief service up on the mountain top.

So we all ate breakfast in a tremendous rush that morning, as if by bolting our food, ignoring our juice, and not eating toast we could make the eclipse come that much sooner, and after breakfast we picked up our bag lunches from the table at the back of the dining room, and then, bags in hand, raced back to our respective cabins. After one trip to Owl's Head to get my jacket and cap, I had to make a second one for my knife, which I had forgotten; my counselor Bonnie had told me I wouldn't need it, but I knew better than that. I always took my knife with me when I was hiking.

When I slammed back into Owl's Head and dashed toward my footlocker, I saw another Owl, Sandy Scott, still getting dressed. Always late for everything, Sandy saw no need to hurry even for a solar eclipse, and she was laboriously crossing the laces of her hiking boots from one side to the other. She asked me to wait for her, and though I was in a tremendous hurry – having already thrown open my footlocker, located my knife, and buttoned its leather case around my belt – I unenthusiastically agreed, while admiring the splendor of my hiking boots. A hike! We were going on a hike! We wouldn't be camping, but still. We were going hiking!

"Hurry up though. Everyone's waiting, " I said. "The eclipse is going to start at one exactly."

"I know, said Sandy. "Isn't it lucky your parents aren't coming?"

I stood and stared at her in silence, feeling my whole body sinking and wondering how in the world I could have forgotten. We wouldn't be back from the hike until late afternoon, and if I went, I would not be here to greet my mother and stepfather when they arrived in the Mercedes. And while of course the eclipse would happen everywhere, I didn't much care about the eclipse, because I had never seen one and wasn't sure what all the fuss was about; it was the hike that I had been so looking forward to, the hike and the bag lunch which would accompany it, and also the view from the top of the mountain. For a wild instant, I thought of simply pretending to myself and everyone else that I had forgotten that my mother and stepfather would be coming – indeed, I *had* forgotten it, really, and had Sandy not said anything about it, I would even now be joining the rest of the camp down in the courtyard. When my stepfather pulled up, well he and my mother would find that I was gone, and they would just have to turn around and go back where they had come from. But I knew that now that I *had* remembered, I would find it impossible to forget again, and the constant remembering, and guilt, would remove all pleasure from the hike.

In fact, in one swift, sickening moment I realized that I would have to stay behind in camp, where no one was staying except for Seth and the nurse and a sick child in the infirmary. I don't know why it didn't occur to me that there was still time to have Aunt Helen phone my mother, but it didn't, and I walked back to the courtyard merely to tell Bonnie what had happened. Then I watched everyone set off, gaily singing and tussling as they walked past The Barn, past the stables and up into the meadow, and the silence that grew around me was the silence that I most feared and hated, the silence of the last hour of the last day of the summer. To get away from it, I went down to the river to bathe my feet and sort through some pebbles, and on the way I picked some Indian paintbrush, orange and fire-engine red, for my mother. Sitting by the river, with the flowers resting in a pool of water, I took off my hiking boots and socks, and then thrust my feet into the water next to the paintbrush, pretending that I was an Indian brave forgotten by my tribe. Somehow I had to write a message informing my people of my terrible situation. I had nothing, however, with which to write. Ah! Perhaps the flowers? I would squeeze them for their dye and then write HELP on a handy birch tree. No, I had better keep them and give them to my mother. They would provide at least a few moments of conversation.

As I say, it always took a good deal of resourcefulness for me to find things for my mother and stepfather to do, and I generally planned out an elaborate program beforehand Today we would talk about the paintbrush, then we could inspect my part of the totem pole, then I would show then my bread-board, and my new marbled-paper cup. Next, I would demonstrate my sort-of-dive, and then, I imagined, we could all sit and watch the eclipse together, though we campers, as I had discovered, had each been given only enough developed film for one person. I would probably have to share my film.

While I was waiting for my parents, I ate part of my lunch and walked around, going into and out of all the deserted buildings. I left my hiking boots off after the river plunge, putting them by the wall next to the Whatsit, and was sitting by the birch trees when it came time for the parental arrival. Punctual as ever, my stepfather pulled up, turned off the ignition, and climbed sedately out of the car. My mother rushed over to hug me, noticing nothing but me, but my stepfather was more observant.

"Where are all the other little hoodlums?"

This was his usual tone, at least when he was trying to be nice, a tone that was simultaneously jocular and cutting. I told him they were all "at the eclipse. Everyone hiked up to see it. With bag lunches," I added self-pityingly .

"Oh, dear," my mother said to that. "And you couldn't go because we were coming. You should have phoned. We could have come another time instead."

This, of course, made a bad situation worse, as I was struck with the truth of her observation, so I rushed into my program of things to do, listing the breadboard, the totem pole, and the almost-diving.

"How do you *almost* dive?" my stepfather asked.

"I'll show you. And we can see the sheep, also."

I asked my mother what she wanted to do first, and she clearly had had trouble following my list, since she immediately said, "See the sheep," which I had merely thrown in because without it, my program lacked a conclusion. But I led the way over to the barn, and then down the dirt trail to the sheep pen; we had two sheep that summer, one of whom was my friend. Clara was her name, and she always came over to the fence and let me scratch her face for her, a black face on top of a dirty white body, and with translucent ears that stuck out to either side.

I called her over, and though I was afraid for a minute that she wouldn't come just because this time my stepfather was watching, she did; she pushed her head through the fence to meet my hand, and I scratched the top of her bony face all over. Her tongue went rapidly in and out of her mouth as I scratched the area above her nose, and when I rubbed her ears, her top lip curled back to expose her soft teeth. I explained to my mother that this meant she was happy, and that she always did this when I rubbed her ears. Then I patted her one last time, and that was Clara.

I asked my mother what she wanted to do next, and as usual, she was vague. "Whatever you want," she said, so I decided on the totem pole, and the three of us trooped back dutifully – only my mother was even marginally happy – until we had skirted the edge of the barn, and emerged into the terrifying quiet of the courtyard. By now – it was late July – almost three-quarters of the totem pole had been completed, although none of it would be painted until the carving was fully finished, and I showed my mother my part, a groove along the side near the top, ostensibly part of a hawk's face, though it didn't yet much look like it. I carefully delineated it to her anyway, showing her how I held the chisel, and how I pounded on its end with a wooden mallet, and my mother emerged from her vagueness long enough to ask a question the sort she always asked.

"How many campers work on this?"

I picked a number at random – thirty, I think it was. "Thirty!" marveled my mother, quite impressed, and then, as long as we were there, I decided we might as well move on to the breadboard, so we ducked out of the sunlight into the dimness of the woodworking shop. I found my breadboard in-progress hanging on the pegboard, with my name on a label just above it, and while it was not completely sanded yet, especially in the corners around the handle, it was small and square and thick and I was proud of it. With Jo-John's help, I had drilled a hole in it from which it could be hung, and when I pointed this out to my stepfather and my mother, my mother made admiring noises, but my stepfather said, "Are you going to cut bread on it?"

So far, this visit was worse than usual. Wynakee wasn't Wynakee without the other campers, and my sense of being an animal caught in the glare of headlights was magnified by the other childrens' absence until I felt that it wasn't just headlights, it was a brilliant spotlight and it was directed at me alone from the belly of a helicopter flying above me.

I therefore jettisoned the marbled-paper cup and suggested we move on to the diving, and though of course my stepfather said, "You mean the almost-diving," I didn't care, because I got to go alone to Owl's Head to put my suit on. There I took my time, but when I could delay no longer, I took my towel and walked down the road past Netop to the pond; my mother and stepfather were standing near the lifeguard's tower and my stepfather looked intensely bored, but also just a bit faded as if the light around him was dimmer than it should have been. I wondered if the eclipse could possibly be happening already, realizing with dismay that I had left my black film in my shorts up at Owl's Head, but deciding that I might as well do the dive and get it over with. I dropped the towel by the side of the pond and walked out to the edge of the low diving board, and then asked my mother if she was watching, at which she nodded diligently. Next I explained that what I was about to do was considered a pre-dive, since you went in headfirst, though you didn't put your hands out in front of you.

Finally, letting my hands hang at my sides, I bent my head heavily onto my chest and curled my whole body over until my head was level with my knees. With a great gulp of air to sustain me, I lifted my heels from the board and felt my body tipping forward, until my toes peeled off into the air and I toppled forward. The water slowed my momentum, but I continued to bend sluggishly around in a circle in the water until I had almost come to the top again, at which point I whipped my arms through the water and propelled myself to the surface, gasping for air, and calling breathlessly to my mother, asking if she had seen it. She said, "Yes, of course I saw it, Elizabeth," and then observed encouragingly that I hadn't even put my hands out in front of me, and that if you asked her, that was even harder than doing a regular dive. l knew it wasn't harder, but I appreciated her kindness.

And now that the grueling demonstration of animals, artifacts, and skills was at an end, I thought maybe we could all actually relax a little. It *must* be getting time for the eclipse to start. So I rubbed my shoulders with my towel, about to say something about the eclipse, when my stepfather said, "Well, I guess we'll get going."

I was dismayed. When I had been sitting by the river, planning out the day's activities, the viewing of the eclipse had naturally been their high point, and indeed, the only thing that could conceivably have made up for the fact that I had had to remain in camp while every other Wynakee camper except for the sick one got to go hiking. Really, the eclipse was by then not only to be the high point of this particular visit, but the high point of the whole unbearable business of visits in general, since for once there would be something pleasant that the three of us could do together. Of course, I would have placed dry ice on my tongue before I would have said this. So when my mother explained that she and my stepfather were giving an eclipse party, I said merely, "Oh. I'll walk you to the car," and then waved, as usual, as the stench of diesel wafted back to me.

Now was the worst time of all, the thirty minutes or hour that I would be alone, waiting for the eclipse, waiting for the camp to get back to normal, and I went up to Owl's Head by myself, changed out of my swimsuit back into my shorts, and then lay down on the bunk, taking out the cheese in its brown waxed paper. I unwrapped it and put a bit of it in my mouth, letting its sharp taste fill my senses, knowing that I was supposed to be with the camp nurse now, but ignoring it. Perhaps I cried, perhaps I didn't, but I certainly brooded about the other campers, all having fun hiking – I had missed a *hike* for this parental encounter – and then I guess I fell asleep, because when I woke up again there was something really strange about Owl's Head; the ceiling looked strange, the beds looked strange, and the orchard and hayfield looked strange through the window.

I shook off sleep and went outside. Things were even stranger there. The light was pale and diluted, and the world seemed wintry, cold-looking. Was this the eclipse? I decided that it must be and reached into my pocket for the film, sitting down on the marble stoop and looking through it. Where was the sun? The film was very black. But then yes, I saw it – a pale ball, round and small and far away, no burning rays around it. It looked pathetically unprotected, all alone in that black black space. Moreover, it looked as if someone had taken a bite out of it.

So that was an eclipse? That was what all the fuss was about? A big bite out of the sun and the whole world wintry and cold-looking? The sun had stayed in its usual orbit, and yet it had been intruded upon nonetheless – chewed on by a shadow that had no business being there. I knew that the sun had not been harmed, or at least I hoped that it had not, but I couldn't help seeing myself in that darkened, chewed part – and I thought it mysterious that I could be at Wynakee and yet have somehow been stolen away from it, while I could also leave Wynakee and yet somehow remain there.

Nineteen

WHILE the solar eclipse and all that surrounded it was *sui gene-*

ris at Wynakee, hikes and overnights were happily rather common; we had overnights twice a month, and when the trips were announced, midweek, the counselors who were leading them would rise in the dining hall to describe them. Then we campers, most of us eager, would have the chance to volunteer for one, and hope that we, in turn, would be chosen to participate. I was lucky, for I gained a reputation early as a determined hiker and a willing worker. Quite often I was the youngest camper on my overnight. But for me this was no problem, since my major relationships on a camping trip were with the woods, the counselor, and my personal equipment – a sleeping bag, hiking boots, a knapsack, a canteen, and a magnificent, beautiful, awe-inspiring mess kit.

My mess kit! Inside was a metal cup with a wire handle bent over once to keep it from getting hot – that was the theory of the designer, at least, though the practice was rather different, since the cup handle first burned you so you almost dropped it and then grew freezing cold. And the cup was so designed that when it was full of liquid it was, for me at least, impossible to hold, and would tip half its contents onto the ground immediately should I be foolish enough to pick it up. That was even if it *wasn't* particularly hot. Getting to know my cup, and to form a friendship with the thing, took me a summer or two at least, but eventually I discerned that it preferred to be half-full of tepid liquid, and we got along together famously after that.

The cup was just the beginning, though, as the mess kit also had a bowl, which fit over the cup and the frying pan like a lid – and the handle of the frying pan was fastened with a screw and a wing nut, so that it acted as a clamp to hold the whole kit together. And the bowl could be used as a pot if you gave it the same handle, so that the handle, a piece of bent strap metal, actually had a triple chance of being put to use. And bowl, cup, frying pan, pot and handle, together with the wing nut, were, when assembled, only about eight or nine inches in diameter and four inches thick. The whole assembly fit in turn into a cloth case, which was khaki and snapped tightly around the implements, and then hung from your neck by a strap, at least until you discovered that it would be better off in your knapsack, where it wouldn't bruise your knees while you were walking. It was always a challenge to put the mess kit into its cloth case, which had been cut to specifications as exacting as a girdle; there was only one way it would fit, and even then one needed three hands, or two hands and teeth, to squeeze and wriggle it in. Other children might give up, sensibly deciding that if they carried the mess kit in their knapsacks, they didn't need to put it first into its khaki girdle, but on every overnight I spent what seemed like hours putting the whole thing together and adjusting the wing nuts until the tips of my fingers hurt.

As for my sleeping bag, it was even more important. A mess kit is a tool. A sleeping bag, though, is a piece of clothing. The mess kit developed character over the course of years – burn holes, dents – but the sleeping bag was far more impressionable. Mine was green-brown, the same marvelously ugly color as my blankets, and it was constructed with a top and a bottom, the top made of a synthetic satin, the bottom of a kind of rubberized canvas. Anyone who has owned a bag like this will know that it was rectangular, and that it could not be zipped up from the inside at all. The inside, of course, was flannel – in the case of my marvelous bag, a somber brown color – and quilted like a bed quilt. Other campers, boys and girls, had ducks or forests or woodsmen dancing across the insides of their bags. Mine was a blank canvas on which I could paint my own visions of Elizabeth Arthur, hero and woodsman. Tough guy. Modern Chingachgook.

I would know that sleeping bag anywhere, were I to meet up with it – the rubber on the bottom cracked, and the inside flannel worn and nubbly – and I thought it splendid that it could be unzipped all the way around so that it could be spread flat on the ground like a quilted blanket. After any camping trip, whether it had rained while we were out or not – and usually it had, at least a little – we who had returned from the Beyond, like Roman legionnaires, would spread our sleeping bags on the grass, their bellies opened. There they would lie, like brightly colored banners, with ducks and woodsmen and forests parading across their flannel flanks – except for mine, which was that neutral, triumphant brown. Although over the years the satin wore thin, and the zipper less eager to zip, I would not, could not, be persuaded to give it up. To me, it never became less beautiful, and as it was rarely if ever washed, the odor of woodsmoke was always with it, bearing witness; and the witness that it bore, the testament that it made, was that this sleeping bag had seen things few eyes had ever seen. It had journeyed into the mountains, it had lingered within the forest, it had heard the murmurs of the spirits of the trees. And this was no hearsay evidence, this was the evidence of the nose. This was the stunning nasal evidence of time.

The very first night I slept out was on a trip that had been especially designed for beginners, when Karl took some Wrens and some Crows just a mile and a half from camp. I readied myself in the Wren's Nest with what was then my brand-new gear, strapping my sleeping bag onto my rucksack, hanging my mess kit around my neck, lacing up my hiking boots around my newly dynamic feet. And when I set off across the lawn behind Karl, who was leading, and surrounded by my fellow Wrens and Crows, I felt that my body had been transformed by the weight that was hanging on my shoulders and by the way that the hiking boots encased my feet. Why, I was shod now like a soldier, and I leaned forward to ease the rucksack, maybe a sailor pitching his body into a stiff wind; with the smallest of adjustments, I found myself suddenly qualified to understand a whole new matrix of human history. It was the spirit that pulsed with willpower, the temper that coursed with explorations, the genius that carried human beings around the globe. All you needed, I saw, was a rucksack, a mess kit, a sleeping bag, and a good pair of boots. All of these would pump your blood along.

That was one part of camping out – the hiking to get where you were going, the absolutely glorious feeling of power which resulted from traveling under your own steam. The other part was deeper, wilder, and somehow older, and had nothing to do with power at all. It had to do with arriving where you were going, in the deep wood full of mystery, and the night that I was first a full inhabitant of the woods, as opposed to merely a visitor, was, for me, pure magic. Before, when I had wandered among the tree trunks, under the leaves, I had known that when night came I would have to leave them. Now, I was in the place where all the legends came from, also called the greenwood, or the wildwood. I helped set up a tent, struggled for the first time to pound a metal tent stake into the ground with a rock; I unrolled my sleeping bag inside it, every part of me overpowered by the munificence of the smell of canvas.

While Karl and his assistants were gathering five-gallon jugs of water, I was carrying the pot from my mess kit down to the stream, and there, gathering my own supply in that metal so new it looked freshly scoured. We ate hot dogs and baked beans, and for a while it looked like rain, but then the sky cleared and the stars came out brilliantly, so Karl decided to sleep outside his tent. I had never even *thought* of this! Karl and I and five or six others stretched our sleeping bags by the fire, and I blew up my inflatable pillow and placed my head on it cautiously, pulling the flannel bag only as far as my breastbone; it was hours before I slept, and when at last I had calmed down enough to drift off, rain hit me in the face in no uncertain manner. *We were being rained on at night,* and suddenly we were pretty wet, and had to get out of our bags and scramble into the tents where the canvas smell was now absolutely princely, and I was certainly far too excited to go to sleep again right away, what with the sound of raindrops falling on that canvas.

So from then on, and with Aunt Helen's encouragement, I went on every overnight I could, often visiting the same places over again, so that as the years passed I became well acquainted with the entire panoply of Camp Wynakee out-trips. But there are four which might well stand in for all of them: the trips to the Fire Tower, the Ice Cave, the Bat Cave, and the Long Trail. Like everything else at Wynakee, with time the names alone took on for me the resonance of a great mythology.

The Fire Tower was located to the east of Camp Wynakee, on the top, I believe, of Dorset Mountain itself, and even during my own time in the Hollow, the tower was about to crumble, so by now, no doubt it has long returned to the ground. But then, it was still there, and to get to the Fire Tower on the mountain, we hiked for a day through a gradually ascending forest; the distinctive thing about this camping trip was that we never broke through the trees until we had actually arrived at our destination. After breakfast on the day of the hike, we who were going all gathered in the courtyard, while the camping equipment was placed there in the sun, and the counselor who was leading the hike – in this case, Kuhrt Jr. – checked the equipment to make sure it was all there. The food was brought down also – by the cook and some CITs who were still at it, still peeling potatoes, still hoping for glory ahead – and it, too, was placed on hard-packed gravel, while we who were going on the trip studied it hungrily.

Because all the gear that lay there, and all the food that was stacked in boxes, immediately assumed a stature – to us – of genuine greatness; if it was not *quite* as important to us as our mess kits or sleeping bags or rucksacks, it still inspired an instant, deep affection. You might think that most campers would have been eager to carry as little weight as possible, but this was not the case; the weight was unimportant. We all wanted to be the proud bearers of whatever would turn out to be most vital, whatever every single person on the overnight would need. Would we get to take the matches? Or the scrub brush for washing our mess kits? Or the group frying pan? Or the water jug? Or the tent stakes or the ground cloths for the tents? Or would we be given, perhaps, the eggs for our breakfast, each egg wrapped in its own piece of paper and then placed in a special metal egg-carrying case? We waited while Kuhrt Jr. inventoried everything carefully, and then gave us whatever we had won – at which point, thrilled, we raced off with it to pack it up.

I was an Owl by now and this time I had won the frying pan, which was about halfway from the top in the equipment role of honor; it was heavy, which was a plus, but if we lost it, we could make do, and it might even be fun to, say, fry an egg on a flat hot rock. It was not, for example, like a tent-fly, which was also heavy but truly crucial, since a camping trip would be no fun at all if you couldn't crawl into a dry tent. Being wet when you crawled in was quite all right, as was making everything around you damp. A tent-fly was like matches or the shovel, though – and the frying pan was not.

But I took the frying pan by the handle and carried it all the way up to Owl's Head where I could concentrate on finding the ideal position for it in my pack. This period after breakfast when you were packing up your personal and group gear was, for me, a nerve-wracking period at best. I was always beset by the persistent though entirely irrational fear that if I didn't hurry, the trip would leave without me, so I was always rushing to complete my packing, and yet also trying to do it well, to put my lunch and canteen on top, the frying pan on the bottom and my clothes in the middle. My sleeping bag I strapped to the bottom, although I had learned from much experience that it banged on my buttocks there with every step I took. Still, there was nowhere else to put it, so I slung the whole thing onto my back and raced through the meadow down from Owl's Head, sleeping bag swinging. While I waited for the others to arrive – since inevitably I was the first one back – I lay in the courtyard with my head on my pack and my legs stretched out to display my hiking boots; I pitied with all my heart the poor saps who weren't coming with us, but were at regular morning activities like Woodworking and Arts and Crafts.

When we set off, at about ten, most of us were already hungry, since just the anticipation of physical labor can be very hard work, so Kuhrt Jr., in his opening remarks, reminded us that we would be eating lunch not at any specific time, but when we had put behind us at *least* two and a half or three miles. This made us all slightly grumpy, as we set off on the dusty road, but the hike quickly took that kind of grumpiness out of us. By the time we had reached the end of the Hollow, we were all hot and sweating; by the time we had climbed three fallen logs we were exhausted, and we walked long in that daze peculiar to pack-laden hikers, a daze that both deadens and heightens your awareness. You become more aware of the texture and color of leaves as they lie on the forest floor, blown or crunched; you become less aware of sounds, as they echo in the distance. Sometimes you cannot even be bothered to decide what they add up to. If Kuhrt admonished us to do something – like go around a particular tree where two years before someone had stepped into a hornet's nest – I would hear him and do what he had said, but it would take all the concentration I had not to forget what I was supposed to do by the time I got there.

And I became well acquainted with my hands, and the calf muscles of the person in front of me, and the muscles I hadn't known I had between my shoulder blades and across my back; but if someone not immediately in front of me had vanished, just popped out of existence like a soap bubble, I doubt that I would even have noticed. Luckily, I could count on Kuhrt to notice, and to do other things, both important and unimportant. As we ascended higher through the forest, following the paths of dried streambeds, and trying also to "contour," which is to say to never lose altitude, Kuhrt became more and more astonishing, an amazing figure of authority. He achieved this, basically, because he had one ability that the rest of us did not. He could actually talk comprehensibly at the same time that he was walking.

At about noon, after all, we stopped for lunch, by a nice little pool of water in a side stream that had not yet, as most had, dried up, and after several pots of water had been drawn out of it, most of us removed our boots and plunged our hot feet into its coolness. On all camping trips, we were given oranges for the first lunch out, and I always began with mine – as did most of the others – since it would never taste as good again as it did at this moment; I would punch a hole in the orange with the tip of my penknife and then squeeze the rind like a wineskin, sucking out the juice and afterwards eating the pulp. Half of the juice ended up on either my chin or my shirt, but that was part of the fun of going for a hike, and after lunch – two sandwiches, a candy bar, and water, in addition to the orange – it was also fun to lie on the ground waiting for Kuhrt to tell us to get a move on. We campers were in no hurry, and neither was Kuhrt, as it turned out, but at last he gave the command and we put on our socks and boots, reshouldered our packs and started heading again toward the Fire Tower.

In the afternoon, even in the forest, it was hot. Not just hot but dry hot: the heat lay around us like a piece of birch bark carefully cut and ready to be set to flame. And that was strange. It was like an invisible wall, a force field that had real mass and resistance, and as we were going toward the Fire Tower, the heat of the day and our destination melded together in my mind. Although the Fire Tower had, of course, been built to avert fires, it now seemed a literal column of fire towering toward the sky, and the whole world transformed into heat and conflagration. We were hot, we were dry, we hikers were the wood, and the day around us was the flame. We would go through fire to arrive there, at this mythical place, and the smoke it gave off would be a great burning.

So when we broke through the trees, late late that day, and saw the wooden tower in the clearing on the mountain, I was for an instant disappointed at the shaky, pine pole foundation, the odd little cabin perched on top like a clown's crushed hat. This drooping wooden structure was hardly the tongue of flame that its name had ignited in my imagination – but then I looked beyond it, through the heat of the late summer day, to the Green Mountains, and the blue sky, and the winding valleys. We threw down our packs and climbed higher, higher than anything else we could see, and the haze that hung over the landscape was like smoke. The earth was baking, and we were baking with it, and the actual wooden structure which was the Fire Tower was not important. What *was* important was that here on the mountain we ourselves were towers, and we could launch a kind of rocket of perception; our eyes could connect with all that lay before us, and as far as we could see, that all was *everything.* As we set up the tents, searched for the hidden spring, and carried rocks to build our own small fire, we did it on a promontory from which we could see the light change to evening, the green grow darker and bluer and more glaucous.

By the time the sun set, and we were scrubbing out our plates and laying our sleeping bags on the grass ready for the night time, the hills had passed from blue-green to porraceous to almost black. And yet you could still imagine all the other greens within it. I remember lying on that mountain, not far from the friendly sag of the Fire Tower, looking up at the stars as something set a match to them, and feeling, for just that evening, that there was not a single circumscription or flaw in the life that I had been given. I had never been so high above the unimpeachable earth, had never dreamed that the verdure of the hills could be so emerald, and had certainly never imagined that the world itself was a kiln, and that all things, including me, were fired in it.

Twenty

THE TRIP to the Ice Cave was quite different, as different as water is from burning, and on the whole it is the one I found more truly thrilling, because open spaces came naturally to me, while closed spaces often held danger. The Ice Cave was literally dangerous anyway, and also, Jo-John led us there, and Jo-John was my personal antediluvian; he knew the secrets of the earth, and no matter if I found those secrets fearful, not to learn them would have been abominable. As my mind constructed it, the Ice Cave was left over from the Ice Age. It was a remnant of a long and venerable tradition in which under-or-undeveloped *homo sapiens,* who had a little hair still on their knuckles, had cowered, hiding from the onslaught of the glaciers. The Ice Cave, to my mind, must be an ancient dwelling, and outmoded though it must seem to those of us who lived in houses, it was important to journey with Jo-John, our very own ancient, to this traditional refuge for humans. Although I cannot imagine that at ten I knew a great deal about the Triassic period, I must have had some kind of elementary school introduction to the wonders of the dinosaurs – and to the great ice sheets, which I always imagined were quite transparent, like glass mirrors in which one could see time reflected. And in this primeval dwelling, the Ice Cave we were going to, I would find some of that ice sheet still frozen, and I would look into it just once and see the great corridors of history, stretching away like tunnels.

Well, the Ice Cave was not like that, but while I waited in the courtyard, and was given my trip gear by Jo-John, and while I packed my rucksack, and aired my sleeping bag, and got my orange and my sandwiches in waxed paper, I felt already that I had entered another time. I was going to the Ice Cave, and it was as if I was going to be preserved there. Also, I was nervous because Jo-John's trips were selective, and this was my first one, and I had heard that he had very high standards; I was afraid that I would somehow make a fool of myself, and not live up to my own Jo-John standards, and thus destroy forever my chances of someday being Wayaka Huya. Generally an hour or two with Jo-John was plenty for me to be on my best behavior, the most amazing all-around ten-year- old camper in the world. Two days seemed rather a lot, and I fervently hoped that I would be up to it, and that I would be able to fully appreciate this great chance to see life as it was in the Ice Age.

The Ice Cave was farther away from camp than the Fire Tower, but it was not as difficult a climb to get there, since it lay on the side of a mountain not far from the floor of the valley. To get there, however, we could not set off on foot unless we made an extra day of it, and so we began the expedition by piling into the camp truck, and as we drove down the Lower Hollow Road, we all stood up in the truck, clinging with daring arms to the wooden slats in the sides. From a standing position in the cow truck, we could see all the actual cows, in the farms we passed as the truck went on its way, and we could smell the marvelous manure, and see the farm dogs break from their cover in the shade of their porches and dash along after us, barking deep throaty barks. Our packs were at our feet, our hands upon the railing, and we could see all that was to be seen, which was a gentle, domestic culture of red barns with roosters and weathervanes. Not fancy farms, but real working places, where vehicles lay rusted in the fields and the shiplap on the chicken house had holes in it.

Somehow, it made it more exciting to be going to the Ice Cave, to what I thought of as the very birth site of the entire human race, by way of these scenes of animal husbandry and agriculture, by way of all that had evolved when the ice sheets receded – farmers who shaded their eyes as we passed, children who waved and waved, women who nodded politely while they snapped green beans into baskets; these people I truly pitied because *they* were not going to the Ice Cave. They would never experience the full scope of the protohistoric.

We turned off the Lower Hollow Road, and the farms and pastures vanished. Now we were driving through a corridor in the woods, and the trees met over the truck, joining the tips of their branches, and somehow urging us all to let go of the side slats and sit down on the truck bed. We sat on our packs or our rucksacks, being careful not to crush our sandwiches, and we felt the chill of the woods, which was the first and best promise of the ice to come. We took roads that I had never been on before, and finally came to a stop at a gate, the posts of which were the ends of two stone walls, long sinuous jumbled rock piles running away into the forest. The engine cut off. There was great silence, and we looked right and left at the ancient walls, walls that had run through pasture when they were built, not through forest; they were evidence of the inexorable movement of time, the cold snaps of a century, and perhaps even the final futility of all endeavor.

We walked in relative silence, with muttered warnings and questions passed back in line, all of us treading the mantle of quietude that Jo-John laid down before us. By now, it was clear that this trip to the Ice Cave was not exactly going to be *fun,* though in the end I expected the trip to be worth it; I would not say that the atmosphere that Jo-John created was precisely ice-cold or glacial, but it certainly suited the mood of our present enterprise. And as we started to ascend through the trees, first on a road that was barely visible and then on a path that vanished into a track that vanished into a rumor, I had to wonder whether I was really up to this sacred journey – after all, I was still just a child. But by that time it was too late to do anything but go with it. By the time we sat down to eat lunch, though, hiking itself had worked its usual wonders by heating up the body and pressing the mind into acquiescence, and while we all ate lunch and took off our hiking boots – no water here, but it was nice to cool the feet anyway – some of us decided to sing, to break the silence. Usually, on our camping trips, if we sang, it was while walking, and we sang songs like "Swinging Along the Open Road"; here we entertained ourselves by singing rather hushed songs, and we ended with the old favorite,

Peace, I ask of thee, oh river,
Peace, peace, peace.
When I learn to live serenely,
Cares will cease.
From the hills I gather courage,
Visions of the days to be,
Strength to lead and strength to follow,
All are given unto me.

Peace, I ask of thee, oh river,
Peace, peace, peace.

Although not all the campers joined in, except perhaps for the final chorus, the song seemed to have hit the right note for the trip, and after it we all felt equally virtuous. So when we put on our boots again and picked up our rucksacks and started off for the second lap of our journey, we were all more relaxed, less nervous about what was expected of us, full of serenity, vision and courage. And when, halfway through the afternoon, we were making our way along a narrow trail that suddenly became even narrower, just as it threaded its way above a cliff – and we all had to pass along it, just a foot or two from the cliff edge and its fall of twenty or thirty feet – I still had the song with me as I paused on the near side, trying to summon the will to take this narrow way. Jo-John was standing at the other side, urging us one by one across, and even with the song I almost failed this unexpected test, but then Jo-John thrust his hand out and met me halfway across, and his hand was warm and strong, and pulled me to safety. His hand clasped not just mine but also the words of the song, and I felt the strength to follow, and visions of the days to be.

The trip to the Ice Cave, because of the narrow trails, and the cliffs that lay in the area around it, was considered the hardest hike that Wynakee had to offer, and by the time it was over I knew why. That first cliff crossing was not the last – a fact which, had I known at the time, might have stopped me from making even the first one – but by the third dangerous crossing I was almost inured to the danger, and by the fourth I felt that I almost liked it. The fourth crossing was the last; after that we passed into a high valley, where the cliffs were on both sides of us rather than below us, and where the trees were sparser than normal because the soil was so barren and rocky. By five o'clock we had reached the Ice Cave. We didn't race into the cave to investigate it, not yet. That was not the way of things when you were with Jo-John. We set up our tents first, then gathered wood and water, then we were allowed one initial trip of exploration.

The Ice Cave had a mouth in a cliff that was maybe six

feet high, and at the most ten feet from side to side – not a very impressive cliff, and the mouth was even less so. My first reaction to the Ice Cave was that it was *small*, hardly large enough to have been the primordial dwelling I was convinced it must have been; after all, it was guarded by a series of natural cliffs that were as good as the shield walls of any European fortress. We had to take turns standing in the cave mouth, and we could see that just beyond it, the cavern proper narrowed even further. While it was too late to really explore it, I could make out, even in the dusk, that getting into and out of it would be no easy undertaking. Perhaps the people at that time, those many years ago, had been midgets, to be able to live here. But that didn't mesh with my image of their hairy knuckles or their mighty necks. I was going to have to revise my ideas, I could see that.

But for now, it was too late, and I was tired, and glad to help build the fire so that Jo-John could cook some macaroni and cheese for us, after which we cleaned our plates with pebbles, as we somehow had not brought a scrub brush. I used moss as a second, buffing, implement. Then I climbed willingly into my tent, along with two other campers. This was one overnight on which I had no desire to do otherwise; I was glad to have the tent laces drawn tight from the inside, and to be surrounded by canvas and by other people breathing.

When I woke up, it was hot, as it always was in those canvas tents when the sun beat down on them and their flaps were drawn. I found we had all slept late, and when we clambered out of our sleeping bags, the uneasiness of the previous night had all but vanished. We had a terrifically large breakfast, with scrambled eggs and bacon and numerous pieces of dry bread toasted on sticks and then smeared with marmalade, and then at last it all came together, the quiet, the courage, the dismay, the small cave mouth. We were going to explore, not a dwelling, but an ice cave.

We all had long pants and sweaters on, since we had been informed that it would be cold, and we had all been told to bring our own flashlights. Jo-John himself had a rope and a lantern, and we lined up behind him in single file, as we prepared to enter what I now knew had been an ancient icebox. Yes, by now I had found another explanation for the existence of this cave, and thought that if it had not been a dwelling, then surely it had been a primitive ice plant where haunches of venison were stored for weeks, and cheeses laid out on shelves, and cabbages, or whatever they ate then. Lying on slabs of rock-hard ice, the food would keep almost forever, and in times of hardship would be there for all who needed it. The only problem with this new fantasy, as I was quickly to discover, was that the Ice Cave had no ice at all in it.

Of course it had no ice. I have since discovered that all caves are always more or less the same temperature, about fifty degrees, I think, which is obviously far too warm for water ever to freeze in them. We went into the cave, and we were all allowed to explore the arms that reached back from the main cavern, while Jo-John took the rope and stretched it along a descending corridor reaching about thirty feet down to the second level. There was rough rock both above and below, and it was at the bottom of this corridor that I still expected to find the ice. Had I known that there was no ice there, I would never have made the descent, for I felt breathless and stifled by the rock walls' closeness.

But at the bottom, in the second cavern where we had all gathered on the floor, and where stalactites and stalagmites grew above and below us, I completely forgot about the ice when Jo-John lit three or four candles, placed them on the floor, and told us to turn off our flashlights. The candles actually flickered as in a subterranean wind, and by guttering, grew a little bit smoky; but except for the cold drafts blowing, the place was so very still that all previous stillness seemed unworthy by comparison. If it hadn't been for the candles, we would have been in a dark world like the closing jaws of some great animal. But because we had light in the darkness, everything was radiant with beauty, beauty glimpsed truly, and beauty merely imagined. The stalactites and the stalagmites, those icicles of rock, didn't tell me as much as I had hoped they would. And yet the very austerity of the place, its asceticism, perhaps – though iceless – was nonetheless somehow historical. This was the bare beginning, or the root, of something. What, I didn't know, and I still don't know, completely, but now I can make a guess at it. Not the beginning, or root, of human beings, but the essence of a world where we are superfluous – a world that would still be itself if we had never appeared to trouble it.

Twenty-One

IN THE CONSTELLATION of camping trips, though, the overnight at the Bat Cave was the brightest star in a crowded sky; to me, it was a camping trip about which everything was perfect. The group. The terrain. The weather. The destination. The food. And maybe most of all, the leader, Karl Wieneke. The Bat Cave, actually, was considered one of the easier overnights, partly because it began behind a farm in the Hollow, and partly because the approach to the cave was mostly on old sugaring roads which crisscrossed that farm's outlands. As a consequence of its easiness, it attracted a mixed crowd rather than the hard-core campers who went on the trip to the Ice Cave. In a mixed crowd, also a young one, I was a lot more experienced than some of my fellows, and certainly tougher and fitter than many of them. So I knew from the very beginning that I would need to set an example for the younger campers, and this was not hard, since I was troubled with no great expectations about what the Bat Cave would be like. The one thing I was sure of was that it would have no bats in it.

The farm from which we left for the Bat Cave was owned by Mr. McConnell, and lay only a half mile or so from Owl's Head, so we didn't have to go there in the cow truck. We Owls could just start off from our own cabin. When you participate in an expedition on foot, and its starting point is literally your own front door, the feeling of freedom you experience is just incredible. You sit in utter comfort, hiking boots laced, walking stick at your side, while all the other campers straggle toward you in motley fashion; *they* have had to leave from the Crow's Nest, or from Mohawk, miles away, and they are already hot and thirsty and ready for a break, while you are still leaning your head against the screen, and maybe whittling on the knob of your walking stick. Then you rise casually to your feet, clip your Barlow closed with a snap, place it in your pocket, and sling your rucksack onto your shoulders. As a person who is fresh and unhurried, and who lives at the very point of departure, you are received, of course, by the newly arrived group as an expert on the coming journey, and you may, if you are willing to, choose to share some useful observations with these neophytes on the facts about the hike that is now starting. The approach to the McConnell Farm is along a road which everyone in camp knows, and where everyone has walked at least a hundred times, but this is a little bit different. Shall you walk to the left side or the right? You, the expert, recommend staying at all times high.

When we set off for the Bat Cave, it was an absolutely perfect day, not too hot, but certainly not chilly either, with the sky a deep deep blue, with a few puffy cumulus clouds. It was late July, and the wild roses were in bloom, so there was a sweet perfume in the air. The next farm down, not the McConnells', even had a rose arbor. When we set off, with Karl at our head, we straggled all over the road – on a hike led by Karl, there was never any of this business of single file – and a lot of campers crowded around him, trying to stay as close as possible to his friendly aura and his fascinating body. Some of us surged down the road, passed by the arbor, and headed toward the McConnell farm, leaving Karl and the others behind us, and swinging our handmade walking sticks. They felt like part of our arms. Thwup! Their tips hit the dust. Thwup again! We had legs, we had arms, we knew how to use them.

When we got to the McConnell farm, it seemed almost too soon, we had been having such fun, but Robert McConnell was already at the end of his driveway to meet us; he not only owned the working part of his farm, he also owned the whole mountain above it, and thus the Bat Cave where we would be staying. We all knew this, and so of course we thanked him for permission to camp on his land, which he dismissed, urging us to have a "whole lot of fun," and not to drink the water in the cow pastures. For those of us who had forgotten to fill our canteens, he offered the use of the hose at the side of his barn, or the hand pump near the house, which had to be primed at least ten times before it released its water with a great gush. As I saw some other campers trot off to take Mr. McConnell up on his offer, struggling to undo the caps to their canteens as they walked, I had a pang of deep regret that I had been sensible enough to think ahead, and had filled my canteen with regular tap water.

But then Karl arrived, with his very heavy pack, and we all regrouped and finished being polite to Mr. McConnell, admiring his sheep and cattle when he led us to one of his gates. He reached behind it and unlatched it. It swung out, that is, toward us, and after we had all passed through it he pushed it to and latched it once again, so that we felt a delicious excitement as we moved into the pasture; it was now just as if we, too, were cattle! In fact, the first part of our hike led us for miles through lower and upper cow pastures, and the cows also seemed interested in this question of whether we were new companions, come to share their grass and clover. They regarded us with doubtful eyes as they thought about it. If we were other cows, as we might be, then why were we so strangely foreshortened, so that from no angle could our hindquarters be truly seen? Yes, we had humps on our backs, as they did, which indicated that we *might* be small cows. But the lack of hind legs threw the matter into a fair degree of doubt.

As for us, we were by then engaged in the semi-charming, semi-horrid task of avoiding the numerous cow-plops that dotted the pasture; some were dry and could be picked up like Frisbees, and crumbled between one's hands to reveal mostly straw, and it was mighty hard to resist picking them up and crumbling them. Others, the very newest, one could easily avoid, since they were still steaming like hot mudpacks in the grass; it was the plops that were several days old that posed the greatest danger to the unwary walker, for they had formed a crust on them which was quite deceptive. Like the crust on a snowladen field, it might be thick, or not thick at all, and you really couldn't tell which until your boots had broken through it. When they did, you went right into the wet stuff, which squished up as far as your boot laces. Then you stepped boldly into the stream to wash it off.

The whole thing was thus delightful, hiking with walking sticks through cow-plops, standing in streams, and being treated by cows as possible equals, so that when the first part of the hike was over, and we had reached the old sugar road under the trees, we were all – at least for an instant – a little sorry. But the old road had its own treasures, mushrooms growing through the long grass, puffballs that had dried and could be stomped on with a booted foot. The spores flew out in a cloud, as from a minute subterranean explosion, and gave you a feeling of true creative energy. And the sugaring road was laid out sanely, since it had once been negotiated by horses pulling a sugar wain, and therefore wandered back and forth up the hillside, never getting too steep or too hard, never getting too dark or too narrow. And this was old forest now, with hardly any significant understory.

Since this trip was led by Karl, there was no sense of urgency to get where we were going, and we stopped not only for lunch, but several other times also. Moreover, we sang as we hiked, which made for frequent pauses, especially with young campers, so the approach to the Bat Cave could not have been more gradual. It was only perhaps three miles from the farm gate to the cave on the hilltop, but we managed to take most of the day to get up there anyway, collecting fungus if we saw it, stopping to play with a toad, and turning around constantly to admire the places we had come from.

As I say, I imagined that the pleasures of this camping trip would be in the route and the crowd and Karl, and the last thing I expected was that the cave itself would turn out to be anything much. But when we arrived and threw down our packs, launching our walking sticks to the ground after them, I saw that the Bat Cave was huge, with a vast entrance that stretched like a slash across the hillside. And since this was Karl's trip, we didn't even think about setting up camp yet, but raced immediately to this slash, and then inside it. And I was awestruck. Now *this* was a cave. I mean, this was really a *cave.* A cave, as in the phrase "mighty cavern."

The Bat Cave was entirely unlike the Ice Cave in that it did not possess any underground chambers, and everything it had, everything it was, was right there at ground level, with the hillside hunkering above it. And what it had was three large rooms, all with vaulted ceilings, and all with packed earth floors, and a pond in the front chamber. *A pond entirely covered with fine green scum.* To us Bat Cave neophytes, it was this otherworldly, scummy pond that first captured our ardent attention; had there ever on earth been such a *very* scummy pond, of such a *very* yellow-green color? Some campers ran outside to get their walking sticks to move the scum around, but I was lucky enough to find a stick right near the cave mouth, and then, stick in hand, I crouched by the pond edge, which was a shaley, slatey sort of rock, a gradually descending ledge. This ledge made its way down to the unseen depths below. Balancing on my boots on the ledge, I extended one of my hands and dipped the tip of my stick into the scum – algae – to try and probe it. I found that the scum was thick, although it could be stirred and shoved, and when disturbed, gave off a noxious odor. The odor was just a bit different from anything I had smelled before, and seemed to emerge from bubbles that popped when you touched them; the whole thing looked a bit like that Jell-O which has been beaten full of air, except that it was an indescribably bilious green color.

The scummy pond was quite large – I would say about a hundred feet in diameter – and the back of it lapped right up to the back wall of the cave's front chamber, so that it was impossible to get completely around it, although there was a small ledge that extended for some distance, and many of the braver boys walked out on this ledge, keeping their hands on the rock behind them. They studied the scum in awe. Truly nothing could be more disgusting and at the same time more wonderful than this uncontrolled and primitive form of life. It imparted a noisome and obnoxious gladness, a sort of unsavory exaltation in all of us who were privileged to see it. It was water and it was food, in food's most basic possible form, and though it was noxious it was also somehow enchanting. We traced words in the scum with the tips of our sticks and the words would linger for a moment, as in skywriting; then the clouds of algae would close about the letters, and all would be as it had been before.

After a while, though, we tired of the pond scum, and got up to explore the rest of the cavern. The main room, to the left, was the largest and the lightest, but didn't have anything in it quite so fascinating as the algae. It did, however, have walls that were smooth enough and light enough to have inspired people to write their names on them in charcoal, and I studied these names for a while, beset by a feeling of curiosity, particularly about those people who had written their names very large. Williams and Thompson and Punch Johnson; Sue Jensen and Jamie Trillin and Dina and Debbie. And the love notes, with hearts and arrows and flowers. Many of the words and symbols were fading, because in those days everyone understood without talking about it that to write your name on a rock would be a sin if you used anything more durable than charcoal. Indeed, even though I knew the charcoal letters would all fade finally, it seemed to me then, in the virtuous state which had developed in me as I participated in this so-far-absolutely-perfect-camping-trip – anyone fortunate enough to be on it must be covered with virtue, the way gold pans are covered with gold dust – it seemed to me that writing your name here even in charcoal must be something of a sin, an unwarranted display of ego. I would never write my name here. What good would it do? Besides, there really weren't any blank spaces left that were big enough.

About this time, there was shouting at the cave mouth as the word spread that it was time to make dinner, and those of us still inside went back out to do our assigned chores – mine was usually, as it still is, gathering wood. I loved to run around under the trees, going farther and farther back and farther and farther away from the rest of the group, in the quest to find the perfect piece. I would search for wood by sizes, first selecting the smallest and finest of twigs, occasionally taking them off the bottom branches of a standing spruce or pine tree, and then breaking them until they were no longer than my fist, a lovely spray of tiny twigs like the flower called bridal veil. I would accumulate quite a pile of these twigs before I moved on to the next size, sticks that were perhaps as wide around as my forefinger and as long as my forearm. Again, I would roam far and wide in my search, and again I would gather quite a pile, selecting only the smoothest and driest wood for the fire.

Of course, while I was engaged in my organized rounds, some other children would be dragging back whole logs, dead limbs which contained every size that could be needed right upon them – but to me, this was like picking apples by cutting off the branch they grew on. Other children got more wood. Other children got wood quicker. But I doubt very much whether other children enjoyed wood gathering quite so much as I did. I took great pride in the fact that with this, as with nothing else in my life, I understood the advantages of order and method.

The truth of it was, though, that with Karl as our leader, I needn't have gotten any wood at all, since Karl was a mighty wood gatherer, and used to bring an ax to cut the largest logs, making such a towering stack of them that we had enough for dinner, for the evening, for breakfast, and to leave some for the next campers. Karl was in charge of the fire, and when I had finished my wood gathering rounds, I came back to find him bent over a pile of twigs, crouching down with his knees in front of him, and bent over very delicately for such a large and muscular man, his head tucked forward, puffing ever so softly at the flame growing in the twigs' cavity. The pile of twigs themselves looked like a tiny cave, and the fire was like a campfire in the cave mouth – though our fire was actually well outside the cave mouth so that the smoke from it wouldn't blacken the roof. We were slightly disappointed at this, but we had learned from long experience that anything Karl decided was right, and in this case, he said that the fire wouldn't only blacken the cave roof, it might well end up frightening the bats. The bats! What bats? We hadn't seen any bats! Oh, there were bats, all right, Karl told us. They would come up at night, and they would swoop around our heads, and we could only hope that they didn't drink human blood.

I wanted to go back into the cave to scan it for bats, but Karl forbade any more cave trips until the morning, since by now it was getting dark and while the pond might not be deep, he didn't want to have to make any Tarzan rescues. So instead we put the tents up, and then unrolled our sleeping bags, and Karl cooked dinner with some help from the older campers. I myself didn't help. I wasn't fond of cooking. I appointed myself junior firemaster. While Karl was busy with dinner, I kept the fire going at the perfect temperature for boiling by feeding it thumb-sized sticks, and when the dinner, beef stew, was ready,

I helped to break the fire apart and rebuild it, preparing it for the large logs that would burn on it all evening. The sun had by then set somewhere beyond the hills, and beyond the trees – we hadn't actually seen it do so – and it was getting cold, really cold, as it often did in Vermont in summer, particularly after these days of perfect weather. Instead of making us wash up our mess kits, Karl had us pile them dirty under a tree where, as he said, we would *probably* find them in the morning, and then we all climbed into our sleeping bags right there at the edge of the fire, Karl having decreed that it was unlikely to rain during the night that was coming.

By dint of extraordinary contortions, and lots of "Oh, excuse me, I didn't mean to do that," I managed to get my sleeping bag positioned next to Karl's, so that when we all stretched out later for the night, I was right there, sleeping beside him. In the meantime, I was in an ideal position to listen as he told scary stories. I also continued to feed the fire, giving it all sorts of crucial attentions, and the other campers watched this fire with unflagging interest until someone screamed, "Bats, there are bats!" and we all looked over to the cave mouth to see the bats emerging like smoke and then curling like wind. When the bats first appeared, Karl was talking, and he stopped in mid-sentence to watch them; he was as silent as the campers were noisy until maybe a hundred had flown out, and the screaming stopped and he could talk again.

I screamed, too, though I was not really scared, since the house I had been born in, and had lived in until I was five, had had a colony of bats in its attic, and some of my earliest memories featured these wonderful creatures. They would come out at dusk from the eaves of the attic, just as these bats were now coming out of their cave. They made a sound that was almost like distant singing – actually, it was the music their wings made in sailing, and it lasted only until they dispersed, each to pursue its own insects; the bats from the Bat Cave were now diving and swooping and gliding into the darkness. Looking up from underneath them, I felt almost that they had been choreographed.

Everyone knows now, of course, that bats are wonderful, but since not everyone knew back then, and I did, I felt that I had a special responsibility, and I tried to educate my shrieking friends when their shrieking had died away, something that unfortunately Karl didn't try to help me with. He was far too amused at the inevitable outcome of his plan, which was that at least half of the campers now went off to get in the tents, leaving the rest of us much more comfortable around the circle of the fire. Before the other half left, though, I did my best to say my say, to tell them about bat sonar, and that bats will never hurt you or touch you or bite you. I pointed out the beauty with which they flew, so different from the flight of birds, and how valuable it was to everyone to have them eat insects. In this mood, I was not a popular camper, and so was quickly suppressed, leaving the air free for Karl to tell more stories, and for more shrieks to ring through the night, though this time at the beloved story of a man who had a hook instead of a hand and who killed couples parked on lonely byways. A pair of lovers listening to their car radio heard a news report about the man, and drove quickly home, only to find a hook in their car door, a *hook with blood on it.*

I myself lay back, sleepy, watching the dancing bats and wishing that just once, one would get confused and land on me. How fun to have a bat perched on your shoulder, the membrane wings furled, the ears large, the eyes curious. How fun to reach out and touch that dry, whispery leather, and to feel those feet, clinging like gentle staples. Of course, if one had landed, it would have been uncomfortable until I had put a stick along my shoulder, so that it could swing upside down, as it was designed to do whenever it wasn't flying. I would hold the stick very steady, until the bat fell asleep, its toes curled tightly, its eyes closed, its ears drooping.

We stayed up late that night, those of us still by the fire, while Karl piled more wood on it, talking, soothing those who had really been scared by him; when we finally stretched out, I was very sleepy, but not too sleepy to retain my place next to Karl. I got as close as I could to his side without exciting any comment, and then I turned over to sleep, not away from, but facing him, and I do not think it was just coincidence that when I fell in love with my first husband, it was in precisely this same sleeping bag situation. When Karl saw where I had placed myself, he smiled and said, "Go to sleep now, Arthur." Go to sleep now, *Arthur!* It was almost too exciting. No adult had ever before called me by my last name alone, and it was the perfect end to a perfectly perfect day. Ever since, I have been a sucker for people who call me "Arthur." Particularly men. I always think it means they love me.

We all slept late in the morning, since the sun didn't reach our hillside until maybe seven or even seven-thirty, and when it did, we saw the impossible, that it would be another perfect day like yesterday. The sky was blue, the air was crisp, and the smell of yarrow was sweet in our nostrils as we stretched and clambered out of our warm sleeping bags. One of the older girls who was with us – a rather poetic Netop named Melanie with whom I had contested silently, secretly, but fiercely for the privilege of sleeping next to Karl – decided to start the morning by reciting a poem to impress him, a poem that I would certainly not be able to remember had I not come across it since. Striking an attitude, Melanie said something about what a beautiful day it was going to be and then recited:

I dreamed that I went to the City of Gold
To Heaven resplendent and fair,
And after I entered that beautiful fold,
By one in authority there I was told
That not a Vermonter was there.
We give them the best that the Kingdom provides;
They have everything here that they want,
But not a Vermonter in Heaven abides;
A very brief period here he resides,
Then hikes his way back to Vermont.

Although I wholeheartedly agreed with the sentiments expressed in this poem, I thought it rather an icky way to start the day, and Karl apparently agreed with me, since he asked me – *me,* not Melanie – if I wanted to go get some water for breakfast. As soon as I had struggled into my brown corduroy shorts and my short-sleeved cropped cotton shirt with the little checks on it, and had laced up the leather thongs on my now lovely, crunkly, worn and smelly hiking boots, I grabbed two pots and took off for the stream just as the others were crawling out of their tents. To my dismay, by the time I came back with the water, Melanie had attached herself to Karl's bicep, and he was attempting to lift her off the ground.

Still, nothing could ruin this particular camping trip for me, and after breakfast and the massive clean-up which followed, but before we had rolled up our sleeping bags and packed up our rucksacks, we all took off once more for the interior of the Bat Cave. This time, we found the bats; they were easy enough to find once Karl had led us to the back of the right-hand chamber and pointed toward the far corner of that chamber's ceiling. There they were, maybe a hundred of them, sleeping sweetly as they hung upside down from their toes. They looked as if they had been attached to the stone with some kind of powerful Krazy Glue, or alternatively, like small bundles of dried sticks wrapped around with a scrap or two of leather. We watched them for a while, but since this was their time for sleeping, there was little action on the ceiling, except for an occasional bat disattaching and, after crawling up the stone with its wings spread out to either side as balances, reattaching itself.

I took one last tour of the Bat Cave after I had rolled up my sleeping bag and packed my pack, and I ended in the third, westernmost chamber, where all the names were written. As I looked at them this morning, I felt differently than I had the night before, neither disapproving of the name writers, nor puzzled by them. Now that I had seen the Bat Cave's bats, not flying through the wild night, but all clustered together and hanging from the cave roof for safety, it seemed to me that these names and the bats had something in common – the way they were clustered, the fact that they huddled close, each unique and yet all together. And just as the bats, with the passing of the years, became different bats, but lived in the same cave, so people, as the years passed, became different people, also; the Daves and the Jims and the Johns and the Susans gave way to the Karls and the Elizabeths and the Wendys and the Jo-Johns, yet the very cave that we shared tied us together.

And while I was here now, this moment, standing in the Bat Cave, a Wynakee camper, someday I wouldn't be, I would be gone, and others would have followed me; maybe it was important that as time stretched forward, there was the continuity that was rooted in naming, and in the places where names found their reason for being. So I went outside into the sunshine, and found a large piece of charcoal, and then chose a clear place on the wall of the third chamber. With extraordinary precision, I drew just six letters, two feet tall. ARTHUR they said, just ARTHUR. I stood back and looked at them. And as I looked at them I seemed to see, many years hence, another freckled child standing in the Bat Cave, looking at my name, the letters now quite faded. I imagined her wondering who I was, and whether, like her, I, too, had been fascinated by pond scum, and had wished I had a bat perched on my left shoulder, its large eyes curious.

And as we walked back down the mountain, I was happy to think of my name there, behind me in the Bat Cave, testifying to my experience. But I was happier that the Bat Cave had had bats; it had had bats before I got there, it would have bats after I left, it would have bats forever, or so I hoped. For what would the world be without bats, after all? A place where the rumor could not become fact, and fact could not be transformed into rumor, and where darkness and daylight were not drawn together by the music of wings, sailing. Upside down, bats saw a different earth than we, a place where writing made no sense, but where the tribe endured because of truths far more invisible.

Twenty-Two

FOR CAMPERS who had really learned their campcraft, the ultimate reward at Wynakee was supposed to be taking a trip on Vermont's Long Trail; if you could put up a tent that would stay dry inside in the most shattering of summer downpours, and light a fire with a single match, then you might have a chance at it. Of course, you would also need to be good enough to pack your rucksack in just five minutes, and to do it so well that nothing on it would come loose until you loosened it yourself in the evening, and you had better be prepared to peer at the map when the counselors got it out as if you knew at every moment just which squiggles meant something. In my first three years at Wynakee, every summer there was a four-day trip in which those campers who had convincingly mastered (or faked) all these skills got to participate, but I myself was far too young to be taken on the famous Long Trail, until I was ten and a novel idea was introduced to us.

That year we had a new counselor, Tommy Stevenson, and he was rather feckless, absolutely good-hearted and good-natured but without a lot of solid horse sense. He assisted Karl in teaching swimming – which appeared, in the camping trip on the Long Trail, to be a skill that we who were on it were lucky that he was possessed of – and he was always having bright ideas about how to revise some Wynakee tradition, like the one which reserved the Long Trail for the older campers. This time, he was going to lead a Long Trail Short Trip, and we would be dropped off and picked up at two different spots entirely; unlike the older campers, who took a circular route on a part of the Long Trail several hours north, we could pick it up just forty or so minutes from us.

Well, when this announcement was made in the dining hall, and volunteers for the trip were called for, of course my hand shot up. Two days on the Long Trail! It would be like growing two inches overnight. There was nothing those two words, Long and Trail, did not evoke for me. In fact, they evoked things I had barely heard of, things that existed at the fringe of my conscious mind, things like the Death March of Bataan, and the Long March of the Chinese Communists. They called forth the word "trial," so similar to "trail," and all the freight that went with it – *trailing clouds of dust, trailing a wounded bear, her voice trailed off into silence.* Beyond that, if you took a trip on the Long Trail, you must be setting off on a journey that was probably not just long, as they claimed, but endless; once you had set your feet upon it, picked up the part near your boots, you were committed. Who knew where it would take you?

In order to get to the Long Trail we had to drive north, as I say, for almost forty minutes, and while normally when going on a camping trip, leaving Wynakee was no problem for me, this time the sheer distance made me uneasy. We were again in the back of the cow truck, and Tommy Stevenson was there with us, since Seth was driving and Tommy didn't need to be up in the front with him, and while we drove, Tommy told us stories of other camping trips that he had been on; they had one absolute constant, he told us laughingly. And that was that no matter what the weather was when he left the place he was leaving from, by the end of the first day out it was always raining – and not just raining, but *raining,* hard and long and drenchingly. He was sure, however, that this wasn't going to happen this time.

Tommy had a funny face, with a shock of dark brown hair that was so coarse that it almost always stood up on the top of his head, and his eyebrows were very bushy, but short, like two dashes over his eyes, so that his face had a surprised expression that matched his personality. Since Karl taught me swimming, I really knew nothing about him, but even before the truck had stopped at the road head, I was wondering whether I had been wise to leap so blindly at this overnight. The Long Trail might be hard enough without Tommy Stevenson in charge of leading it. And though the day had been clear and sunny when we set off from the Hollow, by the time we had started hiking it was dark and threatening, and yes, storm clouds were gathering.

Well, we set off on the Long Trail anyway, and I noticed immediately something strange about it, which was that it didn't start climbing upwards, as did all the other trails I was used to hiking on, but instead just meandered along by the side of a river. It went through a stand of pine trees, which seemed hopeful on its face, but then on the far side of the pines there were some birches, and then there was the river again, and the trail slouching beside it. By this time an experienced old camper, I was used to trails that were decisive; the Long Trail, however, seemed not to have the least idea of what it wanted. Here was a river and we walked along the river, and then we left the river and climbed along a hill. But then here was the river again, the very same river, and I found myself getting disconcerted; I wanted to start climbing, so that we could get to our destination. And what was that destination, anyway?

I had signed up for the Long Trail, I realized at this point, without even asking where we would be camping, but I had assumed that it would be at a window or a lookout, if not actually at the top of a great mountain. By the time we stopped for lunch, and I was digging into my orange with my penknife, and leaning against a tree staring at that river, I was beginning to get the feeling that we were never going to start climbing, and that this, around us, was all the Long Trail was. And while the phrase *the Long Trail* still had a remnant of its old resonance, I was now thoroughly reexamining it, and qualifying my approval, and adding some definite stipulations. For one thing, I wanted some markers on this Long Trail, like the knots on the Tug-of-War rope, markers that would tell me from time to time how far I had come on it; for another, I wanted the assurance that once I got off it, I would never have to get back on it, but would be protected from it, as by an inoculation.

I was not the only camper who was already beginning to tire of the Long Trail, although we had been on it then for less than four hours. Some of the others asked Tommy Stevenson where we would be sleeping. Would we start climbing soon toward a lookout? No, we wouldn't be climbing at all, chortled Tommy merrily. The Long Trail had been laid out, in this section, so as to stay low and close to the water. And that was unusual, because in Vermont most of the bottom land was taken. But he, Tommy Stevenson, had searched and searched the maps until he found this one place on the Long Trail where you gained no elevation – that was because we were beginners, and as for where we would sleep, we would stop when we got tired. *Beginners?* I stared at him malevolently, wondering why the Wienekes had ever hired him. And as he finished giving us the bad news, the first drops of rain began to fall.

So when we started hiking again after lunch, we were all encased in hot, sweaty plastic, and the rain, though not hard, was drumming deafeningly on this plastic, and while back at camp I *loved* rainy days, and even on camping trips I didn't much mind them, I preferred it if the rain waited until evening, when the tents were already up, and we could toss our packs inside and dive in after them. By midafternoon my boots were soaked through and by five o'clock most of my clothes were also, and I and the others could only hope that our sleeping bags, under our ponchos, were still dry enough to sleep in. Ahh, here were more pines. And now more birches. More river, and now a little hill. By the time we stopped, we felt we hadn't gone anywhere, and we set up the tents feeling out of sorts, almost rebellious. In fact, we were genuinely grumpy, and wished with all our hearts that we had decided to go on a different camping trip, and the fact that Tommy was singing and grinning merrily in the rain didn't help us feel any more contented. If we had gone to the Bat Cave, well, then, even if it was raining, we might be sitting right now in the mouth of the cave, and if we had gone to the Fire Tower, we could be huddling beneath the tower, watching the rain clouds move across the valley. And if, by some miracle, we had gone to the Ice Cave, we could even at this moment be down in the underground chamber instead of standing around by this river, trying to put our tents up in the rain, and having to listen to Tommy singing.

By the time we got to bed, the rain had stopped falling, but its aftereffects were still with us. My sleeping bag *had* gotten wet in one bottom corner, and I slept all night with my knees pulled up to my chest. When morning came, it was raining again, though intermittently, and in dispirited silence we rolled our wet things into heavy packs, and all I wanted in the world was to be back at Camp Wynakee, going to Woodworking, or the Whatsit, or Arts and Crafts. Right now I could be working on the letter-opener I had just started, which had been sawn but had yet to be chiseled, or I could be feeding two of the rabbits with shreds of lettuce and watching them wiggle their noses at me warningly. Instead, I was walking along, in the opposite direction from Dorset Hollow, and with a whole day and another night to get through, somehow, before I could even hope to climb into the back of the cow truck and head back to the place I should never have left to begin with. What a fool, fool, fool I had been, really, to become enamored of a set of words, two words, two *stupid* words, long trail, and when a few of the Mohawks who were with us suddenly veered and started walking in the river, I felt just disgruntled enough to follow them. I was already so wet that a little more wet wouldn't hurt me, and at least walking in the river would provide a change for a while; Tommy Stevenson, when he saw this, grinned and laughed, and amazingly, joined us, and I lost all my animosity toward him. And then he *really* redeemed himself by making us all gather in the river, and as we stood in a circle, ankle-deep in water, listening to him, he suggested that it was quite a noble tradition on camping trips to get "rained out" – and that he thought we should just go back to Wynakee.

I wanted to hug him. I loved him. What a man! And he grew even larger in my estimation when he explained that he had not the slightest idea where we were, and that the only way to get back to Wynakee was to strike out across the open country until we came to a farm or a town where he could use a telephone. Suddenly, what had been a huge grind, a great, disillusioning disappointment, became instead an adventure. We were wet, and standing in a river, and we were *lost,* and now we had a goal, which was to get back to Camp Wynakee. So we splashed through the river until we were wetter than ever, and then we struck out on its other side, and our beeline across country was far more decisive than any decisions that had ever been taken by the Long Trail. Before long, it became clear that the meadows we were passing through were the outlying meadows of a large farm, and they took us to a fence, which we climbed over with as much glee as if we had been breaking out of prison.

Then we were on a hard-packed dirt road, heading west with the sky beginning to clear and the morning light behind us, and the broken promise of the Long Trail, which was that forced marches could be somehow fun, gave way to another phrase and a more satisfying set of connotations. We were now on the Open Road, and it was surrounded by the two open flanks of a wide, green, classic Vermont valley, and the mountains which we had so missed as we stumbled along through the pine trees were now high and elegant green arms that were enfolding us. I had no idea where we were – I knew that we were not in Dorset, and not in Pawlet, and not in Rupert. We were in a Vermont valley which I had never seen before in my life. What I found truly amazing was that this beautiful valley, unnamed, had been there, not far from us, all the time. And as we walked along, getting hotter, passing no houses as yet and with no cars coming up behind us honking, or traveling toward us with their undercarriages rattling on the uneven road, I thought I had some idea of what it must feel like to be a genuine explorer, and to pass into country which had never been mapped, but merely rumored. I felt catapulted into a fine tradition, the same fine tradition that had sent Toad of Toad Hall out a-journeying with his friends the Rat and Mole; yes, this was the life, the only life, especially as the sun came out and transformed the world from gloomy and wet to dry and full of color. The puddles in the dirt steamed lightly, we stopped and stripped off our outer clothes, and now we were in every way world travelers and explorers, since a truck rattled by us, just as we had taken off our rain gear, splashing muddy water up to our thighs, or even further.

Rarely in adult life do you ever find yourself lost without finding it also worrying, but as I think back on the feeling that we all had as we marched along, I know that everyone should try this, at least a few times a year. Being safe and in the sunshine, and not too far from help but technically "lost," brings a feeling of incredible freedom, as you disattach from all expectations, and thus from all potential disappointments, and have the luxury of really being able to see. I saw Vermont that morning as one might see a totally foreign country, a place I had never even *heard* of in my entire life; we passed ranks of corn that were so symmetrical, and so green, and yet so various that it was astonishing to think they were not art, but just a foodstuff. Some of us walked inside the rows of corn, passing down between stalks until we were hidden, and then staying very still, and listening to the silky rustle; if we had not known better, we might have thought we heard the corn stretching with pleasure at the recent rain, and now at the sun that followed after it. We passed a small stone bridge over a river, and we all went to its end and dangled our feet from it, looking out into the distance; who had been the amazing artisans who had crafted this bridge from rock and thrown it here across the living river? While we sat, a cow came to drink near us, at first apparently not noticing we were there, and when she did, staring up with huge eyes, and then looking away, as if embarrassed; she had an udder that was half full of milk, and the teats hung under her like pink fingers, except that if you looked closely, you could see the hole in the tip of every one.

When we got up and went on walking, we came to a place in the road where it was slashed right through by another road just like it, and because the land on all sides was fenced, if you stood in the middle of this crossing you could see eight fence lines, going in eight different directions. There was something amazing about this, and we stood there for quite a while before we voted on which road to follow, and then we turned right, or north – all of us delighted with our choice, as we would have been had we selected a paper in a hat lottery. At last we passed a farm that had an occupied farmhouse, as we could tell from the dog lying lazily on his front porch regarding us; he *thought* of getting to his feet, but was really so very comfortable that all he did was raise one of his hind paws so that he could chew on it. But we didn't stop at the farm, because by that time we could see up ahead that the next four corners marked what appeared to be a tiny village, and we went on, by now a little footsore, until we came to that breathtaking object which was a single gas pump, with its rubber hose coiled in the dirt beside it.

The four corners also had a telephone, and a post office, and a tiny store, and while Tommy used the phone, the rest of us walked up the cool wooden steps, very broad and worn, into the building, which had large glass windows reflecting the sun brightly in them. In this building, an old- fashioned Vermont country store, where there were winter boots on the shelves even at the height of summer, fishing tackle and tools lying side by side with denim overalls and cans of beans and hams, there was also a counter that held penny candy in glass bottles, and the arrival of ten children thus created a sensation. Or the Vermont equivalent of a sensation, which was a rather subdued equivalent; still, the man who ran the store actually went to get his wife so that they could both look at us, together, and we selected penny candy with a blithe disregard for how to pay for it, in which the storekeeper was kind enough to indulge us.

However, when Tommy was done calling, he followed us in and settled the bill without even telling us that we should have asked him first, and I have to admit that he now rose so high in the estimation of all of us campers that he could have brought a personal rainstorm on us that afternoon and we still would have liked him. We had about two hours in the village before the camp truck arrived to pick us up, and we parked ourselves on the greensward as if we had simply grown there, experiencing for the first time the unmatchable sensation of being dressed for the wilderness and fresh out of it, but sitting in a place where all sorts of people got to see us. Cars went past, going to a distant market, and farm trucks laden with produce, and one man on a horse rode by, stopped, and then rode on, but our arms never got tired from waving, and if the Vermont we saw then still exists anywhere, it must be in that valley, which I never saw again, nor learned the name of.

When the truck carried us back to camp, we were singing and shouting all the way, thoroughly delighted with the greatness of our adventure, and though everything we had brought with us was still soaking wet, who cared, because at least the clothes on our backs were dry, and the rain and the Long Trail were, for the time, just a distant memory. The rain actually gave us an extra dividend, for we got to lay all our equipment out on the grass near the birches, and to proudly display the degree of our rain suffering to all the campers who had not gone on the trip, and who must think we, who had, were really something. To have gotten *rained out* on an overnight! The thing was almost unheard of! And on the Long Trail, too. What they didn't know wouldn't hurt them. So we took apart our mess kits, and laid out our trousers and sweaters and shirts, and let everything roast for hours in the sun, in the sight of everyone – and most especially, we dried out our sleeping bags by unzipping them all around and placing them at the precise angle to the sun that would benefit them most. And once they were unzipped it was impossible to resist stretching out on top of them, and closing our eyes, and feeling the soft flannel, as comfortable as people had ever been, and as happy to be home, at Camp Wynakee. We had brought the odor of woodsmoke back with us, and that was enough to remind us of the great world that was like a kiln, which fired all things, including us, within it, but which didn't require any human beings, and which was stitched up by sleeping bats, and which tempted us to draw our names on it in ash and then come home again.

SOMETHING WORTH CRAWLING FOR

Twenty-Three

BEING PART of the Camp Wynakee family, and considering Camp Wynakee my home, was unquestionably one of the most satisfying things I've ever shared with other people. And of all the activities I enjoyed at camp, it was those that occurred in the evening that made me feel most wanted, or needed, or accepted by my fellows. In the evening, the whole camp gathered to play Kick the Can, or Messengers and Interceptors, to go on a hayride, to attend a play, or to create a Council Fire. I loved them all, as I loved the square dances, but if I could have made one petition to the Wienekes, it would have been to cancel what were called, at camp, the "social dances."

Maybe it was partly their setting which made the dances seem to me so disorienting. They took place on the boards of the Hayloft Theatre. On those boards, just a week before, I might have been a farmer from Iowa, or a pirate, swarming up ship's rigging. Now, right here on the same stage where I normally got to explore all the multitudinous people who inhabited my body, I had instead to dance in a funny way, dressed up as a little girl with freckles, and that meant dancing with boys, and dancing wearing a dress.

Wearing a dress! Wearing a *dress?* And at Wynakee, for which I had spent months getting properly outfitted and clothed – preparing my spare, simple, uniform. Of course, we wore dresses on Sundays, when we went to services in the library, but somehow that seemed different, more reasonable. Whether or not you could imagine exactly who or what God might truly be, it might be seen as rude not to put on a dress as a sign of respect when you went calling. But to wear a dress to a dance . . . well, who were we trying to please? I saw the fact of the matter clearly enough. We were putting on dresses for the Wynakee boys.

Yes, we put on dresses for the boys. I had a lot of friends who were boys. But it seemed absurd to ask me to put on a dress for them. For some girls, perhaps, it was no trial, but to me, dresses simply seemed like handicaps, bottomless sacks

– as items of clothing, baffling. Perhaps they would have made sense if the main concern was to mask your torso from the sight of someone floating in the air above you – someone like God, maybe, who would have had the necessary powers. Boys did not float above you, though, and so dressing for dances seemed extremely stupid, especially when linked to the perpetual general admonishment to be sure to keep boys from looking at your underpants.

Still, I wore dresses, as we all did, and a half hour before the dance we would go to the closet and pick out one to wear. Most girls had two with them for the summer, but I actually had three, it being my theory that the more I had to choose from, the less loathsome would be the result. I would spend a tormented ten minutes trying to decide which dress was the least awful, but I would always pick the same one, blue, with white piping and a white sewn-on belt. I would put this on, and my shoulders would sag, and my face would take on the most woebegone expression, and then I would slump off through the field, thinking bitterly that, like all of them, this dress, too, would reveal my underpants. Would reveal them, that is to say, to anyone lying on his back either in the field, or on the floor of the Hayloft Theatre, which luckily no one ever did at our Friday night dances, but even so, there was always the chance of it, and so, no matter how lovely the evening, it was never fun to walk across the bridge in my moccasins. I and some other Owls might linger at the bridge, and from there we could hear the sounds of the record player already scratching out its ancient dance tunes from the direction of the Hayloft; after a while we would have to get on with it. Climbing the ladder, for some girls, was the worst of it, since after it was done with, you had basically disposed of the underpants question, but for me the worst of the dance had at that point just barely started, because when I saw the Hayloft Theatre with balloons thumbtacked to its roof, and streamers hanging from its rafters, it made me genuinely sorrowful.

Oh, I was a little excited, too, in a sick sort of way, excited in the way you are when you have a feeling you may behave very badly and you really don't want to, so you become extremely self-conscious about every move you make, every smile, every facial expression. The stage had been pushed back, and the props tucked out of sight, and the place was absolutely crawling with sudden strangers – Netops in high heels and stockings, boys in dark suits with shiny shoes, Karl actually wearing a tie, and looking very uncomfortable. Whereas usually on this stage, with all eyes truly upon me, I felt that I was invisible, in a way, had lent my body to another person, now – with no one much caring whether I was there or not – I felt that the eyes of all were absolutely riveted upon me. "Elizabeth in a *dress?*" I imagined they were all thinking. "Well, that certainly is a bizarre sight, isn't it? I bet I could see her underpants if I lay down on the floor!"

Why couldn't I, as I normally did here on the Hayloft Stage in the Barn, just pretend that I was someone else – say, a little girl dressed in a blue dress with white piping? Why couldn't I feel freed by the opportunity to be released into another world? Why couldn't I just put up with it and live with it? Because I had the terrible suspicion that no matter how I might feel about it – how I might feel about it then, how I might feel about it later, how I might feel about it ever – that *this,* wearing a dress and standing around waiting to be asked to dance, was thought to be some kind of preparation for adulthood. *This* was considered by someone – though not, I didn't think, the Wienekes – to be the real thing, which is to say real life, while all the rest of what we did at Wynakee was just playing. And if the rest of what we did was playing, and this was real life, I wasn't about to help anyone out by enjoying it.

Johnny B. and I usually danced together, which was some recompense for having to do it, since Johnny B. hated the entire business as much as I did, and we had one of two modes, each of them a form of quiet rebellion; either we danced much more vigorously than the music called for, or more commonly, danced much less so, holding hands and standing off to the side and shuffling our feet a little. In this mode, we could drift off in thought, no one "leading" and no one "following," but both of us together absenting ourselves almost entirely. Unfortunately, someone would always come up to us and suggest that we dance with other children also, since the Wienekes didn't think it was healthy for young people to "go steady." "Going steady" pretty much describes it, the steady way we avoided doing what we were supposed to, which was to learn the waltz, or the fox-trot, or the twist, when that had been invented. And "going steady" also describes the way we moved steadily toward the ladder, down which we would escape as soon as we were able.

After half an hour to forty minutes of shuffling around in a corner, or, for variety, dancing fast to a very slow dance, Johnny B. and I and several other couples would have a meeting to discuss our departure, and our planned meeting, in a little while, near the wheelhouse. If it was a perfect evening, this was particularly pleasant – this sneaking out of the dance early, which we had to do by staggering our disappearances – but even if there was rain in the air, the relief was indescribable when we pretended we had to leave to go to the bathroom. Our whispers and giggles floated gently into the night, while the music was still blaring out behind us, and the night air, in these circumstances, made me quite exhilarated. The cut grass was now wet with dew, so I would kick off my moccasins and carry them, listening to the night hawks buzzing like wind in invisible wires. Together, I and whoever was with me, maybe Johnny B. and Jack and Wendy, and four or five other children, both older and younger, would make our way to the wheelhouse, and there walk underneath the bridge, where in revolt and outrage and relief, as well as pleasure at the night air, we would have a kissing contest.

Now, the kissing contest was something that I myself had invented, and Johnny B. and I were usually the champions. It involved kissing competitively – one couple against all the rest – while an objective observer counted to see how many times in a row we could kiss one another. You weren't allowed to stop for breath, and if you paused too long you were disqualified. Of course, you understand, this wasn't *French* kissing. At ten or eleven, we modeled our kisses on the sort of thing you did with your parents, so a kissing contest was pecking a boy's lips over and over, until your lips got almost numb, as if you had been to the dentist and he had given you Novocaine. Johnny B. would happily have stopped, I think, before his lips actually got numb – if I had let him, he would even have sacrificed being kissing champions – but the dances always left me feeling so strange, and so full of the need to prove myself, that once we were under the bridge, Johnny B. was in for it. As the years passed, our record grew, and we went from being the winners with a mere thirty kisses to achieving over two hundred, and while this kissing was, needless to say, not fun, it was in its way very satisfactory, linked as it was to our premature exit from the dances. It was on the order of a sober duty, a solemn test of determination that I needed to pass, and having passed it, the slate was wiped clean. Yes, I had gone in a dress to a dance, but I had more than made up for it by standing under the bridge and kissing Johnny B. over two hundred times.

Twenty-Four

FAR, FAR BETTER, though, in the great scheme of Evening Activities, was a game called Messengers and Interceptors, a game which involved the whole camp, and which was partly a military campaign, partly a puzzle, partly a race, and partly a treasure hunt. As the game began – and it was generally held on fine nights, when the light would last long, and the darkness would come as late as possible – we all gathered in the meadow where the flagpole was located, and were divided into two teams of thirty players. Each team captain, generally Kuhrt Jr. and Karl, would be given eight slips of paper, each slip containing a fragment of the total clue, and if the team put the slips together and figured out what the whole rhyme or riddle meant, it would lead them to the one and only treasure, usually something like a large bag of lemon drops. So it was not the reward itself that inspired teams to action, but rather the triumph of having met a lot of different challenges, and all in the course of two evening hours.

The game began with each team captain selecting eight of his team members as Messengers, and giving each one a slip of paper to hide somewhere in his or her clothing, someplace where the paper could be discovered by a visual inspection.

When the game began, the Messengers started from opposite sides of the camp – one team on the far side of the pond, the other down at the Council Fire – and it was their task to try and bring their clues back to their own team captain, waiting by the flagpole. As they did, the team and the captain would try to interpret them. The Messengers were to avoid getting caught by the Interceptors from the other team if they could possibly avoid it, but if they did get intercepted, that is, run to a stop and tagged, the Interceptor would have just thirty seconds to do a visual search of them. Hardly anyone carrying a clue who was stopped in this fashion felt confident that he would get away with his clue untaken, but there was always hope because the challenge was to hide the slip of paper somewhere on your person in such a way that, like the purloined letter, it might be mistaken for something different. A bit of a white barrette, or the white lace on a white moccasin, or the corner of a handkerchief sticking out of a pocket; there were a surprising number of ways in which you could obscure the plain truth of the matter which was that yes, indeed, you were a Messenger.

Eight team members were real Messengers, and another seven or eight were decoys, whose task was to *pretend* they were carrying messages, and therefore to distract the Interceptors of the opposing team from knowing which of your mates were truly carrying clues. The other fifteen team members were, of course, the Interceptors, and their mission was to search and find, and then, once in possession of a message, to bring it straight back to headquarters. Sometimes an Interceptor might read an intercepted message prematurely, and it didn't really matter, because by then it was his own team's clue anyway. But it was absolutely forbidden for a Messenger to read the clue he or she carried, since this would ruin the whole game for everyone. In all my years at Wynakee, I was never assigned to be an Interceptor, so I cannot speak from experience on what it was like to be one; the biggest and fastest boys got to be Interceptors, and I always imagined that it must be rather dreary being the counterforce rather than the force. And those campers who were good Interceptors had to be a tiny bit sadistic. We who wanted to be Messengers were, on the other hand (and depending on how you looked at it), possessed of either high ideals or delusions of grandeur, and having, in some quantity, both, I always begged with all my might to be allowed to be not a decoy, but a real Messenger.

I remember two games distinctly, one when I was a decoy, and another when I was genuinely carrying a clue. The second one was in sunshine, but the first was in a light rain, and was perhaps during my third summer at Camp Wynakee. It wasn't raining when the game started, since, if it had been, the game would have been called and we would have retired to the library or The Barn for the rest of the evening, but it was damp, and rain did threaten, so the general energy of the camp was a little lower than it usually was during a game of Messengers and Interceptors.

When I wasn't chosen as a Messenger, I was relatively disappointed, but I knew from experience that it could be fun anyway to be a decoy, and indeed the whole process for both sides was actually an elaborate psyche-out. So while the rest of Kuhrt's team was being assigned their roles, I took a quick trip back to Owl's Head and put on an unusually elaborate costume, with the equally unusual decorative touch of about fifteen slips of plain white paper. This was not, as far as I knew, forbidden, and yet I had never heard of anyone doing it, so I got great delight from the entire procedure. I put on a shirt that had two pockets, a pair of shorts that had four, all buttoned, and my moccasins, which had leather and beads and laces. Then I clipped all the barrettes I had in my footlocker to my very short blond hair, and I put a slip of paper everywhere that I could fit one. Two went under barrettes, five or six in the buttonholes of the pockets, one on each side of my shirt, three in my shoes. I was littered with paper. And each piece was a little more visible than it would have been had it really been a message. Then I ran back to my place near the pond with the others.

Now, from past experience, I knew that as a Messenger it was best to get a late start leaving your outpost and trying to get to headquarters, since the assumption was that the Messengers who were actually "carrying" would try to get back to headquarters fast. Only thus could they be sure that their messages would be useful. So, in the past, when I had been a true carrier, I had chosen to start quite late, as if I hadn't a worry in the world, and couldn't care less if anyone caught me. This time, therefore, I did the opposite. I started immediately, like a bullet from a gun. If I had to be a decoy, at least I would be a good one.

When the bell rang to start the game, and I began it at a dead run, I naturally caught the attention of the other team and its Interceptors; their strategists pegged me as a true carrier, and a pretty stupid one at that, and they sent Jonathan, one of their fastest runners, after me. I ran until I was sure that he was bound to catch me, and then I stopped, not wanting to waste my breath for no reason. Jonathan grabbed my arm, and gave me a visual check, found the paper in one of my barrettes, pulled it out, and ran off to his headquarters without opening it. I walked on, but in a slouch, as if I were the most unhappy person alive, but I sauntered toward the shelter of the woods, so that by the time the strangled shout came from Karl's team headquarters, I was out of sight and running again. I knew they would send someone else after me, and they did, another fast boy who caught sight of me as I emerged from the woods just above Netop, and then stopped, standing there passively.

The boy caught up with me and shoved me rather hard, and then examined me visually for more paper; while this was going on I counted aloud to thirty, as one always did in these circumstances. While I was counting, the boy, Mike, found eight pieces of paper, all of those that I'd put in my pockets; he didn't find the rest, and the rules forbade him to delay me, so I emerged with five pieces of paper still in place. I was off like a shot, but Mike had learned from Jonathan's experience, and instead of running back to headquarters he unfolded all my papers on the spot, and when he discovered they were all blank, he threw them to the ground and then went back to report my perfidy to Karl. At this point, I suppose one of two things might have happened. Karl might have concluded that I was a decoy. Or he might have concluded, as he did, that I was actually a carrier, who had created dummy messages to draw attention away from the real one. No longer trusting his Interceptors, and sure I was carrying a real clue, he decided to come after me himself, so as I was continuing on my way toward my own headquarters, where Kuhrt Jr. was gathering in clues, I saw Karl appear below me.

I knew there was no way I could outrun Karl. Good grief, *nobody* could outrun Karl, and I was still only nine. But if I didn't at least *pretend* to want to get away, he might guess that I was just a decoy. And I knew, as well, that for every minute I took the attention of Karl or any of the vital members of his team, there was a minute when one of my own team's real Messengers might be making it in to headquarters. If I could hold Karl's attention for a minute, two minutes, four, a clue carried by a teammate might solve the puzzle for my team, and I would have done my part to make it happen. By now it was starting to rain, and I gave a large start of fear toward Karl, acted totally panicked, and then turned and ran back the way I had come. When Karl was twenty feet away, I turned again, since we were on a hill, and I ran back down it as fast as my legs would carry me; I don't really know how I knew it, but it seemed to me that as a kid, with more flexible knees, I would have an advantage on the downhill.

Except for once, in another game at Wynakee, I have certainly never run faster than I did as I was flying away from Karl down that hill, and the sheer ferocity of my run convinced him that I was carrying a message, so he ran just as ferociously. I ran as if I would be executed on the spot if caught, and indeed, I think I almost believed it in that sixty seconds. And though this delayed the inevitable outcome by maybe half a minute, it was half a minute in which I grew by half an inch, since I was running from a grown-up, and not just a grown-up, a big man, and not just a big man, but Karl Wieneke, and he was putting all of his attention – *all of his attention* – into the sole purpose of catching me. If I *had* been executed at the end, there would have been this to say for it: for sixty seconds I had experienced glory.

Of course, I was not executed, but as I put on a last gasp of speed, Karl reached out and grabbed me with his arm, and so forceful were we both that his flying tackle, though it wasn't a body tackle, knocked me entirely down onto the ground. It was joyous, better than I could have dreamed, to feel the power and the rush of action, joyous to have used every resource that I had, joyous to have believed it mattered, joyous to have competed with someone so much stronger, and surprisingly, not unpleasant to taste defeat. Because to be defeated at the hands of a master is not really defeat at all. It is recognition, approval, a savage kind of love.

But Karl was so embarrassed at having accidentally felled me that he spent at least fifteen seconds apologizing, fifteen seconds during which I was counting to thirty just below my breath, and when he was done saying he was sorry, I was already on sixteen, seventeen, eighteen. He found the other paper in my barrette. Twenty, twenty-one, twenty-two. He found the paper under my wristband. But he never found the papers in my shoe.

And so the end of it was that I made it back to my own headquarters still carrying three pieces of blank paper, and experiencing the mixed pleasure of having had my scheme work, and having had it work so well that I had to regret not having carried a real clue. Though my team lost that night, I had the singular honor of having a new rule created for the Wynakee games – no carrying (in future) blank slips of paper.

&

THE OTHER Messengers and Interceptors game that I remember very well took place on a lovely sunny evening, when the whole camp was bursting with high spirits, in keeping with the long cool shadows and the patches of bright sun on the mountains. That game I was on Karl's team, and I really was a Messenger; it was in the era of no blank slips of paper, so it must have been my fourth summer at camp; I don't remember the game because of *my* part in it, however, but because of the behavior of another Messenger. I got my clue, folded it up very small, and put it in the best place that I had found, which was the channel where the lace went through my moccasin. This was really such an excellent hiding place that although I was stopped by several Interceptors, I made it all the way back to headquarters without having my clue taken from me. And at headquarters, I discovered that we were having a pretty good night, since we had five of the eight clues, and three carriers still out; there was a great deal of buoyant anticipation, until our sixth carrier came in to say that he had been apprehended and relieved of his clue. And then came our seventh. And then, alas, our eighth.

So we were stuck with just five clues to try and solve the riddle, and common wisdom had it that five clues was not enough. Moreover, the order of the clues that we had salvaged made it particularly hard, since we had 1, 3, 4, 5, and 6. The missing 2 was no problem, since it was always a promise of treasure, but without either 7 or 8 we were basically sunk, though we still had a chance, since the other team wasn't yet all assembled. We had taken at least two of their clues, which had duplicated ours, and if we just put our heads together, maybe we could do it. The puzzle ran something like this:

1. If lemon drops are what you have in mind, 2. (A bag of them, perhaps, is what you'll find) 3. And if you want to change, or you want to redeem, 4 You can plant a garden, if you only dream, 5. First, seek the way to the largest door, 6. And second, proceed to the secret store, 7. ? 8. ?

You can see our problem, and though all of us who were then in headquarters sat around in a large circle vainly trying to provide an additional two lines, and throwing out, for our mutual consideration, every place in camp that might conceivably be connected to change, redemption, gardens, doors or stores – as you might imagine, thus coming up with basically every single place in camp – it was more than clear that we were axed, we were sunk, we were lost, that unless we simply went out and started blindly searching the entire camp, we didn't have a chance of finding the treasure, with the other team also working against the clock, and already, as we could see, now actually beginning their physical search. Karl in particular was frustrated because it was generally understood that he was better at body work than at brain work and he always loved to have his team win at Messengers and Interceptors, to prove that he was a well-rounded human being.

As I had brought in clue number 5, "First, seek the way to the largest door," I had a natural affinity for that particular portion of the puzzle, and I was convinced that if I could only stretch my brain wide enough I would be able to find the treasure using that clue alone; I was therefore not participating as much as I might otherwise have done in the group discussion, but was thinking to myself, over and over, "The *largest* door. The largest *door.* *The* largest door," and so on, never coming any closer to a solution than to think of the big double door on the animal barn, and relatively convinced that the secret store must be in the hay in the underground portion of that barn, or perhaps in grain bins, and I was, in fact, just about to sneak off to root around in the grain bins when I became aware that a whisper had begun in the circle somewhere off to my left and was making its way around to me. 1 was told, in a drawn and rather frightened subtone, that Mark Lager had read his clue, number 8, before it was taken away from him, and should we tell him to tell Karl what it said?

Mark Lager was not our brightest camper. Had he been smarter, he would never have admitted that he had read his own clue, but would have found a way to introduce into the conversation some of the ideas it contained, until the puzzle seemed so inevitably to point in the direction of his clue that it would be entirely forgotten who had first introduced the notion, and in the excitement of the discovery of the treasure, would never be remembered again. Had I read my own clue, that at least is what I would have done, and it seemed inconceivable to me that anyone, even Mark Lager, would do anything as dumb as actually admit to someone else that he had read his own clue, and still without revealing what was in it. Had I been sitting next to him, and been the person he first asked for advice, I have no doubt that I would have made him tell me the clue, and then myself innocently introduced the concept into the conversation. But I was right on the other side of the circle from him, and at that point so many people on the team knew that Mark had cheated that there was no way to keep this secret. The only question was, would we tell Karl, and would he let us use the clue?

We told Karl. I don't remember who broke it to him, but at last someone said that he had heard that somebody had read clue 8, and did Karl want that person to reveal its contents? I could see Karl was sorely tempted, but though I believe that he, like me, would have used the information had it come to him privately, there was really no way he could do so when it had all been made so public, not if the game was ever again to be played at Wynakee. No, the only problem now facing him was whether or not to ask publicly the identity of the culprit. It was one of three people, that much was clear to him, and the dilemma that now faced him was tricky. If he didn't reveal the culprit, the other two children would forever be under a cloud of suspicion in the matter, but if he *did* expose him, the child would be disgraced, and that wasn't fair, since he had trusted his own teammates. Karl may not have been famous for brain work, but his solution was a great one. He made the dilemma into another game. First, he said that we *would* use the clue to solve the puzzle, though we would have to give the other team the treasure. Then he told the three Messengers who had been relieved of their clues to go off and consult. When they came back to the group they all, in unison, recited the missing clue. One of them had read it. But which one? Karl would never know. And that was the way he wanted it. The two innocent Messengers, as it turned out, loved this, feeling that they had caught a delightful tinge of wickedness without having actually *been* wicked, and when they came back and said in unison, "And the treasure will be behind the garden book," every single person on the team, even those who had never read *The Secret Garden,* seemed to know immediately that the treasure was hidden on a shelf in the library, and that even though the riddle did not make perfect sense – what did? – the "largest door" was clearly the door to the imagination, and the "secret store" was the world of books, and the clue that was missing was so simple that we didn't need it, presumably something like, "And when you're there just give a look." When we rushed off to the library to find the bag of lemon drops in order to present them to the other team, we were all, I believe, even happier than we would have been if we had actually gotten to eat them ourselves.

Later that evening, as we again gathered into a circle, this time to sing our camp song and then taps, arms crisscrossed in the darkness, I tried sleepily to think what it was about Messengers and Interceptors that made it so agreeable to me. It wasn't just the running, and it wasn't just the puzzle, and it certainly wasn't the treasure at the end of it. It had to do, instead, with the messages, the pieces of paper which alone were enigmas, but which together created an entire history.

Twenty-Five

STILL, MUCH as I loved Messengers and Interceptors, Capture the Flag was finally more satisfying, as it was more elegant, involving just one activity. Prizes and puzzles, slips of paper, none of these came into it. What did come into it was the opposing team's red handkerchief. That, and the lawn and fields and woods, even the mountains surrounding Dorset Hollow, because there were no artificial limits to the playing fields in Capture the Flag, as it was played at Wynakee. Except for the line down the middle of the lawn, on either side of which the flags were set, the only boundaries
lay in the imagination. The flags, as I say, were red handkerchiefs, tied to pointed sticks so that they could be planted, but in their way, they had a Klondike Stone quality to them. This was reduced, however, by their public exposure, and even more by the fact that if the flag was grabbed, it was generally removed from the hands of the grabber in less than five seconds.

In fact, although the purpose of the game was to carry the opposing team's flag back over the center line, what this meant, in practice, was that about ten different people had to carry it three feet each; while the *official* job of the defense was to touch-stop any opponents who came within flag range, their unofficial job was to tackle them and throw them to the ground before putting them in jail. That was the bad part of Capture the Flag, being put in jail, particularly if you were one of the first arrivals; then you sat all alone, with your personal, bored jailer. You looked out enviously on all the free campers, one of whom might, or might not, think it worth his time and trouble to come to your rescue and let you join the game again. If a big, strong camper was caught, or a fast one, he was inevitably freed – you could be freed by having one of your own team members touch you – and when they saw a rescuer approaching, everyone in the jail joined hands and stretched out in a line, a line of thick paper dolls, or beseeching semaphores.

On the particular Capture the Flag night I best remember, the whole camp gathered, as it always did, at the end of the lawn – near the porch – for the team selection, and I myself sat in a wicker rocking chair, holding a plucked fern in my hands and running my fingers over the spore caps underneath it. Out on the lawn, Uncle Kuhrt used a chalk gun to draw the line, and then he planted the flags, while the excitement mounted among the rest of us; team selection didn't take as long as you might imagine, even though we had sixty campers and ten counselors, since the team captains had had years of practice in expeditious selection. And what was good about their method was that it was not only fast, but also honest, since they each started by picking the best all-around male athletes they could find, then moved on to the best all-around females, then the specialized males, who might be slow but tough, or very good at throwing. Then they chose the specialized females, generally girls who were shy and awkward, but had incredibly good eyesight, or were very tall, and finally they chose the small and weak of both sexes, in matched sets right down the line, and to everyone present this all seemed very sensible. Even the small and weak, whose ranks I had left by the time I was in my third summer, would not have wanted to have the teams formed any other way, for the Wynakee method of selection ensured that their own team, when they finally joined it, would be as strong as it could be, and they would be part of it.

That night, for some reason, Karl was missing, and Jo-John had taken over as team captain, so it was a much more important game to me than most, and when he chose me, my heart beat faster, and I threw down my fern, and double-tied my shoe laces, then said good-bye to Wendy, with whom I had been chatting. When the whole team had been chosen, we all gathered together in our own territory, which was the pond side, and had a lengthy consultation. The defense and offense had to be arranged, and among the offense would be people called Long Runners, campers who would go far up into the woods on either side, and then, when they had been forgotten, enter the opposing team's territory from an unexpected direction – or, as we all called it, from Deep Cover. I myself was generally a Sprinter, someone who made short incursions into the other team's territory, distracting attention and using up manpower, since as a member of the defense, I had proven ineffective in the past, with a tendency to wander off in thought if not much was happening. But the aura of romance that attached to the Long Runners had always called out to me, and neither Karl nor Kuhrt Jr. had ever indulged it, so on this particular evening, even though my hand went up when volunteers were asked for, I didn't have much hope that Jo-John would select me. In fact, I was sure he looked at me as if he thought my volunteering was crazy – there was little purpose in making it to Deep Cover and having the tactical advantage of surprise if you couldn't run fast afterwards – but for whatever reason, he looked gravely at me and then nodded, and I was, for the first time ever, one of the lucky campers who would be taking to the woods.

As the game started, with a signal from Aunt Helen, who reigned as queen of the ceremonies from the vicinity of the porch, and who would call the game when it was over, I just stood easy while most of the other Long Runners set off hotly, as they always did, for the protection of the trees on either side of us. They were paralleled, equally hotly, by guards from the opposing team, each obvious Long Runner loosely assigned to a pursuer, so that half the camp hit the woods immediately, while the other half stayed on the lawn, the Sprinters beginning their task of sprint and distraction. I myself had had an idea, which I thought comparable in its ingenuity to the idea of hiding multiple slips of blank paper; I would pretend that I was a Sprinter until the other team wasn't thinking about me, and then I would wander off the scene with elaborate casualness. I made a quick run over the line, was chased and made a quick run back, engaged in some banter with a few members of the opposite team. Then I took out my penknife and a stick, and whittled, pretending to be bored, while some of the most eager Long Runners managed to get themselves captured, and were thrust into the dreary grass jail, where if they were unlucky they might spend the entire evening, a fate I had no intention of risking or sharing.

After ten minutes, or a little less, of whittling on my stick, I sauntered off toward the pond, which lay about a hundred yards behind me; I felt sure that anyone who was watching me would be convinced that I was just withdrawing from the game, as the pond was in the opposite direction from the flags and the center line. And that was exactly what I wanted, to make everyone on Kuhrt Jr.'s team think I was out of the game entirely, so that when a curious member of his defense called after me to ask what I was doing, I said that I wasn't in the mood to play, and I was going to go lie down somewhere. Then, sauntering, I made my way to the embankment, climbed up it and looked down at the pond, sitting on the diving board for a minute to really strengthen my little drama. Finally, I lay back in the grass, which would conceal me completely from sight, and would make it look as if I were doing exactly what I had said I was.

Now, I could take some real action, and I closed my penknife and slipped it back in my pocket, then rolled over and over in the uncut grass above the pond until I came right to the edge of the woods there, and now, I lay on my belly, so that without raising my body from the ground, I could crawl into the trees until I was concealed by them. At last, cautiously, I got to my feet, and peering around me in all directions, felt convinced that I was out of danger of being immediately seen.

I started to walk uphill, as quietly as I could, and not in the direction of the battlefield, but catty-corner away from it, and also from that portion of the woods which by now would be absolutely packed with Long Runners and their pursuers from both teams. I was in my own team's territory, so if I met some opposing Long Runners, technically it was they who would have to run and not I, but I wasn't about to capture them, and if they escaped back to their own team and side, they might carry the news that I was loose here. No, I wanted to get quite away, maybe a mile or so above the camp, before I started doubling back toward the flag and the invisible boundary, so I took my time and went on a fine hike, getting farther and farther away from the others, getting higher and higher into the hills and more and more confident all the time. I really did feel like a soldier in the midst of a military campaign, and with a maturity of understanding that had just come to me that very evening, since for the first time in my life I saw that the best way to reach a goal might be to take not the straight way, but the long way around.

I moved as quickly as I could, but I was careful to make little noise, and I stopped several times to look back down through the woods behind me; I could see no movement at all, not of people, though there were birds perched in the trees and they were singing, preening, and preparing for the coming night. The higher I got, the calmer I felt, so that it almost seemed unimportant for the moment that I finish the job I had begun, and it even seemed a little sad that I could be so easily forgotten by all those people whom I had once thought were my friends. No, it was amazing how quickly you weren't missed – or so I thought at this juncture of my journey – and I was almost tempted to shout or bellow to those down below, just to let them know how far I had gotten.

So I crossed over, about a mile above the camp, and started wending my way into enemy territory, and when I got to woods that I considered were surely "theirs," I found myself in a state of renewed excitement. My heart was pounding, my paranoia growing, and my hope that this would work getting ever stronger. I was so far behind the lines, and we were by now so well into the game – probably an hour had passed since Aunt Helen had called "Start!" – that it seemed impossible that I would run into enemy scouts, particularly since no one could suspect that I was even there. I was heading for the gully, which in the spring before camp started was a rivulet of water leading down from the hills, but which now, in midsummer, was almost dry, though it might be slimy, and would certainly have rocks covered with moss. By lucky accident, the gully came out directly behind the place where the other team's flag was planted in the lawn, but no one ever used it as an approach to that flag, since it was well guarded, at least early in the game.

When I got to the gully and slid down into it, my heart now pounding continuously in my throat, my main concern was to make certain, as I started to move down, that my head never became visible above the banks. Dusk was starting to fall, and that made me a little nervous, because the game would be called if it got too dark, but I knew that having come this far, I couldn't rush it too much at the end, or everything that I had done before this would have been for naught. From time to time I heard shouts, and as I got closer to the lawn below me, it was clear that most of Jo-John's team had now been thrown in jail, where they were calling out piteously for rescue to the few remaining team members who would have been capable of rushing in and touching their hands. It was strange, but the closer I came – and sometimes I got down on my hands and knees and crawled, when it seemed to me that the banks of the gully might otherwise reveal me – the closer I came to the lawn, and to the jail and the flag and my teammates, the more genuinely terrified I became. I knew this was just a game, but it no longer seemed like a game, and I feared that now, at this late date, I might be caught like my fellows. Almost on my belly, I crawled to the edge of the woods and peered out to assess the situation thoroughly.

My teammates were obviously dispirited and waiting for the game to be called, since there were too few people still loose on either side for things to change much now; the jailer had wandered away from them and was talking to one of the girls from our team who was standing right at the line, just barely on the proper side of it. Most of the enemy, also in jail, were a good distance away, near the pond, and as I peered toward them I saw that the light was truly fading, since I couldn't quite make out exactly who was in jail, though I would have liked to, to see which opponents had been thoroughly eliminated. While in other circumstances it might have been reassuring to see most of the other team in jail, and the flags both still planted well within their own territories, in fact it made me quite worried: I was under the pressure of passing time, and I had to move, now or never.

And then I had another idea. Instead of going directly for the flag, which I probably didn't have a chance at from the edge of the gully, perhaps I should try to slip into the jail first, and then work all the way around its edge, I hoped unnoticed; for this, everything depended on my team understanding instinctively what the plan was, and not, for heaven's sake, calling out to me. Would they understand what I was trying? Or would they blow the entire thing by letting the guards know where I was when I appeared? There was only one way to find out, and I stood up, put my hands in my pockets, and strolled casually toward the jail. I walked ten feet, fifteen, twenty, then twenty-five, and thirty, and I was there, and not a single teammate had said anything, though by now, all of them had noticed me, and rather than being bored and depressed, they were galvanized at the sudden prospect of victory.

The jailer was still standing chatting with the girl, the flag guards were still standing around the flag waiting for the bell to ring, and my teammates were reaching up to me, pulling me down to sit among them, whispering fiercely and patting me on the back to congratulate me. They saw the possibilities as clearly as I did, and when the jailer glanced back toward us and looked at me with all the others, he obviously did not remember that I had never been put there, but was free. Ten or fifteen people were whispering to me simultaneously. Whatever they were saying, I would do it. Free them? Of course. Capture the flag? Naturally. Take it over the line? Well, I couldn't see any argument against it. They joined hands as innocently as possible, so that I could free them as I took off, and they kept saying to one another, "Now, we've got to wait to scatter. Let her get really near, first."

So I stood up, and then touched someone's hand, which freed the whole group of them at once, but they stayed where they were until I had had time to amble forward, while the flag guards incuriously watched me, wondering what someone was doing so far from the rest of the people who were in jail tonight. Now, it was really now or never, and I was standing, I was walking, I was running, and then I was running flat out, my life condensed to a single lance-length; I was running toward the flag, and I was lifting it and picking it up, and I had it, there was no doubt about it, in my hands. Through the haze of my sudden speed, and the adrenaline rush which was driving me, I saw my teammates erupt and scatter behind me, and I saw the flag guards as well, suddenly spurred to desperate action, and three of them coming at me from two different sides.

The flag guards were big, big sixteen-year-old boys, and I had twenty feet to go to get to the line, but I knew, I just knew, that I could make it, and already the cheering had started. The flag, the flag, the flag! Everyone was shouting and everyone was running, and I was pumping my legs up and down like pistons, the flag guards were closing around me, and I could feel the wind of my own passage, and I held the flag to my chest as tightly as possible. It was ten feet, and now it was eight, and I was still running, and I was still uncaught, though the boys were looming. Then they were upon me, and they were toppling me to the ground, and it felt as if my face was being securely planted there. But just as I fell, toppled by the boys, I summoned the last remaining ounce of strength, and I threw the stick with the flag on it as far as I could away from me. I didn't see how far it flew, or where it ended up, and I was tasting grass, and the iron tang of blood in my mouth.

Now the boys climbed off me, abashed, as they were not supposed to fell runners, and certainly not if they were little, and also if they were girls, and so they lifted me up and dusted me off, while Aunt Helen picked up the flag, which had landed, point-down, exactly on the chalk line. It hadn't crossed the line – I could see that just from looking. No referees were needed to call this point. But no one in the whole camp seemed to care, not the other team and not my own team and not even Aunt Helen, who was usually most particular about such things, in the interest of fairness.

The game was won, that was the consensus, and Jo-John's team had won it, and both the winning and the losing team felt (as they always did) proud of the flag carrier, but strangely enough, I was not proud of myself, not at all; I didn't care that I had captured the flag, now that I had done it. Oh, I cared that the flag had been captured, since there was nothing worse, as far as I could see, than a game of Capture the Flag in which the flag remained permanently planted, but anyone might have done the capturing if they had just had the same opportunity as I had, and had gained it by following the same procedure. No, what I *really* cared about was the way that my teammates had understood, without having to have it explained to them, what the plan was; I had joined them in the jail, pretending to be a jailbird, and instead of being envious of me, or calling out only for their own freedom, they had understood that the good of all required each of them singly to remain patient, and wait for the time when they would be able to be free again. I had a feeling of incredible warmth toward them for having come to this conclusion on their own, and not just some of them, but every single team member – in fact, I felt an inchoate sense of hope, and affection for the species that I was part of, which could, when the occasion demanded, truly work in concert.

Twenty-Six

NOT ALL of the Evening Activities had a competitive structure or edge to them, and in fact, two of my favorites seemed to have been designed purely for pleasure, because although they taught us some lessons about life, their intention seemed merely to allow us to enjoy the world together. And I have to admit that if I had the magical opportunity to go back to camp for just one evening, I would choose an evening during which we either went skinny-dipping in the pond, or went on a hayride in the Wynakee hay wagon by moonlight. I guess skinny-dipping was, of all the Evening Activities, the one that might appear to be the least group-oriented, since once you had slipped into the dark pond, and were surrounded by the dark world, you were in a state which was not unlike the state of dreaming. I myself have had water dreams all my life, some of them frightening and some of them enchanting, but none of them so wonderful as the dream I lived when skinny-dipping in Dorset Hollow, and I guess part of what made this swim so dreamlike was that it was actually sanctioned by grown-ups – not just sanctioned, but overseen and organized. "Skinny-dipping tonight," our counselors would announce, and repeated experience did not make hearing this less wonderful; had our counselors said, "Flying tonight," or "Floating above the treetops after dinner," it could hardly have struck us campers as more extraordinary.

I flew in my dreams, too, and while flying was more

amazing, the water dreams and the sky dreams had a lot in common; they both proffered states of being that I had never really felt in life, a peculiar mixture of deep peace and exhilarating transcendence. Never really felt in life, that is, until the first time I went skinny-dipping in the Wynakee pond, with the encouragement of Uncle Kuhrt and Aunt Helen, those relatively stern adults who had never been seen to swim, much less to swim – as they now urged us to – without suits on. I was never one of those children who suffered from undue modesty, or had been taught that nakedness was something shameful, but even so, I found this group skinny-dipping to be as intimate as anything I'd ever done, and it was an intimacy not so much of the body as of the imagination. Looked at from the point of view of grown-ups, it served no useful purpose – we all swam at least twice a day anyway – and it taught us no needed skills, gave us no models to emulate, especially exercised neither our minds nor our bodies. It was not advertised, either, in the Wynakee brochure and I don't think it was mentioned to parents. As I say, it seemed to be solely for pleasure. And so while it might appear to be an activity that was not group-oriented, there was something so conspiratorial about the sense of freedom it brought us that we who swam could all have been part of a secret society.

On the evening of a skinny-dip, we had no other activity after dinner, but had free time until we gathered for an early good-night circle, after which we returned to our cabins to pick up a towel. Skinny-dips were organized age group by age group and cabin by cabin, so that it was Crows, then Wrens, then Mohawks, then Owls, then Netops, with the last cabin to swim always being the Mettawees, which the rest of us felt was rather unfair. Each cabin had fifteen minutes, which meant the whole thing took an hour and a half, and it ended, for the oldest campers, in real darkness; as an Owl, I was a dusk skinny-dipper, and that was great, but going last would have been even better, since the Mettawees stayed in a lot longer than fifteen minutes. While I and the other Owls were waiting for the Mohawks to be finished, we all sat on the porch behind the library, and from there we could hear the shrieks and screams of pure joy that rose from the pond while the boys cavorted in it. These shrieks were inarticulate, and rose high in the scale – it was rare that an actual word was spoken in the English language – and when the boys finally cleared off, and it was our turn to have the pond, we were as silent, walking toward it, as they had been boisterous. We had on our regular clothes, and no swimsuits were anywhere nearby, so we knew that if we were going to swim, it would have to be naked – it felt extremely odd, though, to be walking purposively toward the pond in long pants and shirts and maybe even sweaters.

When we got there, we were counted, and each given a number – this varied from the usual practice of buddies, since it was easier to hear a count-off in the darkness – and then we were told, "All right, fifteen minutes, girls. You can get in whenever you want to." We would stand barefoot in the grass, our feet already freezing, knowing that when we took our clothes off we would get even colder, but knowing too that when we jumped in the pond, the water would seem as warm as a bathtub, though during the day, and the sun, it always seemed to be filled with ice cubes. Whenever we took off our clothes, we had better be prepared to launch forth, as the air temperature was then about fifty degrees. I was often one of the last ones in, for I wanted to savor that moment while I was stripping my clothes off slowly and folding them under a tree.

Around me, there were naked girls already, their bodies gleaming in the dusk, not white perhaps, but certainly a glowing pearl color, and as none of them had breasts yet, you could easily, in this light, have mistaken them for boys if you hadn't known better. They had slender arms and legs, mostly short hair and trim, flat chests, and the good divers would launch in headfirst, their arms linked as if in victory, while their feet flipped up behind them, as they insinuated themselves into the water almost exactly like mermaids. Then the nondivers would jump, one knee cocked up toward their navels, one hand holding their noses, their short hair flying, and as they hit the water, whether in dive or in jump, they would make sounds, and I could see them going under.

When I got in myself I neither dived nor jumped, but went to the place where the embankment fell off sharply, and there would half slip and half fall in, trying to make no noise at all; I thought it a challenge to see if I could be silent when the water took my body. When it did, I never could be, instead always letting out a yell, a yell of surprise and joy – could *anything* feel this wonderful? – at the pond which was like black velvet stroking every neuron, every fiber in my entire body. I would feel the water close around every part of me, all at once, so that in itself it became a magic garment; there was no slow infiltration of meaning as the water made its way between my flesh and the flesh-protecting cotton. All at once I would be wet, all at once I would be caressed, all at once I would be in the arms of my first lover – that was the difference between swimming with a suit, a great pleasure in itself, and swimming without a suit, in what I thought of as "the gloaming."

And once I was in the water, and the warm hands had clasped my body – clasped my chest, clasped my thighs, clasped my buttocks – I would launch myself forward, and then dive under the water and stay there as long as I could without surfacing. Under the water, in the dark, I might bump into someone else, another naked girl doing the same thing I was, and we would slither off one another's bodies, feeling as lithe as if we were fishes, and watching the brief glimpse of white blur off into shadow. I would always do the breaststroke, whether on the surface or below it, and I would always do it slowly and very forcefully, imagining my body as it might look from above, seeing the arms slide forward and then apart, the hands cupping, the arms drawing down, the legs kicking lightly. The usual meditative pleasure of simply being in the water, having my body move in response to my unspoken fantasy, was made greater and far more mystical by the absolute lack of restrictions, which, except for other nights skinny-dipping, I must have felt last when I was in utero. And if one can fly in this world other than in dreams, it is surely thus, naked, in dark water. Now, when I dream of flying, it is always the same, I am not floating or soaring. I am swimming. I am doing the breaststroke in the sky.

I guess what made skinny-dipping so intimate was not just that we were all naked, and in fact nakedness was just incidental to what it finally asked of us, which was a subliminal understanding that we – all of us there in the water – were feeling the same thing, though we didn't have words to talk of it. The girl we had a crush on, the girl we secretly despised for being a cry-baby the girl who had strange nipples that grew inward instead of outward, the girls with innie belly buttons and outies, the girl who was stocky and the one who was tall, all of these, all of us, were alike swimmers. We had all passed into the gloaming, where we had learned the bliss of bodies, and the deep comfort of forgetting, for the time, our differences; we were all on the same boat, having embarked on the same voyage, and we none of us knew where we would come to anchor.

Twenty-Seven

BUT IF I *really* had to choose which of the Evening Activities at Wynakee to return to, I guess there is no question that it would be a hayride, because I still have the occasional skinny-dip, and there is something constant about water, but hayrides now seem part of the world that is vanishing. The pleasure of a hayride was in the tractor, the hay wagon, and the hay – as well as the full moon that often shone down upon them – and these days when I hear of "hayrides" that meet none of those conditions, I find it hard to imagine just what is left that might seem like celestial navigation. Always when there was a full moon, and sometimes when there was not, the whole camp would go on a hayride, in a first shift and a second one. Since only about thirty people could fit upon the hay wagon, the younger campers would go first and the older campers afterwards. As an Owl, I got to choose which shift I would be on, and of course I held out for the second, in order to stay up past my regular bedtime.

The Wynakee hay wagon was an ordinary wagon, of the sort that one still often sees on farms, with four widely spaced rubber wheels smaller than those required by cars, and with a solid flatbed bottom made of wide plank boards nailed longwise, from back to front. The hay wagon's flatbed was probably twenty feet by eight feet, and it had four two-by-fours at the front, sticking twelve feet into the air, with two cross-pieces of lumber, and a larger cross-piece of plywood to hold the hay back on this crucial side. It also had side and back railings, which didn't go quite so high into the air, and which were sometimes almost obscured by the hay bales; these were arranged creatively by campers who volunteered for the task, and who always took it on as an artistic challenge. Some bales *here* and some bales *there;* some bales down low and some bales up high; loose hay on top of bales and underneath them. The end result was a huge piece of furniture, which had sections and subsections and further subsections, connecting hay chairs and hay love seats and hay couches.

Once loaded, the hay wagon was yoked to the smallest of the camp tractors, an old one which would go no more than five miles an hour, and then driven down to the river by Seth, who loved these occasions, when he was indisputably the star. The first shift would go off while it was still light, and we felt sorry for them as we waited for their return and the sinking of the sun; then the first shift would come back, and we others would greet Seth, and wait for his permission to swarm on. More than with any other activity at Wynakee, placement was important on a hayride, and thus at this point there would be frantic muscling for position – particularly frantic because it had to be invisible, since any overt shoving or interference would have sent the culprits right back to their cabins. When I was a Wren, the frantic muscling was relatively uncomplicated – we all wanted to get as close as possible to the front of the wagon, where the hay was piled highest, and where you could sink into it most deeply, and look back with a certain satisfaction at all those behind you. When I was an Owl, it was more complicated, as in addition to getting near the front, we all wanted to be seated next to someone special, and whether this person was the same sex we were, or the opposite sex, affected how hard this was. The same-sex pairings had a distinct advantage. They could clasp hands as they clambered on, or, if boys, one could grab the other's bicep, but the boy-girl couples had a desire to be subtle, and thus often got separated in the throng, after which they were pretty much stuck with it, unless they wanted to announce to the world that they were going together.

And while I wouldn't like to compare the clambering

onto the Wynakee hay wagon with the desperate evacuation of a village just minutes before the advance of an occupying army, the two occurrences did share a common feature, which was total, single-minded devotion to getting one's body on the road at any cost. During the hayrides I remember best, I wanted to sit next to Johnny B., but though we were openly friends during the day, at night things took a different course, with part of the pleasure of our dependable partnership arising from not fully admitting to it; thus we tried to end up *accidentally* next to one another. Somehow, more often than not, Johnny B. and I did end up sitting side by side, if not at the front, then in any case somewhere, and when we landed, we would pretend to be surprised as we found ourselves bumping elbows, surprised and pleased. We had found our spot for the hayride. And it really didn't matter that we weren't right at the front, as we sat on a couch that could hardly be surpassed for comfort; in the end, wherever you sat on a hayride was by definition the best spot, a feature of the ride that we somehow always forgot beforehand.

After a while – too long for my taste – when all of the campers were settled, and the counselors had checked the railings to make sure they were still sturdy, Seth climbed back onto the tractor, and turned the key to start the engine, and it made its loud put-put sound in the night. Then the tractor would, with a large resistance, tug forward against the rubber wheels, and pull away from the lights of the central compound, chugging off into the moonlight without headlights of its own, carrying us wanderers and gadabouts. With that first movement of the wagon, as we lay looking up at the stars and feeling the enfolding magnetism of the hay all cradled around us, it was as if the tractor were a fulcrum, and the hay wagon being levered right out of the stable world to another world where we were all pilgrims and nomads. The tractor moved slowly, not much faster than we could have walked, and that was what made the whole ride so *credible* – that it was attached to the familiar earth, which it was like and yet not like. Just enough had been changed, or shifted. In other circumstances the tractor was a piece of farm equipment, and the hay would feed the horses in the coming winter, but now they had been pressed into the service of pure pleasure; we were a movable piece of reality that had just pulled loose from its mooring and was lurching and rumbling off, forcing us to take new bearings. The comfort was so extraordinary and the haloed moon so very beautiful, and being next to Johnny B., in these circumstances, was strangely comforting; I felt warm with my forearm touching his forearm, and our eyes gazing in the same direction, as we looked at the moon together for a while and then at the overhanging trees.

Or we might turn slightly, having discussed this, and peer over the edge of the wagon to see the road moving – dignified – underneath; we would be drawn back at once when the singing started, as it always eventually did. Then we would lean back together in the darkness, closing our eyes and listening for the tune, pleased with our own gentle, watery voices, as the rambling tunes wafted on the breeze into the night.

Gypsy rover came over the hill,
Down through the valley so shady,
He whistled and he sang till the green woods rang,
And he won the heart of a laaaaa-aaaa-aaaa-dy.
Ah, de-do, ah, de-do, data-day,
Ah de-do, ah, de-day, oh,
He whistled and he sang till the green woods rang,
And he won the heart of a laaaa-aaa-aaaa-dy.

When that was done, and someone proposed, for example, Drill ye tarriers, drill," our voices would grow far less gentle and watery as we belted out:

Early in the morning, at seven o'clock
there were twenty tarriers a working on the rock,
And the boss comes along
And he says kape still
And come down heavy on the cast iron drill,
And drill, ye tarriers, drill.
Drill, ye tarriers, drill!
And you work all day for the sugar in your tay,
Down behind the railway,
And drill, ye tarriers, drill
And blast and fire!

Our voices would remain stern and long-suffering as we moved on to "Sixteen Tons," where we could further elaborate on our wretchedness as manual laborers; reluctantly we would return to a gentler mood and a more watery voice when we became stricken cowboys as we walked out in "The Streets of Laredo."

While we sang, the hay wagon would be traveling down the Hollow, the lights on the tractor still shut down, and as long as we were heading away from the camp, everything on the hay wagon was simply wonderful. The sweet smell of alfalfa, the night owls hooting over the tractor noise, the moon making her slow way across the sky. We were riding as in a cradle that was rocking us not to sleep but to a state of greater wakefulness; though we might get sleepy, we were sailing too close to the wind not to fight to keep those inner eyes awake, and we were straddled against the hay like iguanas or lizards, come out from beneath their rocks to take the air and bathe themselves in the celestial light. We gazed at that moon above us as if we had never seen it before, as if in taking its rotund and stately path across the sky while we took our lumbering way across the earth below it, it was there especially to make our acquaintance, a fellow vagabond. And we were always aware, all of us, that hayrides were short, that they never went on long enough for us to really learn the moon's secrets, but instead went on just long enough to remind us that there was much about the night we normally missed, because sleep usually overtook us like a blindfold.

So we strove to take it all in now, to savor every moment of the hayride, every moment of the night, which we wished would last forever – and then it would happen, the tractor would stop and turn into a pasture, making a great swooping circle, and then coming about to start the slow drift back to camp. And we would lie athwart it, unable to stop this motion, though we had wanted to keep going west for all time. "Oh, not *yet*, not *yet*!" we begged Seth, but his one good arm was on the wheel, and the hay wagon was heading back where it had come from. Now, with the hayride almost over, we would savor the few remaining minutes as if we would never be on a hayride at Wynakee again, and though one day that was true, of course, thank god we didn't know it, and could sing our last songs without too much sadness. I myself would always propose a song like "Worried Man Blues," which few of the other campers knew, and which those who did know it didn't like, but almost always we would pull into camp on a counselor-proposed up-beat note like the one about "This Little Light of Mine," which, as the hayride came to an end, I found almost as sad as another of my favorites, "Maid of Constant Sorrow." So that when the tractor slowly, slowly, slowly, slowed, and the final words of

Nobody's going to put it out,
I'm gonna let it shine.
Nobody's going to put it out,
I'm gonna let it shine.
Nobody's going to put it out,
I'm gonna let it shine.
Let it shine, all the time, let it shine

rang out into the night, I often found that I had tears in my eyes from emotion, as if this normally sappy song had been transformed by the moon, the brightest light around us, into a veritable ballad that summarized in its simple phrases the essence of life itself, and the tragic fact that all hayrides are too soon over.

Twenty-Eight

FOR ME though, it was on Sunday night each week of the summer at Wynakee that the most clearly *important* Evening Activity was held; it was on Sundays that we had Council Fires, run by Jo-John and the Wayaka Huya, and attended by all the rest of us in our role as ordinary Indians. Council Fire was framed by two eminently ordinary events, a cookout before and an ice-cream bar afterwards, but during the time that it was going on, after the Call to Fire was rung, we all entered a world of great wisdom and intensity. The cookout, with its all-is-normal deceptiveness, was held in the field down by the river where we also ate with our parents on the Fourth of July, and where there was a large stone fireplace in which four fires could be built, one at each point of the compass. There, a half an hour before cookout time, fires would be lit, which by supper would not yet have burned down to coals, and on these fires, we campers would cook our hot dogs. We held them until they were either browned nicely, with little bubbles in their skin, or charred absolutely black, and the second result took a lot less time to arrive at, so mine was always charred, just as when we toasted marshmallows, mine always ignited.

But before I got to char one I would need to make a new stick, since mine had inevitably, the week before, burned to ruin, and you were expected to be on your honor about whether or not you could reasonably claim that one of the sticks leaning against the fireplace was really "yours." Some campers were so involved with this business of the sticks that they actually whittled codes on them so they could find the same one and use it every Sunday, but while they were carefully searching for their codes, I and about fifteen other campers would set off into the woods with our penknives. We would cut a new stick from willow or some other soft and handy wood and then whittle it just enough to get it ready; depending on how long before supper we began this arduous process, our sticks might be blunt or truly pointed. If they were blunt, they would punch holes in the hot dogs, which would cause the hot dogs later to break in half, and force us to retrieve half of our meal from the fire; since this almost inevitably happened to me, I was accustomed to eating hot dogs that were not just charred but also covered with cinders.

By the time my stick was ready, the tables were set up near the fireplace, laden with paper plates and cups and real cutlery, which would later be placed in pans of soapy water; in addition, on the table there were great vats of potato salad, and tureens of coleslaw, and sometimes a three-bean salad. Except for the hot dogs, all the food was cold, since it had been prepared the previous evening in order to give the cook a Sunday night holiday; we had bug juice at the cookouts, and there were hot dog rolls, and enormous jars of mayonnaise, ketchup, and mustard. Cookout manners were rather lax, and with all that mustard and ketchup, all those salads, and all those hot dogs falling into the fire, even a relatively fastidious child might well end up a bit buttered, as food seemed to have a life of its own at these cookouts. The little boys loved to demonstrate this with a habit of which they could not be broken, because to pay too much attention to it simply gave it a greater delight for them; they would take a raw hot dog and hold in front of the zipper of their pants, and then run around the girls, their hot dogs flapping. We girls turned away in disgust, which we told ourselves was at the boys' immaturity, their insistent display of their own bodies, but which was really much more about the substitution of an inanimate object for an animate one, something that produced a very creepy result.

The same disgust would have resulted had they stuck a fake hand up their sleeve and hidden the real one, or put false buckteeth behind their upper lips. All these substitutions distorted the tenderness of a real body, and the tenderness that a real body may evoke. Moreover, the hot dog substitution took away in an instant all our desire to ever become more familiar with the actual penis. If it was anything like that hot dog! All rubbery and slick! And didn't it have a slightly *squared off* look to it? Well, none of that for us, thank you, and how wonderful to be girls, and not have *attached* to us that clammy hot dog! In fact, every Sunday evening we were given a renewed reason to be grateful for the bodies we had so fortunately been given, and more than that, a reason to think that boys – who had been burdened with this extra thing that no one could be happy about – must have been commensurately deprived of something more important, like brains or judgment. If you had a growth on you like that hot dog, why display it?

I found it particularly odd that the little boys would engage in this behavior when we were so shortly to be answering the Call to Fire, and I could only conclude that, somehow, not everyone was as deeply affected as I was by the prospect of being an Indian. At Council Fire, we began to be Indians from the moment the bell rang, and although the trestle tables were still near us, the remaining food still resting upon them, all of that seemed merely a kind of test to me; could I ignore their existence completely, while I thought about what was coming, and prepared myself for the games, the chants, and the stories? Now, we had finished eating and placed our silverware in the soapy bins, and cleaned ourselves in the river, if necessary. Most of us were quieter than usual, a little anxious, even, about our part, whatever part that might be, in the coming evening. We were sitting against a tree, or poking the fire with a stick, and we had watched the campers and counselors in the Wayaka Huya leave us – going off, as they did every Sunday, to the Indian Lore cabin to change, and then returning transformed into different people – and we had watched the Dog Soldiers leave also, boys who belonged to the secondary honor society and got to wear ankle bracelets and loincloths as well as great broad beaded armbands, and who beat drums when the ceremonies required them.

We would wait, we would wait, we would wait by the river, and then suddenly the Wayaka Huya would appear, Dog Soldiers behind them, all walking in single file until they reached the field where we waited. At that point they split into two separate groups. The Dog Soldiers were almost naked, and Karl, who was their leader, had a horned buffalo skin helmet on his head; the Wayaka Huya, led by Jo-John, were elaborately clothed, the males wearing fringed leather tunics and leggings, the females Indian dresses, also often fringed, and always beaded right above the heart; whether you were male or female, when you were selected for the Wayaka Huya, one of your first responsibilities was making yourself an Indian costume. A lot of thought and care went into them, so they were often genuinely beautiful, adorned with laid quills or feathers. Jo-John had on his feathered warbonnet, authentic in every detail, with two horsehair tassels hanging at his temples. Altogether, not counting Jo-John and Karl, there might be four Dog Soldiers in any given season, and perhaps six members of the Wayaka Huya – once you were Wayaka Huya you were Wayaka Huya for life – and these twelve people were, to me, as impressive as someone else might have found the twelve apostles.

And there they were, around and ahead of us now, and

the brass bell rang out for silence, for there was no talking allowed on the walk down to the Council Circle, or on the walk back either, for that matter. While the cabin groups were lining up, in single file, and in ranks of age, youngest to eldest, the Dog Soldiers were scattering and readying their drums, and the Wayaka Huya was taking its place at the very head of the tribe. Those of us who had moccasins had worn them to the cookout, and those of us who had headbands had brought them in our pockets, and now, as we stood in line waiting, a little farther back in the tribe than we had been last year, we put our headbands on our heads, tied our moccasins securely, and waited, in a hush, to start our walk. But "walk" was not the word, really, since to be an Indian, it seemed, you had to put the ball of your foot down first and the heel down second; all the way from the fireplace to the Council Circle a half mile away, we Indians walked toe-heel, toe-heel. There was a saying that the Wienekes loved, "Do not judge a brave until you have walked two weeks in his moccasins," and walking toe-heel, toe-heel down to the Council Circle, I always felt that I understood what they meant by this, because to walk two weeks in this peculiar manner would be very difficult, though it might be, in its way, pleasant.

The bell rang, we gathered, we paused, and then the Dog Soldiers started to beat their drums, and the whole camp began its silent and concentrated procession, toe-heel, toe-heel across the river, toe-heel, toe- heel through the meadow, and toe-heel until we got to the edge of the forest, at which point some campers would start to walk regularly, since the path got rather rocky, and coming down on your toe on a rock could be quite painful. But the rest of us kept up the toe-heel, and followed the paths that we ourselves had cut, paths marked with white rocks from the river for our return along them in the darkness; finally we broke out into the large sawdust arena that had been cleared and lined in the tangled forest floor. Toe-heel, toe-heel, and now the drumbeats grew suddenly a little bit more rapid, and in response to their urgency, we sprinted across the sawdust and climbed the hillside on the far side of it. There, half-logs had been set, as seats rising in tiers. We rose with them, cabin after cabin, until, all standing, we were in place and the drumbeats rose to a crescendo, and then with a final BOOM fell silent.

By now, the Wayaka Huya were also standing in their places, facing the camp across the wide expanse of sawdust. Behind them were the totem poles. Jo-John stood in the center, his arms crossed on his chest, and a huge chair carved from a log behind him. The other members had benches to sit on, but for now they stood, as we all did, waiting while Karl gave the order to the Dog Soldiers to light the fires, and two Dog Soldiers kneeled on one knee before two fires, which they had laid themselves earlier in the day, and took out a single match. With a single match they lit them. The fires did not roar into flame then – there were no pyrotechnics or tricks – but to those of us watching from the tiers of logs, the fires did something even better. They caught slowly, sweetly, confidently, first just a small tongue of flame, then a fine crackling, then the first smoke pushed its tendrils upwards; after this, while we watched, the fires were ablaze, and Council Fire had started just as surely and confidently as its emblems.

Now Jo-John lifted his arms, and the Wayaka Huya sat down, after which the whole rest of the camp did, too, and from there on, every week the program varied. Sometimes cabins prepared special dances or pantomimes. Sometimes there were stories. Sometimes we learned new games. But I will have to let one particular Council Fire stand in for all of them. And I think that I will choose the night the Wayaka Huya itself performed a ritual, using the masks from the Indian Lore cabin.

These masks were mostly made of papier-mâché – a few of them were carved from wood – and Jo-John had made almost all of them, over the course of his many summers, but while we knew that they were the result of his artistry, we knew, too, that they now belonged to the camp, the way the totem poles did, or the Crow, or the snapping-turtle rattle. No two were identical, but when they were finished they were mostly painted black or red, or black and red, and they had disproportionately large eyes, which were made of leather. The noses, like the nose of Eekanyw, were long and protuberant, and they ran right down the face to the mouths that were wide and sometimes upturned at the corners. A few of the masks had huge teeth showing through parted lips. I remember one mask that had a tongue sticking straight out at the viewer. The lips often seemed to leer, and some of them were swollen forward like shelves; others had lips puckered as if their owners were whistling. All of the masks, however, had the same long hair attached to the back of them, horse hair taken from the Morgans' tails, and then wound about with yarn. It was amazing how much more horrible this made them.

And there was something truly horrible, too, about this ritual that I am remembering, in which the seven members of the Wayaka Huya took seven of the masks, and then, with no narration – no speech of any kind – acted out a drama for the tribe, a drama about a sick girl who was cured by the masks. Ginger Wilson was a Netop, maybe fifteen years old, and she had been in the Wayaka Huya for two years now; she was slim and tall and pretty, with shoulder-length brown hair and the most extraordinary green-and-gray-colored eyes. She was shy and seemed quite incapable of ever making an enemy, but she had a lot of friends, since she was kind, and she never put on airs about being Wayaka Huya, or seemed really to think about it much at all. Although she was pale, she really looked like an Indian when she had on her Indian dress and an elaborate beaded belt that she had made to wear over it. Also, on Sundays she wore her hair in two short braids, and these braids were tied with feather bands, so that the feathers blew whenever there was any breeze.

That night, Ginger was to be sick, though, and while the Wayaka Huya got ready, her face was painted with charcoal and ash, and the feathers on her braids removed; she walked forward into the Council Circle clutching her stomach and miming pain, doubling over and then clasping her face with her hands. She had no mask, as the others did, and she lay upon the ground without a headrest, just lay out flat, like something that had fallen in the forest and would probably never rise again. The whole camp, watching, felt slightly sick also – Ginger! Why *Ginger?* we all felt – and then, from out of the woods into which they had disappeared, the rest of the Wayaka Huya came running. The men had stripped to the waist and all of them were masked, all of them bearing gourd rattles except for Jo-John, who carried the mighty snapping turtle; they ducked and reared and danced, and then swarmed, *en masse,* to the prostrate Ginger, who did not seem even to notice their coming. Some of them blew in her mouth, some of them rubbed ashes into her hair, some of them spread their arms above her, and all of this was in total silence. In total silence also they shoved and lifted and appeared to drop her, with a combination of tenderness and roughness. The boy who wore the tongue mask seemed to be everywhere at once, leering and tonguing not quite at Ginger, but beyond her. The girl with the shelf lips seemed beseeching, and altogether it was clear that these masked figures were doing their best to drive forth the evil spirits.

Eventually, they did. When Ginger rose to her feet, looking a little bewildered but somehow well again, the chanting started, led by Jo-John, and then the spectators were drawn forth into a circle dance around the ill person who had been made healthy. In these circle dances, whatever their context, we all grabbed the hands of the campers beside us, and inexorably, snakelike, the whole camp was uncoiled from the hillside and led down into the sawdust while the Dog Soldiers beat their drums again, this time in a rapid tempo which grew more rapid the longer they sustained it. The camp danced, now low, now high, twisting its collective, sinuous body, until the recovery of Ginger had been thoroughly celebrated. As I danced, my body, too, twisting, I got some close-up looks at the masks of the Wayaka Huya, which made me feel that they really might cure any sickness. They were *so* horrible, *so* leering, and the horse hair was so wild and harsh that it seemed no mere weakness would want to stand in the way of them; even a weakness of the body would probably be driven forth, not to mention a weakness of the spirit.

Later on that same evening, there were Indian games, as there usually were, and some of these were also harsh, like the masks. One involved a snapping rope, one involved many blindfolds, one was a complicated game of chicken. But as dusk fell in Dorset Hollow, and the fires died down to coals, and the games were carried out to their conclusion, they did not seem to those of us watching as anything more than harsh. They did not seem cruel, so particular was their context. Certainly they were unlike anything we normally did in camp, where empathy was stressed in all group activities, but just as certainly they did not seem savage for savagery's sake, but rather reminders of what normally went unremembered. That in any palette, there were bright colors, and there were dark ones, there were blacks for whites, purples for yellows, and reds for greens, and for every beam of sunlight, there was a similar shaft of darkness that would cover the light if it was not taken seriously. On this night, those frightening masks, so stiff and unyielding, so false to the tenderness that was a real face with its wide expressiveness, were a lesson in the fact that we didn't want to become like them, frozen for whatever reason into a single expression. And during any Council Fire we were forced to realize that some things worth having – like health, like happiness, like being part of a dance of celebration – could require a degree of real sacrifice, moments of pain and terror; if we wanted to be Indians, if we wanted to be *people,* we might have to suffer for it.

After the games, there would be chants, and then the Council Fire was over for the time being, and the Wayaka Huya stood in their places and lifted their arms up to the hills, and we followed suit, listening to Jo-John pronounce an Indian blessing. The walk back to the camp from the Council Circle was always carried out in single file, and again in silence, this time without any drumbeats. Since it was dark now, it was left to each camper whether he or she wanted to walk toe-heel or not. I always walked toe-heel until I had crossed back over the river.

BALL LIGHTNING

Twenty-Nine

MY LAST SUMMER at Wynakee I was eleven years old, and the summer began for me with an event that at the time seemed very strange. Perhaps in light of later events, it acquired for me an extra significance which it would not have acquired had it happened in an earlier summer. But whether or not that is true, what happened was most unusual, and that it happened at camp, on a rainy day, could not help but make it seem more wonderful.

I loved rainy days at Wynakee. Rain did not prevent us from doing anything important. Only Physical Activity was usually eliminated, and as that was my least favorite part of a day, no matter what, there was always a sense of holiday about missing it. Of course, if it had rained on one of the days of special events, or hard enough right before an overnight to keep us from leaving, that might have been a different matter, but it rarely *did* rain on such important occasions, and thus rain was generally a treat. Even before we were quite awake, we who were lying in our beds would be aware that the weather had unexpectedly shifted, and that sometime during the night, the clear skies we had gone to sleep with had vanished. Now, it was raining, and the air smelled of relaxation and sweetness.

It was not that we had been tense before, of course – god knows life at Wynakee was not stressful – but as we lay there in the early light hearing the rain hitting the windows, we noticed the soft susurrous way that it slithered on the panes, and we felt utterly and completely peaceful. If I myself had gone to bed with the window beside me open, then the windowsill might be wet – and perhaps even a bit of my blanket – but that was nice, in and of itself, and unless the rain was really driving in, I would leave the window open and watch the drops as they hit the glass, beaded, and then scurried down. And there was a breeze, always a breeze, when it rained in Dorset Hollow, so that I could see, through half-opened eyes, the leaves of the apple trees, the whole orchard bending and bowing and fluttering in the wind, not as if it was being pummeled, but rather, as if the leaves were showering.

And before I even got out of bed, as I lay there in that deep peace, every part of my being going through a process of unwinding, I could smell on the wet wind the joy of every single plant in the Hollow, as they all sent their delight in the rain onto the blowing breezes. There was the smell of hay in the air, now mostly timothy and clover, and there was the smell of ferns and hollyhocks from outside our own house, and roses from the farm down the road; I could also smell humus, from the deep woods on the mountains, and the Indian paintbrush in bloom almost everywhere. Warm and sleepy, my friends and I would just lie in bed as the bell began to ring to tell us the day was here; we noticed that it was much darker than it normally would have been at seven, and the mood of the world was so muted that although nothing was really changed, everything was different.

So instead of leaping from our beds, as we did on clear and sunny days, we took our time in getting up, keeping the covers tucked to our chins longer than usual. We shared a conspiracy, we Owls, but it was the very nicest kind, because there could be no one who was not a conspirator. It was not a conspiracy of sloth, nor a conspiracy of cleverness, it was just a conspiracy of people who were determined, today, to do things differently. Today, we would take our time, see minutes and hours in a new way, and we would do this all day long, by acting as if the day were made of taffy. Normally, when the sun shone, we knew time for the rubber band it was, always hurtling us forward into the following moment. Now, though, it could be stretched by the warmth of our bodies in the morning, by the rain shushing softly against the windowpanes.

At last we decided to get up, and someone would open the front door wide, the better to let in the delicious smell of the wet wind. We dressed perhaps rather hastily then, because it was just sixty degrees and the damp air chilled our bodies more quickly than usual. There was never any question when it was raining that it was time to get out long trousers and wear a shirt and a sweater as well as a raincoat, or in my case, a poncho. We also all wore shoes, and socks, or perhaps even boots, though of course whatever footgear we put on would be soaked through by breakfast. I knew from experience that going barefoot in the rain was wonderful, but only for about ten minutes, after which it chilled me right to the bones in my forehead.

So boots it was for me, and then I made my bed and the other Owls made theirs, and we agreed, without talking about it, to wait until everyone was ready; usually we left for the flagpole in twos and threes but today we ran for the flagpole together, helter-skelter through the meadow, one girl in a green trench coat, another in a see-through raincoat, another in yellow. I also was in yellow, and my poncho had a silly plastic hood which wasn't big enough, and seemed designed to expose my face as much as possible, so that by the time we got to the flag raising, water had trickled in around the hem, and I could feel it start to dribble down my sweater. By the time the flag was up – we raised it even in the rain – the water would have soaked through my shirt and sweater. By the time we got to breakfast, where we shed our wet coats in the lobby, there would be a great wet patch from my clavicle to my navel.

But who cared? It was raining, still raining. This wasn't going to be one of those disappointing days when it rained a bit in the morning and then stopped, and everything was dry by lunchtime. No, it certainly looked as if this was a rain day, not too much rain at any one time, but a steady shift and change, a steady breeze, a steady sheeting. In the Barn, you could hear the rain on the roof as you waited for the breakfast gong to ring, and in the dining room you could hear it hitting against the windows, because the noise in the dining room was subdued today, with everyone in the place half listening. Indeed, the rain sounds were distinctive in each different building. In the Whatsit, which could not be closed, the rain might come in and soak the dirt floor, and to be in the Whatsit in a rainstorm was to be more outside than if you'd been outside, because the earth smell and the animal smell and the floor smell, as well as the fungus smell and the toad smell and the beetle smell were mixed together more completely, creating a more unified impression. You were in a cave, it seemed, when it was raining, a cave somewhere in the deep wet woods, and you felt lucky to be in a cave with all the other animals. When the time came to leave, and you put on your poncho, you stood for a while under the eaves of the wide doorway, feeling that the rain was something that, as a cave dweller, you should know better than to brave.

But you did brave it anyway, and when you got to the Arts and Crafts room, you found that the rain made the paint there smell more acrid; in the Indian Lore cabin, on the other hand, it softened the smell of bone and leather, and made it richer and yet a little less overpowering. It was nice to go to the library, because when it was raining, then in the library the books themselves smelled very tempting, like safe old houses; on rainy days, the library, so often quite neglected, drew children to it with an unarguable force of character. Before lunch, there might be ten of us there, curled up in armchairs or sitting on the floor, half reading and half listening to the falling water.

The afternoons were somewhat different. It wasn't that we wanted the rain to stop, since we didn't, at least not really. Give up this gentle soothing smell? Give up this newfound state of daytime togetherness? On the other hand, you couldn't spend the whole day in the library. And with archery and riflery canceled, as well as all the ball sports, it was necessary for each child to decide on a special activity. The children who liked games simply went up to the Rec Room in The Barn and whiled away the hours playing Monopoly or Parcheesi. The children who liked boating went to the pond, to canoe or kayak in the rain, and some campers would go for a second time that day to Indian Lore or Woodworking. I myself generally chose to be in a play, to do some extra theatre practice or some improvisation, because it gave me an excellent opportunity, while I was waiting to take the stage, to have a memory feast.

This wasn't the kind of memory feast that I would have when I got home, when I would start nibbling at the very beginning of the summer, and it wasn't the kind of memory feast where I thought about the big things – Klondike Day or Capture the Flag or the Wayaka Huya. It was the kind where I thought about the small things, the things that were simple and happy, like the rain itself, or a hayride, or working on a crafts project. Whatever I thought of, I thought of it slowly, my back against the wall of the loft, and the air around me sweet and soft, like the velvet nose of a horse who, when you touched it, would snuffle at your palm. The air suggested that time was there for me to move into.

After the play rehearsal was over, and the children in the Rec Room had packed up their games, and the children in Woodworking had hung their chisels back on the pegboard, the bell would ring, as it always did, to announce that it was time for free swim, although on rainy days not very many people showed up to go swimming. I myself thought it was one of the best swimming times, second only to skinny-dipping, and when the bell rang I would run through the rain to get my suit, splashing my feet in any puddles so that the water flew out with a *splat!,* because my boots could not really get much wetter. Before I reached the pond, both my suit and towel would be soaked through, and I had to notice, now that I had no footgear, that the grass was *cold,* and the driving rain, even when it was fairly gentle, would jab my shoulders and arms with ever-sharper needles as I got closer and closer to the pond and safety. When I was there, I wasted no time, but as soon as I had shanghaied a buddy, would cannonball into the water, which felt warm and, compared to the rain, almost dry.

On rainy days, I found it fun to do one of two things, either stay as long as I could beneath the surface of the water, swimming in the darker-than-usual darkness of the pond like one of the larger breeds of freshwater fishes or – a special treat – climb up and sit on the pond's spillway and let the force of the water rush over me before it fell down the wall. On sunny days, we were forbidden to do this, since there was a small element of danger – it would be possible, if one got careless, to fall backwards over the wall – but with so few people in the pond, and those who were there the most earnest pond fanatics, Karl turned a blind eye to spillway climbing. I, and a friend, perhaps, would tread water in front of the spillway, with our backs against the slimy, mossy wall, and we would let the water pound our chests, our upper arms and necks, while the rain from above did acupuncture on our heads. Then we would put our hands behind us, and treading upwards in the water, grab the spillway with the palms of our back-turned hands, and with one successful venture, get our fannies to carry upwards until they landed on the eight-inch-thick concrete wall. Then a sudden shift of the hands, and we would be clinging to the wall fingers-forward, and the rain would be doing a tapdance all over our upper bodies, while the pond water, sluicing out, would massage and caress our legs and buttocks, and we would feel – well, we would feel wet, wet, wet.

I got bluer than usual during free swim on the days when it was raining, and on several occasions was told afterwards to take a special shower. We had a shower over the claw-foot bathtub in Owl's Head, and I would stand there under the drizzling hot water until I was baked hot again, and quite pink, like a good strong sunrise. Then I dressed in fresh clothes, as my old ones were damp through – the breakfast wet spot had spread outwards in all directions from clavicle and navel – and at that point, just before supper, it would have been quite all right with me if the rain had decided to stop. But as it didn't, I dried the inside of my poncho with a nice clean towel from the bottom of my trunk, making sure that every speck of dampness was removed from it, and then I put on the poncho again, this time trying to get that hood forward so that the rain wouldn't leak inside, as I knew it would.

We had Personal Inspection, as usual, and lowered the flag, and went in to supper – by now those campers who had *not* gone to free swim and had a hot shower were looking pretty bedraggled – and we hoped that the rain would stop soon, and were glad when we heard that the Evening Activity was to be a sing fest in the library and that there was going to be a fire. The fire had already been lit – we could smell it when we left the dining room – and everyone wanted to rush over and sit by it right away, but we had to wait until seven o'clock, at which point we jammed in like an army after a battle, one day of rain having made us feel like Napoleon's troops on their winter retreat from Moscow. Just when it had happened, it was hard to say – and there was no question that rainy days were wonderful – but we could hardly wait to get to bed, and out of this damn rain and have our hair, sometime during the night, get dry again. After we had sung all our songs, many of the same songs that we sang on the hayrides, we cautiously peeked out of the library to find that the rain was lessening, and then we walked off to our cabins where we toweled our heads vigorously, and went to sleep on a self-dampened pillow. We felt a continued sense of togetherness as the lights went off, and the rain finally stopped just before we slept. We were all survivors of a day that had been sweet and splendid and that we now were very glad was done with.

&

WELL, THIS DAY was different. It had rained a good deal in the morning, and as this was the first week of camp, and we were preparing for the Fourth of July, we all found it a little bit frustrating; also, the weather was thundery, and there had been lightning on and off in the distance, and rumbles as if a whole second storm system was coming. I loved storms as much as plain rain, but this storm had a strange kind of edge to it, and I had found it difficult in the morning to keep enthusiastic about the float we were working on for the great parade. While most of the other Owls went off to the Barn's lobby to wait for lunch, I decided, for some forgotten reason, to go up before lunch to Owl's Head. It was not raining at the time, but the air felt very lowering, very tense and charged with storm that was still unexpended.

For some reason, this lowering weather, with the oppressive shifting of air pressure, made me walk much more slowly than was usual for me during the summer; in fact, I was dragging my feet, my poncho thrown over my shoulder, kicking a pebble along the road in front of me with my shoe tip. I was wishing that the storm would either vanish, or break and really *storm* and be done with, rather than hanging around over the Hollow, unable to make up its mind, and I was thinking that our float wasn't shaping up well. I got as far as Netop, thinking all this, and then I stopped. A tiny spring was on the edge of the road there, with a little bubble of water, and I had passed it a hundred times before without ever thinking about it. Now I stared with hypnotic attention at the water, which bubbled and bubbled and bubbled. While I stared I suddenly had the strangest sensation. It was as if I were being watched – there was a flicker of felt perception – and I looked quickly behind me to see who might be coming up the road. But there was no one. Everyone was in The Barn. I looked uneasily into the woods beside me. Was it possible that there was someone up in them, hiding?

No, that was ridiculous, but I started walking a lot more briskly until I stopped dead, maybe twenty feet farther along the road. Yes, there *was* someone near, I knew it, and I turned back and looked down the road that I had come from just in time to see that someone appear from the woods; only that someone was not a someone, it was a something, bluish, not quite translucent. About two feet in diameter, it seemed to be rolling about a foot above the ground. Not that it was really rolling, which would be turning end to end, no, it was floating. It moved no faster than a person might walk, but it moved with, seemingly, a good deal more purpose. It was stately in its perfect symmetry. A globe is always a dignified form, one which takes no risk and invites no comments.

But this globe was a lot more than dignified. It was obviously extremely dangerous and gave off an electrical message not to touch it, not to hinder it, not to come too near it, and while it was like nothing that I had ever heard or read of, there it was, a ball of blue fire, a ball of lightning, a perfectly formed ball of electricity. It was moving under its own power, traveling wherever it willed, and it passed me on the road as I stared at it, utterly dumbfounded. It passed me no more than ten feet away, while I backed away from it toward the woods, and then it moved down the road in front of me toward Owl's Head. I followed it, just keeping up with it, and with no inclination to get closer, yet drawn to it, as the ball continued dispassionately on its journey, first keeping to an imaginary center line on the Lower Hollow Road, and then, just before Owl's Head, pausing as if in thought. It hovered for a moment in place, and when it started to move again, it was rolling down the field, the surface of which was uneven; but this made no difference to the lightning ball, which stayed always exactly a foot from the ground and was now moving at a faster pace than before.

I thought that the ball was very beautiful, and very perfect, and somehow very *lucky* to be made, as it clearly was, of pure electricity, guarding itself with a protective force field as efficient and resolute, as symmetrical and simple, as a pure idea. To me it seemed to be full of purpose, as full of purpose as any human being – though it was composed of the skeletal essentials, matter and energy, movement and repose – and yet, unlike human beings, it was utterly independent, choosing its own path and then proceeding to follow it. The ball, in fact, seemed like pure mind, unencumbered by any body, unencumbered by time or space or anything else, existing in its own dimension, which had touched ours for just that morning, but was normally somewhere alongside it, and would probably exist forever, long after ours was gone. I turned into the field to follow it, and as I did, it began to move even faster, and now turned west so that it was heading toward the woods with the Council Circle. I wanted to run, but my legs felt very heavy. The ball was outdistancing me without any trouble. It now had a head start on me that I would never overcome.

The last I saw of the fire ball, it had paused at the edge of the woods again, and now turned south and vanished, while my legs were finally freed and I ran forward to where it had been. Then I stopped. It was gone. I would never see it again. And what would I have done, anyway, if I had caught up with it? What *can* you do if you are confronted with the thing which I later discovered is called ball lightning? You can't touch it, you can't hug it, you can't toss it, or move it, and much as you would like to, you can't ask it questions. "How do you know where you are going? How do you decide where to go? And how do you come into being to begin with?" Those are the questions I would have asked it. I stared vainly into the woods. It had come out from them and now had returned there.

When I got back to Owl's Head, there were several other campers, changing their shoes or combing their hair for dinner, but though I wanted to tell someone what I had seen out on the road, I found it hard to share with just anyone. So I waited, thinking I would tell Wendy later on, or maybe Johnny B. during Evening Activity, or perhaps even Aunt Helen, if I could get her all alone; she might know what it was that I had seen. I sat with Wendy at lunch, and with the din of the dining hall around me, three times I tried to tell her what happened, but three times I began to whisper, "Guess what I saw on the road just now?" and three times I got no further than the first two words "Guess what?" "Guess I'll have some more bread." "Guess what?" "Guess the storm is really over."

Her comical face more comical than ever, Wendy stared at me.

"Guess what?"

"Guess you wish I'd just shut up."

As for telling Johnny B., I couldn't do that either, and I didn't even try to tell Aunt Helen, and the story didn't get told, not that summer and not for a long time afterwards, because the more I thought about it, the stranger it made me feel, and the more desperately I tried to understand it. At home, I went to the library and looked up lightning and storms in the encyclopedia, but all I found was a reference to Saint Elmo's fire, and only in later years, when I was not looking for it, did I at last come across some references to ball lightning. That was the thing that I had seen, then. Of course. Ball lightning. I learned that Jesse James had made a sighting; so had a sailor with Columbus, on the *Santa Maria;* so had a soldier in Wellington's army; all of their stories had been discounted as pure fabrications. Now, the existence of ball lightning had finally been recognized.

But it was recognized almost grudgingly, because it was exceedingly rare, and consequently, few human beings had ever caught a glimpse of it, and I was the first one to say, "Why me? Why had I gotten to see it?" And what was I going to do with it, now that the sighting had been given to me? Eventually, I arrived at the conviction that if only I had followed the lightning into the woods, all would have been explained to me. I would have understood its purpose, and its ability to decide things, and why it had paused as if in thought at the edge of the meadow. Actually, if only I had followed it, it would have brought me to the site of the Klondike Stone – the ball lightning the rainbow, the Stone the pot at the end of it. And I couldn't imagine why I hadn't run, run down the meadow, run through the trees, run to wherever that blue ball of fire might have taken me.

Thirty

ONE MORNING later that summer, the Morgans got loose, which was not an uncommon occurrence at Wynakee; what was uncommon, this time, was that they ran in both directions, up the valley toward the mountains and down the valley toward Dorset. Usually, when the horses were loose, the whole camp was told at breakfast that we should gather near the pond at nine o'clock, and then, breaking into factions, take the road deep into the Hollow and spread out through the woods like human netting. I liked these occasions a lot, since Uncle Kuhrt was always so serious, his bald head gleaming as he rubbed it nervously, the tops of his pants hanging over his basketball sneakers with a particularly determined look, his muscled arms waving widely in the air. I also liked these occasions because they were the only time that I can remember when Aunt Helen would actually put on trousers and boots, forgoing her costume jewelry and her dresses for the great trek through the forest after the horses. Finally, I liked these occasions because the counselors who could ride would mount the horses *bareback* once they had caught up with them, having carried bridles with them in the chase, and then vaulting onto their backs, and riding back to camp in fine style. How wild they looked, how primitive, with their legs dangling down to the horses' knees, and the fit of their thighs just draped over the horses' withers, particularly in the woods, where they reined the horses back and forth quickly, in an effort to avoid the snapping of the tree limbs.

This time, however, it was different, as the camp had perhaps thirty horses, and only half of them were suspected to have gone up the Hollow, while the other fifteen had been seen sneaking toward the woods around the Council Circle, where it would be a good deal harder to catch them. When the herd was up the valley, it was in dense woods which never ended and was held by the hands of the flanking mountains, but with part of the herd in the opposite direction, both roads lay for their taking, and any alarm would surely send them bolting off down the valley.

At breakfast that morning, therefore, the camp was divided into two contingents, with Uncle Kuhrt pointing to one half and then the other of the dining hall, and I happened to be in the half that was chosen for the down-valley horse brigade, which was to be under the leadership of Megan, the head riding counselor. I had always admired her a lot, because she was so slim, and her face was so stern, with her dark hair always pulled back in a ponytail, and of course because when *she* had been little she had done exactly what she was expected to, which was to love and understand horses. But I had never before seen her do anything like organizing thirty campers to efficiently capture fifteen horses loose in the woods, and I was surprised when, having gathered at the river, we searchers were given the brief instruction that we should follow her and try to keep together.

She then mounted the little pony that was the standby for these occasions, since, being fat and lazy, it never ran anywhere, and – her feet almost reaching the ground – led us down to the trees past the Council Circle, signaling us to follow, which we did with a fair amount of difficulty. We hadn't seen any horses, but we assumed Megan knew what she was doing, and that this was the way to get errant Morgans. I was walking toward the end of the line, with maybe three or four people behind me – the rear was my preferred spot, for obvious reasons, when it came to horse searches – and soon I got hot and tired because there was absolutely no sign of any horses, and the woods we were passing through had a lot of dead logs in them. I wouldn't have done this on a hike, but as we were only on a horse hunt and as I had no desire to meet horses in the wild in any case, I thought a little rest would be nice, so I sat down on one of the fallen logs, fanned my face with my hand, and fell to studying some fungus. The fungus wasn't big enough for the Whatsit, but it was a most unusual shape, and it grew in clusters at the base of the fallen tree I was sitting on, so after a while I bent down and picked it, and when I looked up I noticed that everyone had vanished and, although I could hear some crashing sounds in the distance, I couldn't see a single person.

I wasn't worried, but I got to my feet, pausing to take off my sweater, then putting the fungus onto it, doubling it over, and tying it around my waist by the sleeve ends; only after

I was all done with this did I set off in the direction of the others, following the route I imagined they must have taken. These were not woods with which I was familiar, and shortly I found myself climbing a small hill, the existence of which came as a total surprise to me.

Halfway up, I turned around and looked back, and saw nothing but woods all around me, woods which were strange and yet also had a strange familiarity. I was amazed at the monotonous repetitions of maples and birches, ashes and beeches, and leaves and leaves and leaves again, and of course, of shade and sunlight, and I was now unable to hear even those crashing sounds in the distance. The woods were dense and very, very silent. I was lost. Oh, I wasn't really *lost* – how could I be lost, so close to Wynakee? – but I *was* lost, and my heart was beating faster because I had never before in my life been precisely where I was now, and I had no clear idea of how to get away from there. I thought about turning around, but then I decided that that would be stupid, since I was at least halfway across this center section of the valley, and if I just kept walking straight, I would certainly hit *something*. There was no way around that, after all. Keep walking straight, that was the ticket.

It might have been, if I could have managed it, but a small voice within me suggested that if *walking* straight was a good idea, *running* straight would be even better, so first I walked faster and faster, and then I broke into a trot, and then I was crashing along, my heart thumping like a drill hammer. When we had been on the Open Road, after leaving the dreadful Long Trail, we had all been together, and we had had meadows all around us, and not knowing exactly where we were had had a delight which I had not realized would not be repeated in circumstances like those which now surrounded me. "Hello!" I called. "Hello, Megan! Where are you? Everybody? Hello!" and trying to shout while I ran made my breath tear in and out of my body. So, making an enormous effort to be calm, I stopped and decided to retrace my steps after all. Dark fancies were now flitting through my consciousness, of being lost here until my bones had actually whitened, and I was on the verge of out-and-out panic at being lost, lost, lost – which had a most dismal ring to it.

Somehow, after I turned, I found my way back to the fallen log where I had picked the fungus – I could see the fungus roots still attached there – and while I hated to abandon the horse hunt, I could see that the only thing to do now was to go back to camp, to which I knew the way from here. I sat down on the log and rested until my heart had stilled, and then I continued on until I found the Upper Hollow Road and almost hugged it. When I got back to camp I discovered that all the horses had returned before me, but that every other member of Megan's search party was still out in the woods somewhere. I put my fungus on a shelf in the Whatsit – so what if it was too small? It was the only thing that I had to show for my experience – and heard someone from the other search party say, "They must be lost. I wonder where they are?" referring to Megan, the pony, and the twenty-nine people who were with her. "Are you nuts?" I wanted to respond. "You can't be *lost* in a crowd that size. You can only be lost when you call, and no one calls back to you."

It was sometime within the next week that we had a Cabin Night for Evening Activity – Cabin Nights were something that we did maybe four times a summer – and the Owls decided to have a cookout in the woods down by the Council Circle, not on the site, but in a firepit near the wickiups and longhouses. I'm not sure exactly why we chose to do this, rather than practicing a skit for the whole camp, or a dance to perform at Council Fire, or even a song for Sunday morning meeting, but we probably were sick of responsibilities and just wanted to have some fun. And what could be more fun than being laden down with food from the icebox in the kitchen? We got to skip dinner, and we were given hamburger, and lettuce and tomatoes, and buns and baked beans and cocoa, as well as milk and marshmallows, and enough cookware to properly prepare all this; each of us had brought a rucksack, and while the bell rang to call everyone else to dinner, we were just setting out for the Council Circle, our rucksacks fully laden.

Of course, what this meant in practice was that by the time we got there we were starving, and we didn't even have wood gathered yet, much less a fire to cook our food on, so we were extremely motivated as we prepared things, some of us gathering wood, some of us going to the river for water, while others started forming hamburger into patties, putting beans in pots, and cutting up the salad. I myself was, of course, a wood gatherer, and I roamed through the woods in my search, though I was careful never to get out of sight of at least one of the other Owls, and after the wood was stacked in piles, I put myself in charge of the fire, first clearing most of the ashes from the firepit near the longhouse. Then I constructed a perfect teepee, with the twigs going first, a rush of fine wood, and the small sticks going next, in concentric circles to form a pyramid, with the larger sticks capping the entire structure. The fire caught, and in less time than all of us had feared, we were cooking hamburgers and toasting rolls and heating up the baked beans, and also congratulating ourselves on what a splendid idea we had had for Cabin Night, since the food tasted extra delicious for having been carried on our backs from the dining room. It seemed that everyone was in a sweet temper, and everyone doing the task to which she had been appointed.

My task was keeping the fire going, which I did with enormous relish, adding wood to it even before it needed replenishing, and after dinner we roasted marshmallows and drank cup after cup of cocoa, once or twice sending somebody off to the river to get more water. The river was a quarter of a mile away, over a little rise and then down its embankment, and we could hear the sound of it if we weren't sitting too close to the fire. It was a very soothing sound, as running water always is, and as dusk fell and some girls told stories of their other lives, I listened more to the fire and the water than to their voices. When night fell, we were sitting by the fire, and I was wishing nothing so much as that we had brought our sleeping bags and could just stretch them out and spend the night right here, when someone started telling a ghost story and then someone else told another, and they were scary – especially the one about the Wendigo.

This was a terrifying Indian spirit, a legend among tribes from the north woods of Canada, who had fiery stumps on the ends of his legs, which burned the ground he walked on. The refrain of the story was the wailing of the Wendigo, as he called in the voice of the wind, "Oh, my fiery eyes, my burning feet."

Soon we were huddled about the fire, which I built up larger and larger so that it roared, taking oxygen from the air around us, but repaying us with a brilliant light that cast dancing shadows on the tree limbs above us, and the night grew later and later, with the moon setting at about ten-thirty. It was then that our counselors Trudie and Bonnie reluctantly suggested that it was time to pack up our gear and get back to Owl's Head. And at that point, we suddenly realized, one, that the fire was enormous, two, that we had no water to put it out with, and three, that although the river was only a quarter of a mile away, that was a quarter of a mile with no moon to see by. Even so, things would have been fine if it hadn't been for the fourth fact, which it took us a while to discover and then to comprehend, which was that among all of us there wasn't a single person who had had the sense to bring a flashlight. Not even our counselors. It had been full daylight when we'd left Owl's Head.

Yet somehow, we had to get to the river to get more water to put the fire out, because we knew that we couldn't possibly leave it burning, and even though we would probably have done just that if we had been spending the night nearby, we weren't. So there was no way around it. The light of the fire itself, which was surely a white man's fire, despite its location near the Indian longhouses, was bright enough to pack up our gear by, and the water issue was put off until that part of the preparations for departure was completed. Still, *someone* was going to have to make the trip in the pitch darkness to get the water, and while this might not have been so bad if we hadn't just been telling ghost stories, we had, and they had been scary, and for me, there was the added fear – a new fear – of getting lost in the forest. But I knew, as I looked around at the Owls industriously scrubbing their plates with ash and pebbles, packing their rucksacks, talking animatedly together, that each one of them had the same thought: "*Somebody* has to get the water. But you can bet your booties I'm not going to be the one to do it."

Even Bonnie and Trudie seemed reluctant, since Bonnie said that she would do it, but she wouldn't do it alone, and Trudie said that she felt one counselor should stay with the girls, presumably to protect them, and it was about that time that I realized that I was in for it, for a variety of reasons. The first one was that I had built the fire to begin with. Not only had I gathered the wood for it, and lit it, and tended it through dinner, but, more relevant, I had kept putting logs on it until it was enormous. Also, I wanted to be Best Owl, and you didn't get to be Best Owl by sitting around the fire letting someone else get water in the darkness. Perhaps most important, however, was the last reason, which was that we were within a stone's throw of the Council Circle, and as far as I knew, you could never get to be Wayaka Huya if you were a coward. Yet I was scared, really scared, of the darkness, and the ghost stories, and, mostly, of getting lost. How much worse that would be in the darkness than it had been in the daylight.

So, suddenly, the evening which had been so enjoyable became bone-chillingly unpleasant, and I wished that we had never even thought of having this cookout, but, knowing what was expected of me and not daring to seem craven, I said to Bonnie, "I'll go with you to get the water." She nodded, as if she had been counting on this, and then we each picked up two large pots and moved away from the firelight in the direction of the river, which we could hear still running as always; the sound alone would guide us, and of course, on the way back, we would have the light of the fire itself to steer by.

Still, those first five feet away from the fire, it seemed that the darkness was as dark as pitch, and I felt that I might as well be wearing a blindfold in the House of Horrors. Then Bonnie reached out to touch me, and I realized with a shock of wonder that she was almost as scared of this dark quest as I was. She was probably nineteen or twenty, but that didn't mean she was all grown-up, and as I sensed her fear, mine, I found to my astonishment, receded, just as it had when I had been with Sarah, and we had climbed down the trapdoor into the Whatsit, and she had cried because of the smell of earth and the tiny hairless rabbits. Indeed, I felt quite maternal toward Bonnie, this girl who was at least eight years older than I was, but who wasn't – as I considered myself – a natural woodsman; I decided it was up to me to lead the way, and to be hearty and jovial and reassuring, so that Bonnie wouldn't ever know that I had known that she was frightened.

Actually, there was something absolutely splendid about

being in the woods in the large darkness, with the river running gaily over the rocks, and the fire burning behind, and my girlish counselor right beside me – and neither of us lost, because we knew where we were going, as long as we had sound and light to steer by. Yes, it was really splendid, this feeling that nothing could hurt us, and that there was no such thing as ghosts – at least not the kind we had been hearing about – and we felt our way carefully among the trees, sometimes stumbling but never falling, until we came to the banks of the running river. There we could see something dimly, since even though there was no moon in the sky above us, there were stars, and the water had a reflective surface, so that it glimmered faintly, oh, so faintly, with the light of the distant suns shining down on it. I could hardly believe my eyes. But it was true. The water was shimmering.

The water was shimmering. Yet the light was so dim, and the night so black, and the trees so enfolding, that it seemed impossible that such a thing could happen. I asked Bonnie, "Do you see the water?" and she said, "Yes," in a hushed, reverential voice, so that I knew I wasn't just imagining it. We filled our pots with the shimmering river and climbed up the bank again, spilling a little water but making our way from light to light with most of our cargo, and when we poured it on the fire, the fire hissed and sputtered and crackled, and sent a huge plume of steam off into the night.

Still, it wasn't really out, and we knew it might smolder until we had left and then burst into flame again when we were all far from the spot, so Bonnie and I made another trip to the river, this time gaily, and we filled our pots to the brim, no longer fearing the Wendigo. That fire I had built could so easily be doused by water, but the water could be put out by nothing. It would glow for all wanderers who came to these banks as long as there were stars in the sky. And this time I almost pitied the rest of the Owls, who were not really any more craven than I was, but who would never get to see this palest of lights, for fear of darkness.

Thirty-One

IT WAS ALSO in that summer, my last summer at Wynakee, that I took my first high jump into the Dorset Quarry. For years, the campers at Wynakee had been taken there several times a summer, but I had always been scared to jump, since the place itself scared me. It lay outside the Hollow, on the main road between Dorset and Manchester, and just about a hundred feet, at most, from the edge of the blacktop, so it was very much part of the world that lay beyond the bridge, and yet it was also, in those days, protected from it. It was protected by a screen of trees, and by the well-known iciness of its water, but most of all, or so I thought, by its reputation; rumor told that people had died there, impaled on old quarrying machinery, knocked unconscious against rock, having sudden heart attacks. The stories were quite grisly, and I'm not sure where I first heard them, but I am sure it was before I ever saw the quarry. When we arrived there my first summer, I saw it through a lens that was already clouded by the reflection of all those deaths which lay beneath its waters.

In fact, so thoroughly did I believe that to swim in the quarry was to risk harm that I was not only scared of jumping into it, I was scared of *being* in it, and this fear was not helped by the fact that to swim in any Vermont quarry, you have to commit yourself totally before you even enter it. The edge is sheer and sharp, and plunges vertically toward the water; nowhere is there a sandy beach, or grassy bank, or graveled bottom. The sides are sheer because they have been sheered on purpose, and the water is deep because the quarry has been delved deep before a hidden spring far beneath the earth rendered further quarrying impossible. The Dorset Quarry was a huge pit of stone, to one side of which marble blocks were piled, and around which there were marble cores from which columns had been pithed. Because it was spring-fed, the quarry was cold, and because of its depth there was little convection, so it was truly icy, colder even than our pond. Also because of its depth, it seemed almost black to the eye, the marble white against the inky pool of water.

So I was scared to swim in the quarry. It looked to me, then, like what it was – or what I thought it was, because of all the morbid rumors. It looked like a dangerous place, and it did not surprise me that it also seemed ugly – striking and dramatic, but a good deal too much so. Of course, I knew that the marble that had been quarried from it had been sent, via rail, to become part of the great New York Public library, but while this gave it a certain charm, the charm was rather abstract, and hard to maintain in the face of the actual quarry. Only when I wasn't there, standing at the edge of the water, could I envision those great marble columns, those smooth marble floors. Only when I wasn't there, nervously adjusting my towel on the rock, could I see in my mind's eye that huge reading room with all the green-shaded lamps in it. Then, when I wasn't near it, but somewhere safely and completely else, I could feel proud of our quarry for having served the cause of knowledge. But when I *was* there, I would merely think of those who'd been impaled upon the same cause, the bodies littering the bottom of the quarry like old bottles.

Well, this day, in my last Wynakee summer, it was hot – very hot for Vermont – and Aunt Helen and Uncle Kuhrt decided that it would be a good day for quarry swimming. Only the Crows and the Wrens were left behind. The rest of us climbed into the camp truck, along with Karl, and most of the other counselors, several of whom were Red Cross lifeguards. This plethora of lifeguards should have been comforting, but it wasn't, since I had always reasoned that lifeguards, Red Cross or not, could do little when you were already impaled on machinery. Many of the other campers leapt into the water immediately after we arrived, and swam to the far side to jump off the high marble blocks there, but Wendy, Sandy and I, who all felt the same way about the quarry, found a nice safe flat spot, well back from the edge, and spread our towels out upon the hot marble. Then we watched the other campers, jumping in, climbing out, jumping in again. We ourselves were satisfied to stay dry, even though it *was* hot. Anyway, we had an activity of our own, which was adjusting our towels and discussing the dead-body thing again from every angle.

For example: The dead bodies couldn't still be there,

could they? The families would have wanted to get them out, wouldn't they? They would want to bury them in a graveyard, we supposed, and put a headstone over the grave, and anyway, the health authorities would have insisted, for sanitary reasons. Yes, all right, so someone had once impaled himself on machinery that we had never seen – and that meant it must be deep, *so deep,* beneath the surface! – but they must have pulled the man out by now. In fact, they had, we were almost sure of it. And besides, if they hadn't, he would mostly be gone now, wouldn't he? Or would he? The water was so cold, and cold preserved things, like meat in an icebox. No, no, no, it would have to be just a skeleton now. And there was nothing awful about skeletons; we all had one in our science classrooms. Well, actually, now that you mentioned it, there *was* something awful about skeletons – the way they dangled, and if they were in the Dorset Quarry, especially.

At last, though, we were really hot, so hot that we had to swim, at least for a minute, so we slipped off the side into the rush of cold waiting there. By this time we were all quite convinced that the body or bodies were still *in situ,* and also that we were about to have a personal encounter with them. We tried to swim holding our feet up, and not pushing our arms out very far, yet we couldn't help but feel how pleasantly cold the water was, and by daring one another onwards, and following some passing Mohawks, we managed to swim to the far side of the quarry.

There, we climbed out near the jumpers, and settled ourselves, now towelless, upon a hot rock, feeling that the return swim could wait until it was time to leave again; we watched the jumping and the exhibition diving, and from this vantage point, close up, the fun the other campers were having was almost infectious. Also, I couldn't help noticing that whenever they leapt off the cliff edge, they cleared it by miles, protected by the laws of physics. One of the reasons I had always feared to jump was that I'd thought I might bump my head somehow, just like one of the bodies in the stories – he'd become a body that way. Even now, my vivid imagination told me that if, right at the edge, I were to slip, I *could* be knocked unconscious. I would jerk back and slide into the cliff like a fish slithering off a platter, and that would be it, it would be the end of everything. It would be the end of swimming, and Wynakee, and Klondike Day, the end of next summer, and the chance of making Wayaka Huya. But Wendy, sitting beside me, and dry now, suddenly got up, climbed the marble blocks and then jumped into the water. I watched her falling, in nervous amazement, watched her comical face concealed by whipping hair, watched her vanish into the water and emerge again. Then I watched her clamber out, all wet and smiling, and saying it was easy. I found myself getting to my feet and following her.

Of course, I wasn't going to jump. I had become older, maybe, that summer, what with getting lost, and Cabin Night, and the ball lightning; but I wasn't totally foolhardy, and just because Wendy had suddenly done it, I didn't have to take the plunge that might impale me. Still, I got to my feet, and then I climbed up the big blocks of marble, and to my astonishment, found that. from up here, the quarry looked quite different. Down There, where I had always lingered, the quarry was stark and jammed with bodies; Up Here, it was cool water set into a landscape. Down There, the water was black, and the sides of the quarry were stark and sheer; Up Here, the sides looked gentler, and it was easier to see trees reflected in the water's surface. They were green and leafy and reassuring, although they were upside down and backwards, and there was blue sky with white cloud painted on top of it. As for the sheerness of the sides, from this new vantage point I could see that there were little inlets which had natural underwater ledges. Up Here – and now I was at the top, twenty-five feet above the water – the quarry looked chastened, more manageable and more trustworthy.

I was intrigued, and drawn toward the cliff edge. I approached it, and then I was upon it, my toes curled, as if I were about to launch them. Karl was below me in the water, and he looked up and called out, "Go ahead, Elizabeth," so I put my thumb and forefinger to my nostrils to seal them. Then, without much preparation, just a sense that everything about the quarry seemed different, I pushed off, and found that I was falling, falling, falling. The wind was a torrent rushing upwards, created by my passage so quickly through the air. When I hit the water, it was like landing in a vat of Jell-O.

I went down, and down and down. My eyes opened underwater, and I could see – see how deep I was, how safe was the water around me. Then I shot up, irresistibly buoyant, to break the edge of the air, and as soon as I could get my breath I actually started shouting. Yes, strangely, I was shouting with joy, at being in the Dorset Quarry, and I swam as fast as I could to the edge, and heaved myself out. Practically running to the top of the cliff, I paused only to grab my nostrils, and then again I was in the air, and falling, falling. The wind was touching every part of me, grabbing me as I raced past it; it seemed to be holding me, embracing me, exploring me. And I had never before felt air like that. It was as if the air had become interested in my being, and now that it was interested in my being, I was interested in its being, also. In fact, I loved the way it felt on me, as I fell through it – its harsh affection. I jumped, and I jumped, and I jumped, hardly stopping. By the time we left, I was pink all over from hitting the water at all sorts of odd angles, and my lips were blue, my teeth pleasantly chattering.

Still, when the truck pulled up for us and Karl called us to gather by the road, I lingered one last time on the high rock, looking downwards. Really, what a marvelous place this was, a place where you could jump through the air such a distance that it was almost like jumping from an airplane. The water had to be there, to catch you safely at the end of it, and the rock had to be there, to launch you at the beginning, but it was the space between the two that really was remarkable, because that space let you *let go,* let you find out where letting go would take you.

And where it took you was to a place where the Dorset Quarry was not ugly, and not frightening, and not a place where bodies lay waiting; indeed, it took you to a place that suddenly seemed absolutely fascinating, like the wisdom stacked in books in the New York Public Library. How interesting that marble could be quarried, right out of the ground, as it were, and that the ground was where marble was always located. How bold and geometric were its angles, how dramatic were its lines, its smoothness, its depth and its purity and the coldness of its spring-fed waters. Altogether, the quarry was amazing, not gentle, but very resonant, an ideograph scrawled across the woods of Dorset. It seemed that truth wasn't something absolute, something fixed from every angle, but that it might have a lot to do with how you looked at it. It was a relationship, not a thing. Neither out there nor inside you. Not the rock you jumped from nor the water you jumped into. No, it was more like the wind – intangible, even noncorporeal, until the moment at which you finally launched yourself into it.

Thirty-Two

ONCE A SUMMER at Wynakee a photographer came, generally during the first week of August, and he took formal portraits of campers at various important spots, like the hay wagon, the porch, the bridge and the waterwheel. I liked the photographer's visit, because I liked to have my picture taken, especially when I was wearing my Camp Wynakee sweatshirt, but it also made me sad, because it was always the first reminder that summer was now more than halfway over. It reminded me of that fact because I knew, being now an old camper, that the photographs taken that day would be presented to us at the final banquet, along with any awards we might have won, any trophies, or feathers or adorned feathers, and I found that final banquet an absolute nightmare. Oh, the Wienekes tried to make it fun, with the photographs and awards and decorations, and the "themes" that varied from year to year according to the tastes of our counselors, but I think that all this achieved for me was to give me a permanent phobia about formal parties, since they have been, ever since, an occasion for anxiety. I went to five final banquets in my five years at Wynakee, and none of them was even remotely bearable, except for the first one, when I hadn't yet experienced the parting that would come after it.

The banquets were truly banquets, with the richest food we had all summer – rare roast beef, baked potatoes that had been opened, split, and mashed, large salads with fresh Vermont cucumbers, and in a separate bowl, bright cherry tomatoes that popped in our mouths like the edible equivalent of cherry bombs. There was soup to begin with – unheard of – and there were rolls that fanned open like books, so that you could peel the pages off individually and butter them, and there was, of course, fresh milk, and water with ice in it, instead of bug-juice, and on the tables, glass containers of both mints and peanuts. As for dessert, it was always the same, a strawberry shortcake that melted in your mouth, with real whipped cream that lay across it soft and lazy. The food at the final banquets might be wonderful but, although I ate it, and almost enjoyed it, it always somehow made me sick to my stomach anyway.

In fact, when I think of those final banquets, which were just the first act of the final drama that ended with me sobbing on a mattress near the ceiling of the Wren's Nest or Owl's Head, I wonder whether they may not have given me a permanent phobia about having people be too nice to me, because the banquets always ended with the awards, and I generally got several of them. And though I thought beforehand that I would like this, in the event, this made me sick also, since it seemed so clearly intended to try to make up for what could not be made up for, which was leaving Wynakee; and it somehow made it worse that each banquet had a theme, and that the themes dominated the decorations.

Because what this meant was that on my final night at camp, when I wanted nothing so much as the familiar, the Wynakee I knew was replaced by some strange contortion of the counselors' imaginations; the theme might be Poseidon's Palace, or Alice in Wonderland, or Romantic Europe or the Rocky Mountains, but whatever it was, I didn't want to go there. No, I wanted to go to the Wynakee dining hall, and have supper, and forget what was coming, but I couldn't, because this banquet had been weeks in preparation, and we campers had to wait in the lobby until the counselors and the Wienekes were ready for us, and then walk inside and be surprised by whatever awaited us. On the night of the final banquet, the tables, rather than being separate, were arranged in an enormous squared-off horseshoe, with Aunt Helen and Uncle Kuhrt sitting in the place of honor in the middle, in the spot which on a real horseshoe holds the luck. As for the rest of us, there were name cards telling us where to sit, and on each table there was an individual menu, which had been devised to supplement the theme and which didn't tell us straight out what we would be eating, but instead covered the food with strange disguises. The tables were also disguised, being covered with white linen, and instead of cheap paper napkins, we had the fancy kind.

We also had glass candlesticks with ivory-colored candles burning in them, and the lights were dimmed so that the candles would seem brighter, and for some children, I am sure, it was truly a moment of wonder when they walked into the dining hall to have dinner there for the last time. As for me, after my first final banquet, I knew that whatever theme the counselors had chosen, it would probably turn me against the whole idea of it for life; if the theme was Poseidon's Palace, I would never again look at a net without feeling my feet curdled by their own private fog. If the theme was Alice in Wonderland, from then on I would feel nothing but contempt for that wretched Alice and her careless White Rabbit; and if the theme was Romantic Europe, I would be permanently uninterested in ever visiting smelly Venice and its stupid gondolas. Those Italians warbling love songs! Those Frenchmen on the Riviera! The whole thing just had to make you sick, or make me sick, anyway, as I sat there peeling my roll's thin pages and watching them disappear into my mouth and into the past, just as the summer itself was about to.

I fear that the menus didn't help much, with their constant alliteration. They seemed to ram home the message much too hard that the summer was over, and that my familiar, solid Wynakee was to become the next night just a memory feast. When the dining room was Europe, we had Romantic Roast Beef, Platonic Potatoes, Gracious Green Beans, Ravishing Rolls and Sensuous Strawberry Shortcake; when the dining room was Poseidon's Palace, we had Rolling Roast Beef, Bounding Main Milk; when we were in Wonderland we had Red Queen's Rolls and Gryphon's Green Beans. In fact, the menus seemed to me arch in a way that was so unlike Wynakee that it was as if someone were trying to break it to me gently that the morning after the banquet I would be leaving basic sanity and returning to a world where the arch often passed for cleverness, just as doggerel passed for poetry, and knowledge passed for wisdom. I would sit there eating that meal, and incredulously read that menu, wondering how sheer pretense had gotten mixed up with creative imagination.

The decorations varied from year to year, depending on who had been in charge of them. Poseidon's Palace was just nets and painted floats and a trident, while Romantic Europe was a positive jungle of "grape vines" attached to posts and painted backdrops of gondolas and castles. Whatever the decorations, the counselors were naturally praised for them, as we knew that they had put in a lot of effort, but while many of the other campers took home decorations from the banquet, I never did. It was bad enough as it was, without extra reminders. And reminders, anyway, I would have, in the form of my scrolls or pins or feathers, both adorned and unadorned, which were what the banquet would finish with. The only good part of the final banquet was if you got one of the big awards, and your name was burned forever on a wooden plaque. That, and the photographs.

Well, the day of the photographer's visit, which was often on a Saturday, by definition dawned that last year clear and sunny, since the visit would have been postponed if the weather had been anything less than perfect. I dressed – as did all the Owls – with unusual care after I got back from breakfast. I put on my crispest shorts, and my whitest socks, and my moccasins were brushed, and I carried my Camp Wynakee sweatshirt over my shoulder, since I didn't want to get it smudged or dirty before the great moment when it would be exhibited in numerous photographs. My hair was too short to do much with, but that year it had grown quite fast, so that by squeezing *very* hard I was able to put it into pigtails, which I thought would look very festive. Actually it looked as if I had glued two paintbrushes to my head, but I didn't see that until it was too late to do anything about it. I repacked my trunk very carefully, and smoothed my blankets until they were flat, and then I walked sedately to the field where we were all to assemble.

There were lots of photographs to take. There would be cabin pictures, and girl pictures and boy pictures, and special interest pictures, like Woodworking and Arts and Crafts and the Whatsit. The most important picture, however, would be the one that got taken last, which would be of the whole camp, campers and counselors sitting together. Each year since the waterwheel had stopped working, we had wanted to have that picture taken at the wheelhouse, and not just at the wheelhouse, but sitting on the wheel, which the Wienekes had never before permitted, as it would create tricky problems for the photographer, and also because it was thought to be somewhat dangerous. But this summer, they had at last agreed to it, and so we were particularly excited about the morning, which would end with such a splendid and dramatic vision. While we waited for things to get started, I played with the camp hound, Bassett, who had that summer had a litter, and who had brought her puppies down to the field from the woodshed. I picked up one of those puppies, and buried my nose in her little tummy, which smelled so fresh and new and hopeful that the doleful expression in her eyes was quite negated. The Owls decided that the puppies would feature in our cabin photo, and when the picture was taken later most of us were holding one.

I always enjoyed posing for pictures at Wynakee, even though the process *did* remind me that the summer was more than half over, because I saw the posing as an extension of acting in a theatre. While the photographer was readying his equipment, you composed yourself into character, and that character was what you displayed to the camera. This forced you to be very self-aware, forced you to try to decide who you were, what was the most important thing that you had thought, or been, or done lately, and so, during the annual photograph session, I was often tense with concentration, thinking that I had to *work* to get my real image onto the photographic paper. If I *worked,* then surely I could manage to come across as more than just freckled and blue-eyed; surely I could show, in my face, that I wanted to be an Indian. Surely I could show that I had recently jumped twenty-five feet into the quarry, with the wind grasping and pummeling my body; surely I could show the way I had gone for water in the darkness. Or the ball lightning that I had followed, and that had imprinted itself on my retina; surely if I concentrated *very* hard, the pictures would see it also.

And that year, though I worked just as hard as usual to make the outside form that the camera's eye would capture display the inward form in what I hoped was its true complexity, I also particularly tried to show my life as an Indian, because while I had no hope that I could make the Wayaka Huya, not that year, I thought I had a chance at the Indian Lore award. There was my trip to the Ice Cave with Jo-John, and the quenching of the fire near the Council Ring, and the long hours I had put in weaving various beaded objects, not to mention my part of the totem pole, and while the final banquet might be a nightmare otherwise, there was something about having your name burned on a wooden plaque that seemed irresistible. So when the photographer went to take pictures in the activities cabins, I pursued him hotly in order to be in the Indian Lore pictures; when the Owls' cabin group was taken, each Owl holding at least part of a puppy, I tried to look as if basset hounds were an entirely new life-form to me; and when the totem pole was photographed, as always, in progress in the courtyard, I held my chisel and mallet with what I hoped was the appropriate amount of enthusiasm. Down by the Council Circle, I insinuated myself into a group that had a log it was carrying on its collective shoulders; and as for the longhouse and the teepee photographs, I managed to be in every single one, though I tried not to be *too* obvious about it.

The photography session took hours, and had a long break in it for lunch, after which there was the all-camp photo; it was about three o'clock in the afternoon when the bell rang to gather all of us together, and we assembled, as prearranged, at the wheelhouse. No amount of familiarity with this marvelous place had ever dulled it for me, and the idea of being in a picture with the wheel was riveting. The only thing that would have been more wonderful would have been to have seen the wheel start up again, and the water once more fly and spray around its iron surfaces, but as that couldn't be, just sitting on the wheel would be eminently satisfactory. At first, while the photographer was setting up his camera on a tripod and with a hood that he could duck under, there was a fair amount of chaos as everyone in the camp tried to get on the stone superstructure simultaneously. I was still in my Indian mode, and I was determined to look bold and brave in the coming photograph, so I waited until the rush had died down, thinking that then I could climb on the wheel itself.

But Aunt Helen and Uncle Kuhrt had other ideas. They called everyone back off the wheel, and then let us file on again in small human doses, with the biggest boys getting to go first, and to climb right onto the topmost part, and then the Netops allowed on, and perched a little lower. The Netops and Mettawees took up the whole wheel, and the Crows and Wrens were allowed to go next, so that they wouldn't be lost in the crowd but could sit in the middle of the picture. They took up the base of the wheel, which meant that we Owls and Mohawks had to take what was left, the two concrete wings that jutted out from the more massive center. From any point of view, this was the least interesting place to be sitting, and I felt disappointed that the photograph, when it was taken, was bound to make everyone in the whole camp look bolder and braver than I did. Or at least at first I was disappointed, but the photographer took so long to set up his camera that I had time to get comfortably settled in my spot, and almost sleepy.

By now, after all, it was midafternoon, and I had put in long hours of effort, and it was very nice just to be sitting by the Mettawee River. The river was sparkling and the pebbles at its bottom were colorful, and it was soothing to watch the water moving, and to listen to it running, about ten feet below me, too far to reach down and play with the pebbles, too far to dangle my feet in it, too far to reach down and get a drink. Too far to do anything but look at it. Wendy and Johnny B. were to either side of me, and some of my other friends were nearby, and I listened to them chatting while I grew sleepier and sleepier. The photographer fiddled with his equipment. Then at last he said, "Look this way," which I did, but without enough time to get ready. I had time just to lift my head and direct my eyes toward his pointing finger, and then click, the photograph had been taken, and click again, and again, without warning, and I had not once in the three pictures transformed myself inside into the Indian that I had hoped to display upon my countenance. No, I knew even as the photographer shot, that *this* time I would look like what I was, no more or less, a Wynakee summer camper, surrounded by my friends and my surrogate family, who were surely in their own way a tribe as unified and bonded as any tribe of Indians. And I would not stick out in these photographs, but would be just one face in the crowd, supremely ordinary, and in that sleepy moment, liking it. Liking feeling the sun on my face, and liking hearing the river on the rocks, and liking thinking of nothing, and being absorbed into Wynakee.

Thirty-Three

I DON'T KNOW if it was that week, or a later week, but it was in that last month, that last summer, that the rumors started flying that the following Sunday at Council Fire two new members were to be inducted into the Wayaka Huya. These rumors, which were flying everywhere, were like threads of milkweed blowing, and they blanketed the whole camp in their delicate silkiness, so that I heard the rumor in the Woodworking shop, and then in the Arts and Crafts room, and then I heard it as I was walking past the showers. By the time I heard it at dinner, and then at Rest Hour back at Owl's Head, everyone at camp must have heard it at least four times also, and content that we all now *knew* that there were to be two new members of the Wayaka Huya, most of the other campers were content also to let the matter rest. Of course, they, too, must have wondered all week who the two campers would be, since whoever they were, they would affect the tone of the camp for years to come, because not just I, but everyone at Wynakee, knew that those souls who stood in front of the totem poles took on an importance that did not stop at the edge of the Council Circle. One boy in the Wayaka Huya was brave, he was very brave, he was known most of all for his bravery, and the Wayaka Huya was brave, because the boy, Brent, was in it, and we were all brave because the Wayaka Huya was really us. One girl was kind, she was very very kind, she was known most of all for her kindness; her name was Teresa, and the Wayaka Huya was thus kind, as were we, the camp that had chosen her. Each member of the society became to the rest of us a touchstone, a way of measuring ourselves not against some abstraction, but against a real person whom we saw all the time, and whose faults were as evident as his or her virtues.

So it was very important, not just to me but to everyone, whom the Wayaka Huya had selected to join them, and what they would stand for when they stood before us and the gods of the earth and sky, of fire and water. Important, yes – but I doubt that most of my fellow campers were as sick as I was that week with fear and longing. I didn't delude myself into thinking that I *deserved* to be Wayaka Huya. But I wanted to be, with a fierce desire. And I felt just as fiercely that if I *were* chosen by Jo-John and the others, I would somehow become better than I'd ever dreamed of, that if I *were* chosen – chosen freely – then I would struggle harder than ever to be worthy of the place that was Camp Wynakee. In fact, if I were chosen, I would die before I would make a single person in the camp regret it, and if desire went for anything in the great scale of the future, then my sheer desire must surely be increasing my chances. This desire to be one of those chosen weighed on me all week like something physical; I had to drag it from place to place as a burden, and it sat on my stomach like food, like the largest meal I had ever eaten; at the square dance on Friday, I found it had moved to my feet, so that I had to sit on a large wooden beam while the others twirled their partners.

By Sunday morning, I had to drag myself into the library, so burdensome had my desire become, but at least by Sunday, there were no more rumors, since we knew for certain that there would be an induction; Jo-John had confirmed it, and so had Uncle Kuhrt, and now all that remained was the waiting. And whether we were waiting, as I myself was, to discover our personal destinies, or whether we were waiting simply to find out whom to admire, we no longer wished to discuss it, or even mention it out loud, as it was far too sacred for such disrespectful bantering. After dinner, I went to the woods garden, and I made a wish on Eekanyw, rubbing his long nose over and over, and I got permission from Aunt Helen to go to the Indian Lore cabin that afternoon so that I could finish an almost-completed headband. Whether or not I was selected, I wanted to wear it in honor of the gods that the Wayaka Huya stood before, those gods who were the perfection of a single feeling, or a single current in the great earth-river. And that feeling, those feelings that were gods, were attached by a gossamer thread not just to me but to everyone in Dorset Hollow; I wanted to honor those feelings which blew through Wynakee like the foundation lines of spiders, picked up by the breeze and then mind-entangled.

The Indian Lore cabin wasn't just quiet – on a Sunday when no one else was there – it was eerie, with its rabbits' feet hanging in bundles, and the porcupine quills in baskets waiting to be dyed, the masks with their tongues and shelf lips and that terrible horse hair. Only five rows were left unfinished on my latest, broadest headband, which was my simplest and most elegant design yet; it was all dark blue beads with a white star shining, a star that would be centered right in the middle of my forehead. Shortly, it was done, and I tried it on and put it in my pocket, and left the Indian Lore cabin, closing the door behind me. The hours passed until cookout time, and I dressed for it as carefully as I had dressed for the photographer, with clean shorts and a clean shirt and my headband in my pocket. And then I went to the river where the fires were burning nicely and the little boys were doing their usual thing with the hot dogs. By now, though, I was past caring, as I floated through the cookout in a trance, not even charring my hot dogs, but roasting them brown, with bubbles. Then I gave them to one of the hounds, and at a great distance I noticed the Wayaka Huya as it left and then arrived in costume, and when the Dog Soldiers, too, had assembled, I got to my feet and put on my headband, and found my place in line with the rest of my cabin.

The Call to Fire rang, and we finished assembling in silence, from the youngest camper in camp to the eldest, as always, and then, Jo-John at our head, we started off toward the trees and the Council Circle, the drums beating with what seemed like special urgency. As I concentrated on my walking I could hear, between the drumbeats, the sound of the river and the leaves rustling in the maples, and a horse whinnying once or twice up on the mountain, and the movement of people's bodies producing little swishing noises. I held my body very steady, and tried to gather it almost as if I were riding, riding my familiar body, toe-heel, toe- heel, toe-heel; as we got halfway down the meadow where the ball lightning, too, had traveled, I felt more and more in harmony with the coming evening. We walked through the opening to the forest, and then on the paths with the rocks on them, and we passed silently by the Wayaka Huya, who stood there awaiting us, as always, with their hands stretched up toward the sky above them.

With the others, I crossed the sawdust – toe-heel, toe-heel, toe-heel – and with the others I mounted the hill beyond it. Then I stood in my accustomed place before the half-log which was always clammy when I first sat on it, and which afterwards warmed to the temperature of my body. I looked down at the Wayaka Huya, at Karl and Jo-John and Ginger and Teresa, and as I did, there in my beloved Wynakee, in my beloved place in the Council Circle, the desire I had been dragging with me all week simply vanished. What difference did it make, really, whether I was the one inducted? The truth was, I was only eleven, and I had many more years before me, and if this year passed, there was always the next one, and the next one, and the next, and anyway, I would still be a Wynakee camper even if I was never invited to join the Wayaka Huya. Being a Wynakee camper should be enough for anyone.

We sat, and had our usual games and dances, and somebody told a story, and then, as the Council Fires burned low, there was unusual movement, with Jo-John walking into the Circle's center and taking with him a long ceremonial peace pipe, which he proceeded to fill with tobacco and then lit with a brand from one of the two fires. He puffed it and set it on the ground, and then announced what we all already knew, that two new members of the Indian Honor Society were to be chosen that evening – and now my temporary peace was gone, and the desire returned stronger than ever, making me breathless and tense, and invading every part of my body. When the Dog Soldiers stepped forth, those two boys who would, by tapping them on the shoulder, signal to the new initiates that they were to descend into the Circle, it sent my heart racing so that I feared it might actually explode, and when the Dog Soldiers crossed the Circle, I was surprised that I was still conscious and breathing.

The Dog Soldiers slowly climbed the hill, aware that every eye in camp was upon them, and making the most of this moment which had been given to them, and then they separated, leaving the central path, one of them turning right to the side of the hill where the boys sat, the other turning left into the side which held the girls. Someone on the boys' side was tapped – it was, I thought, a Mohawk – but I didn't even turn my head to look, I didn't dare, since I was afraid it might come loose from my body. And I wouldn't look at the Dog Soldier on the girls' side, either; he was climbing, in any case, above me. No, he was coming back. He was entering my row. And he was moving past me. Well, that was it, all over, and it was a relief in a way, as the desire drained down toward my toes again, and then the Dog Soldier returned, as if he had somehow lost his way here, or had calculated to a decimal just how to extract the maximum amount of feeling from me before he placed his hands on my shoulder blades, not tapping me, but shoving.

And that shove which the Dog Soldier gave me, those hands hitting me and forcing me forward, telling me that now and forever, I was one of the Wayaka Huya, that shove was an amazing surprise, since this boy not much older than I was treating me as roughly as if this were not an honor at all, but a punishment. And whatever his reasons, he did precisely the right thing for me when he shoved me, for he brought home to me something that I should have known already, which is that honors are not sweet and soft things, they are hard. They make life harder. They are unfabricated and unideal. They are like hands shoving you forward. And if that boy had simply tapped me, it might have been a birth that was a bit too easy. Real births, of whatever kind, are intense and painful, and they are coming and coming, but when they actually happen, they hurt you anyway. I might have spent the whole previous week longing to have just this very thing happen, but when it did happen, I thought, "Oh, God, no, please, not me." I hoped that the Dog Soldier was mistaken, and that he had put his hands on the wrong camper, and I imagined that it was in confusion that he had hit me hard enough to make my back ache. But then he was shoving me ahead in front of him, all the way down through the ranks of the campers, until I had gotten to the circle of sawdust, where he told me to go to the center and kneel. I was shaken, and I almost fell down, grateful to find the ground there, grateful to grasp the sawdust while the Wayaka Huya gathered around.

Drums began to beat, and I was dimly aware of the rhythm, dimly aware when more wood was placed onto the fires. I heard a brief pronouncement from Jo-John, and silence from the camp, which I couldn't see anymore, since I was kneeling away from it, facing the totem poles. There seemed to be smoke, much smoke, and I saw that Jo-John had picked up the peace pipe, and that he was kneeling across from me and my fellow inductee. Robert, I saw that he was Robert. And then the whole Wayaka Huya was kneeling in a circle, and the pipe was passed around the circle until it eventually came to me. Placing the stem to my lips, I sucked at it three times, drawing the smoke into my mouth and then letting it join the air again; though I had never smoked in my life, an inexplicable surety seemed to tell me how to do it, and the smoke tasted strong and acrid as I pulled at it and then let it dissipate in a bluish haze. Bound objects dangled from the pipe, medicine bundles and decorative beadwork, and after I was done with the smoking I held up the pipe as the others had done. I saluted each of the four winds before I passed the pipe to Robert, who did the same.

When the pipe reached Jo-John again, he spoke some words to it, presumably in Seneca, and then he and the other old members of the Wayaka Huya got up. Robert and I remained kneeling, our backs to the rest of the camp, while Jo-John led the closing prayer, and there was a song of thanksgiving. Then there was the final chant, and the camp filed away, toe-heel, toe-heel, off into the night, back to the river and the courtyard, and when they were totally gone, and not a whisper of their feet remained, the members of the Wayaka Huya lowered their arms and came to Robert and me to lift us up. They greeted us, each of them in turn, welcoming us warmly to their ranks, and Teresa, the kind one, rubbed my hands, which she said had gotten cold. One of the boys nodded at me encouragingly. I must have looked as if I were shell-shocked, since that is certainly how I still felt.

At some distance from the two public Council Fires, a smaller fire had been laid, and talking softly, the Wayaka Huya proceeded to this private place, where our real initiation – a very simple one – would be held, and before which Robert and I were asked to promise that we would never reveal what went on during the rite. I took this vow, and now I am breaking it, but I am sure that my fellow members will forgive me, wherever they are, and they are scattered now around the globe. Jo-John kneeled, as we all did, facing the fire, and then with a burning brand he had carried from the Council Fire, he lit this one, which had been so well prepared that it burst at once into flame. I touched the rocks around it and they were cold, but by the time I left they were very hot, since Robert and I sat vigil until the fire had burned down.

First, however, we looked at Jo- John as he spoke to each of us in turn – spoke more words at once than I had ever before heard from him. He told us that after tonight we were no longer Robert and Elizabeth, white people in a white people's world. We were, if we chose to be, members of the Wayaka Huya. If we decided to take on the burden, freely, and without anyone forcing us to, we would be members of an Honor Society, and Indians, and he – Jo-John – or whoever came after him, was and would always be our personal sachem, but we weren't to do as he said just because he said it, since Indians didn't work that way. They gave honor and they expected honor in return. More than that, they sought for truth. If we vowed, we would be vowing to seek always for the truth. We would become Seekers of the Way. And whatever we did, at camp and outside of it, all through life and perhaps even beyond it, we should judge ourselves not as whites, not as children, but as full-grown, enduring souls.

We were children, indeed, but children of the Great Mother, who bore our futures in the bosom of her earth, and as of this night, if we stepped into the Circle, we would be held by her. And the Circle was not our Council Circle, which was an earthly and physical representation of something which was not physical, but existed on many planes. The Circle was a way of being, in which reverence for life in its great diversity was the only absolute. Always love life. Love the dirt and the rocks it carried in it, love the water and the droplets that came out of it, love the spiders who painted their sketches in sunlight against the sky. And if we took this vow in our own hearts, we should write down our white names on these pieces of birchbark, and with proper thought, burn those names to ashes in the heat of our little fire.

He handed us the birchbark, which was thick and white, with little lines of gray; my piece was large and square. It had obviously been carefully chosen, and I was sure that Jo-John himself had cut it, and I held it in my lap, in the light of the fire. I looked at it for a long time, while the Wayaka Huya sat patiently, in silence, each person thinking about what Jo-John had said, each old member renewing his or her own vow; at last I took a twig and then wrote on the birchbark Elizabeth Arthur. I held it on my lap. Then I laid it on the fire. It lay there for an instant on the coals, then the letters sprang out with great clarity, and the bark began to curl. But before it could curl my name shut, it just exploded into flame, and then fell back, exhausted, into white ash.

I had no name. I remembered my name, as it had been before. A funny sound, a collection of letters, letters from A to Z. How meaningless, how arbitrary, that collection of letters had been, and how carefully I had carried it, like a bundle of dried bones. The name that I had lost had come to me when I was born, and had never been modified in any way for my personal soul. The name that I had lost had been as little my own real name as a conjunction or a pronoun or a verb. Indeed, a rock was more my name than the name that I had burned, because I knew rocks, and saw rocks, and some of me went into them, but that name – what was it, anyway? – that I had once had and had no longer, that was nothing. I would have to get a new one. And Jo-John then explained to us that we wouldn't speak again, Robert or I, until the dawn came, and that in the night we would have a dream or vision, and from that dream or vision we would learn our Indian names, and next Sunday at Council Fire we would be asked to tell the story. We would dress in Indian clothing and stand before the whole camp and recount the tale of how our Indian names had come to us. The Wayaka

Huya then left us, and Robert and I sat together in silence until the fire died down to ash and coals.

Back at camp, everyone had had their ice-cream bars, which were the Sunday evening treat, and now they were waiting for us so that we could have the evening circle. When Robert and I appeared, a great cluster of campers gathered around us, asking us questions, touching us, congratulating us and teasing us. Someone had saved us some ice-cream bars, but we both refused them with nodded thanks, both apparently concluding the same thing, which was that it would be safest just to keep our mouths closed. It was awfully strange standing with the rest of the campers while they sang "Dark Green Mountains" and taps without being able to join in the songs.

As soon as I could, I slipped off into the night, and was one of the first Owls back to Owl's Head. I climbed into bed as soon as I got there. I lay facing the opened window while the rest of the Owls got undressed and had fun with what they saw as a new kind of challenge. They were determined to make me speak, and asked me casual questions like, "Have you seen my soap?" or "Did you take my towel?" and they begged me to say just *one word.* Did I like being Wayaka Huya? Did I, did I? Oh, I could tell *them.* Well, all right, if I wanted to be a *snot* about it. Forget it, they didn't care at all. They just hoped that being Wayaka Huya wasn't going to go to my head. At last it was over and the lights went out, and I lay there awake in the dark, too excited to go to sleep for a long, long time.

When I did fall asleep, I didn't dream, and when I woke in the morning, I was aware of two things. I was Wayaka Huya, and I hadn't had a vision. I had burned my white name in the fire, but no Indian name had yet come to me, and I was mightily worried, because I had only six days left before the next Council Fire. If I kept up this dreamless sleeping, I was afraid that no name would come to me, and that in desperation, at the last minute, I would have to simply *make one up* and that not only seemed like cheating, it also seemed to mean that I was lacking something, and that my induction into the Wayaka Huya must have been a mistake.

Days passed and I had no visions. I worked every day sewing my Indian dress, but I couldn't work in the same way at trying to receive a vision, and as the week went on I was driven to talk to Ginger, and then to Teresa, and to explain my problem. Both of them told me that they had actually made their names up. "It's really a kind of vision, though," they said. "You just sit down by yourself somewhere. And then you think about names until you hit one that you like. The story comes out of the name, sort of." I was shocked. But I sat by myself a lot, and hated every single name that I thought of, until Saturday, when I knew that all was up. I had finished my dress and I had my new headband, but without a story I would have to die before the next Council Fire, and I went to the Mettawee River to see if I could think of any other remedies.

I played, as I often did, with pebbles, sifting them through my fingers under the water and then setting them on the banks to dry; and when, drying, they began to lose their color and stopped shining and glinting and sparkling, I carefully set them back. A name. I needed a name. Most of the names were poetic. Morning Star, White Buffalo, and Dark Shadow were three of them. But I needed to find my own name, not some poetic imitation of someone else's. I needed a name like, well, like maybe Bright Pebble. Yes, *that* would be a good name, if only I could have it, like those rocks sparkling under the running water.

Then suddenly, it was clear to me. Bright Pebble *was* my name now, and I would find a story to tell about it, and though it hadn't come to me in a vision, what was a vision, anyway? Wasn't it just a way of seeing something suddenly, and with a feeling you were right about it. So when I went to bed that night, I let my mind wander without trying to harness it. I saw the pebbles lying under the Mettawee, and I saw the sunlight reflecting off of them, and I thought of things that had happened to me recently, that summer. And before I went to sleep, I had had my naming vision. I woke up in the morning wondering whether I had dreamed it, or only "made it up."

The evening came, and for the first time when the Way-aka Huya left the cookout, I went with them to change in the Indian Lore cabin into my dress in the full sight of the masked faces. Jo-John put on his fringed leather leggings, and the Dog Soldiers put on their loincloths, and Karl put on his buffalo headdress with the horns. I put on my new dress and my headband and my moccasins. But mostly, I clothed myself in my new name, Bright Pebble. I walked toe-heel down to the Council Circle, keeping my eyes on the fixed horizon, and being Bright Pebble every inch of the way. After the Council Fires had been lighted, I stood with the others, and then sat on the bench, Bright Pebble, listening to the invocation as one of the Wayaka Huya. We had dances and games as usual, and then the time had finally come for Robert and me to tell the camp the stories of how our names had come to us.

Robert went first. His name was Young Eagle. I didn't hear a word of his story, because I was so intent on rehearsing, one last time, my own – and though I loved acting, I knew this wouldn't be merely acting, because I truly believed that when that birchbark had flamed with my name on it, so, too, had a whole part of my prior life. I wanted my new life, wherever and however it took me, to begin here, in the presence of people I truly loved, and when my turn came I walked forward to the middle of the circle with my hands toward the sky. Then I slowly lowered my hands earthward, and held them outstretched above the sawdust, as I had seen Jo-John do, until I dropped them, and spoke.

"It was at the time of the Green Corn that I was separated from my tribe, O Sachem, and Great Mother, and I was frightened and lost in the wilderness where the wild beasts lived. My tribe had been walking through the forest, in order to gather wood for the winter, as the corn was soon to be taken from the fields and the days were getting shorter. In fact, the autumn was coming, and the winter would be with us after, so we needed much of everything, much corn, much meat, much wood, and with my own sling to carry wood in, I kept going farther and farther away from the others, so that I could get the largest load of wood of anyone. It wasn't just that I wanted to be helpful, I wanted praise for being the finest – the finest wood gatherer in the entire tribe – and it was this which proved to be my undoing, because I knew where there was a grove of beautiful trees, and where many sticks could be found ready for burning, dry and barkless and thick as my arm. But it was in one direction, and the tribe was moving in the other. I went after it anyway, following a streambed up a hillside. When I tried to cross the stream, though, I tripped and fell and hit my head on a boulder. And when I woke, it was dark, and my tribe was gone.

"I wanted to shout, but I was very frightened, and there was no moon, so it was very dark, and the wild beasts, though not very hungry, made strange noises with their claws on the rock. There was no way for me to light a fire, although I had wood lying all around me, that wood that 1 had gathered so greedily in my pride. I was still near the stream, however, and after a time, as I stared at it, it seemed to me that it was carrying the faintest of lights. The glow was dim, but it was reassuring, and I stayed by the stream all night long, and when the dawn came, and the sun rose, I thought I would follow the streambed down through the woods, so that I could try and find my tribe. This I did, leaving all the wood behind me and taking only the sling that I had carried it in, and a waterskin which I filled half-full of water. I knew that when I emerged from the forest, I would have to leave the river behind in order to find my way back to my family's longhouse.

"The day grew long, and I grew weary, and I did indeed leave the river, and struck out across strange country, which was open and almost treeless. Before I left the river behind me, though, I thought I would take some of the bright pebbles that lay in it, because they were so lovely, and for no other reason. I placed them into a pocket, all oranges and purples and greens and blues and golds, and every other color of the rainbow, and then I started across this great open space, all by myself and not knowing where I was going. I hoped against hope that my tribe would return and find me. But as the afternoon turned to evening, they hadn't, and my feet were sore and my heart was aching, and I was hungry, for I had eaten nothing all day. At last, I stopped and sat on the ground and drank some water, noticing that I only had a very little left. As I drank, I heard the pebbles clatter together in my pocket.

"So, thinking it would be nice to see something lovely, I took the pebbles into my hand, expecting the colors of orange and purple, green and blue to soothe me. But to my amazement, the bright pebbles I had gathered that morning were now dull and dry and colorless. They did not reflect light, now. They only absorbed it. And they seemed just as weary as I was, and just as homesick for the place they had come from, and I felt guilty that I had done this to them without even thinking. I had only a little water left, and perhaps only a little time, also. But I thought I would take my waterskin and make the pebbles wet again.

"This I did. And they were transformed. They became once again bright pebbles, glittering in the last rays of the sun which was now setting on the far horizon, and though I now thought I was surely dying, I loved them anyway for their beauty, and one of them, particularly perfect, I held up and let see the sinking sun. It shone like a tiny fire, and my tribe, far across the valley, saw the light of its shining, like a beacon which called them to come and find me. They were kind to me, and fed me and gave me water, and in the morning, helped me back to the river so that I could return all the pebbles to where they had been born. I left them there, including the one that had saved me. I did not know which one it had been. But I am called, myself, Bright Pebble, now."

My hands at my sides, I stood a minute in silence, and then the whole camp erupted into applause, which I hardly heard, since I was hearing something even stronger. It was the thump of my new heart. For the moment that I stood there, *I was* Bright Pebble, an Indian who had been lost and now was found, and who had learned that things shine like beacons if they are left where they belong; for the moment that I stood there, *I was* Bright Pebble, who had learned the dangers of too much pride, and who had discovered how much it matters that you have a tribe to count on.

"And for the moment that I stood there, with the eyes of the whole camp on me, I knew that I wanted to be Bright Pebble all my life. I wanted to stay in my own river, and let the water and the sun shine off me, and be a Seeker of the Way, who had stepped into the Circle. The story had come from my head, but it had come from the part of my head that belonged to Camp Wynakee, and that was fed by the great stream of feeling. My wood-gathering on camping trips had gone into it, and my getting lost looking for the horses, and my trip to get water to put out the fire on Cabin Night. Even my jump into the Dorset Quarry, and the photographer's annual visit, and the unexpected shove of the Dog Soldier seemed to have found their way somehow into its boundaries. But though I could see, even then, where it had come from, the way it had been put together from pieces of what had really happened to me – to me, the white child and not the grown-up Indian – that didn't make it less miraculous; it was as miraculous as the day in late spring when a full-grown fern uncurls out of a fiddlehead.

&

I LEFT WYNAKEE that summer Best Owl, with the Swimming Award, of all things, and having been for four weeks in the Wayaka Huya. I looked forward to the following June as the continuation of my life. But I never went back to my camp in Dorset Hollow. Instead, I found myself sent, for reasons that made no sense to me, to Maine, to a girls' camp on Lake Sebago. I was in Maine for only three summers, though, most of which I have now forgotten, and I will be at Camp Wynakee until my life is over. Because, like all things that are sacred, Camp Wynakee still exists, and will exist even after I and all who went there have vanished – and I cannot help but believe that if only every child ever born could go there, the world would be a healthier, and saner, and better place for everyone. Children, after all, are the first symbol makers. In childhood we invent the world. In childhood we invest all things with meaning. And what we create, though it is always young, is neither arbitrary, nor radical, nor new; it is as ancient as the very stones the earth is built on. We create, in our minds, a Fire Tower, and an Ice Cave, and a Bat Cave, and a Long Trail, also a Waterwheel, and a One-Armed Man, maybe a Quarry. We take what we have been given, and we bake it in the kiln of our own perceptions, until we have formed the symbols that will always nourish us. And any child who can live in safety and with the natural world around her will bear her own symbols the way that fruit trees bear their own fruit. These symbols will resonate like bells, not like bugles, if we are lucky, and if we are lucky, they will show us who we are and who we might become.

In the years that have passed since I left Wynakee, though, I have discovered some things about myself that I didn't know when I was there, when my perceptions of the world were still so young. The one that I feel most ambivalent about is that I am inescapably more white man than Indian, for all that my induction into the Wayaka Huya was one of the most important events of my life. I have a white man's mouth and a white man's ego, and a white man's load of desire, and though I would like to be that bright colored pebble, that natural beacon shining in the almost-dusk, I am still, in fact, the figure wandering farther and farther, in search of greater and better loads of wood, which will weigh me down even if they do not get me lost. For all that I might wish that my white name had really burned forever in that fire, and that I could be on the earth as simply as something still being formed, I cannot help but remember the moment when I stood in the Bat Cave and wrote the word ARTHUR, in charcoal, and in letters two feet high. The word itself has faded now. There is no ARTHUR there these days – though I hope that there is still pond scum, and sleeping bats – but while the name itself is not there, what I felt when I wrote it is still with me. Which is that I am unique, as well as an inextricable part of things. Part of the specific but invisible tribe of all the people who have ever hiked behind the McConnell Farm, and stepped in cow-plops, and ended up in the Bat Cave.

And part of me, like any white man, feels that it is important to continue to try to name things, since white man's naming is all that can be set against white man's strange and gnawing hunger; but part of me, perhaps like an Indian, feels that it may be better to go on a journey without any maps or words to distract you from what is actually around you. I am still afraid of eclipses, which is sometimes Indian, I believe, and my reason may not be so different from an Indian's, either, since when my mother and stepfather came to visit me at Wynakee, which was my home, they took away the sun, and the world grew pale and strange, and I was, for the time being, unmade by it.

But in the years that have passed since I left Wynakee and

found myself living on the far side of the magic bridge, the far side of the wardrobe, back again in Kansas, I have found that such things can be mended, and that the blundering shadow of the moon will pass away from the perfect circle of the sun above us. I have also found time and again that there *is* such a thing as ball lightning, and that it is not imaginary, not a story, and certainly not a symbol. It is a thing, and rolls around the world unencumbered, like a cloud or the wind or a vision, without boundaries, and seeing all that lies before it. Nothing can stop it when it moves, and surely no one should ever try, since ball lightning is not just dangerous, it is deadly. Yet it is also very beautiful, so that though you know that it may kill you, you long for nothing so much as to reach out and try to touch it. You won't succeed. It will keep you at a distance. But the sight of it will never leave you, and you will try to pursue it, hope always for a second encounter. You know that one was more than you deserved, and that anyway, ball lightning is rare. And you are convinced, yes, you are, that it wasn't sentient.

And yet, when the air hangs heavy, and the sky grows dark around you, and the thunder rumbles and the bolts of lightning start to crack like bullwhips, you go and stand in the. courtyard or in the fields if it is Green Corn time, or you wait on the porch with its wicker chairs and its cold marble flooring. And you think, "Well, maybe this time. There's always a chance. Is it as *blue* as I remember it? And why did I just stand there, on the road, gaping after it? Why didn't I run until I caught up with it? Why didn't I run, the way I ran with the flag? Why didn't I run, in fact, for my life, for the secrets of the universe? *Next* time," you think. *"Next* time I'll chase it." And you know, as the rain comes sheeting, and the air is filled with the smell of rich humus, that there will probably not *be* a next time for you, not soon, not ever. But as ball lightning found me alone, that last summer I was at Wynakee, guessed that I would be leaving, guessed the vastness of the coming separation, so I cannot help but feel that ball lightning will once more find me, electrical, basic, blue, inhuman, and charged with mighty resonance.

And in the meantime? In the meantime, while I wait for the coming storm, the storm that will gather at last behind my cornfield, I have something else to do, something other than simply waiting, something more active than merely raising my arms toward the heavens. When I'm not gathering wood, or putting out the fires I have started with it, I'm still wandering the green mountains looking for a chunk of gold, gold that may be right there in front of me – gold that I first looked for when I was at Camp Wynakee in Dorset Hollow and it was the most wonderful day of the entire summer. I had a spoonful of oatmeal in my hand, or a glass of juice at my mouth, and suddenly – where had he come from? – there was Karl, not Karl any longer, but a prospector covered with gold dust, a man whom everyone had called a vagrant simply because his hat was lopsided and his clothes were worn and ragged.

Now he was banging into the dining room, shouting something that could scarcely be heard above the din that was suddenly rising all around him, and he was holding in his hands two rocks that had been painted a bright and shiny gold, and it was impossible to eat another bite of breakfast. It was Klondike Day, it was my day, and I would be the most devoted prospector that this green hollow around us had ever seen; I would get dressed up in my overalls, and I would throw my laundry bag over my shoulder, and I would tromp off at once into the hills. And I would gather gold, indeed, and would exchange it for spondoolees, but the spondoolees would be stuffed, forgotten, into a pocket of my shirt, and I would go off again on my quest, my self-appointed quest. I would stay in the hills until I found the Klondike Stone. And if, as the years have passed, and I have again and again brought my bag home empty, and it might seem that the chances have grown long against my filling it, that's not how it seems to my hiking boots, and that's not how it seems to my overalls, and that's certainly not how it seems to my tattered laundry bag. No, it seems that I'm always getting nearer. That *that* trip I must have just missed it. And that tomorrow the Stone will be there, not a bright pebble, but a great gold boulder. And if it isn't, well, that will be all right also. Because I'll still have my mess kit and my sleeping bag, and I can go back with them into the mountains, and look again, look as long as my feet will carry me. In a way, the more time I spend looking, the better I will like it.

Just hiking through these hills could take a lifetime.

About The Author

Elizabeth Arthur was born on November 15, 1953 in New York City. She is the daughter of Robert Arthur, an accomplished fantasy, horror, and mystery writer and the creator of *The Three Investigators* children's mystery book series, and Joan Vaczek, a Hungarian-American literary writer. She was educated at Concord Academy, the University of Michigan, Notre Dame University of Nelson, British Columbia, and the University of Victoria in Victoria, B.C.

She is the author of *Island Sojourn* (Harper and Row, 1980); *Beyond the Mountain* (Harper and Row, 1983); *Bad Guys* (Knopf, 1986); *Binding Spell* (Doubleday, 1989); *Looking For The Klondike Stone*, (Knopf, 1993); *Antarctic Navigation* (Knopf, 1995); *Bring Deeps* (Bloomsbury U.K., 2003); and also *The Lay of Gilgamesh* (Hollow Tree Press, 2025); and *The Forest of Katyn* (Hollow Tree Press, 2026). Her work has been extensively published in the U.K. and translated into Hungarian, Spanish, German, and Japanese.

Antarctic Navigation – an 800-page epic narrated by an American woman who sets out to recreate Robert Falcon Scott's British Antarctic Expedition of 1910-1912 – was chosen by the New York *Times* as a Notable Book, received a Critics' Choice Award from the San Francisco *Review of Books*, and was chosen as a Best Book of 1995 by *A Common Reader.* In 1996 the novel received the Ohioana Book Award for Fiction from the Ohioana Library Association. These awards came on the heels of two NEA Fellowships, as well as an operational support grant from the Division of Polar Programs at the National Science Foundation – the first ever given to a fiction writer.

Arthur has taught creative writing at Miami University in Oxford, Ohio, the University of Cincinnati, and Indiana University/Purdue University of Indianapolis where she directed the creative writing program. She has been married to the writer and editor Steven Bauer since June of 1982, and the two of them have recently completed twenty-six books in a contemporary *Three Investigators* mystery book series, updated for a new generation of readers.

www.ingramcontent.com/pod-product-compliance
Lightning Source LLC
Chambersburg PA
CBHW020914060726
47591CB00004B/1242
* 9 7 8 1 9 6 9 4 9 8 2 9 9 *